CREATING AN ENVIRONMENT FOR SUCCESSFUL PROJECTS

CREATING AN ENVIRONMENT FOR SUCCESSFUL PROJECTS

SECOND EDITION

Robert J. Graham
Randall L. Englund

Foreword by Judd Kuehn

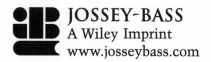

JOSSEY-BASS
A Wiley Imprint
www.josseybass.com

Published by Jossey-Bass
A Wiley Imprint
989 Market Street, San Francisco, CA 94103-1741   www.josseybass.com

Jossey-Bass books and products are available through most bookstores. To contact Jossey-Bass directly
call our Customer Care Department within the U.S. at 800-956-7739, outside the U.S. at 317-572-3986,
or fax 317-572-4002.

Jossey-Bass also publishes its books in a variety of electronic formats. Some content that appears in print
may not be available in electronic books.

Library of Congress Cataloging-in-Publication Data

Graham, Robert J., 1946-
   Creating an environment for successful projects / by
Robert J. Graham, Randall L. Englund.—2nd ed.
       p. cm.—(The Jossey-Bass business & management series)
Includes bibliographical references and index.
   ISBN 0-7879-6966-4 (alk. paper)
   1. Project management. I. Englund, Randall L. II. Title.
III. Series.
   HD69.P75G678   2004
   658.4'04—dc22

                                             2003020186

Printed in the United States of America
SECOND EDITION
HB Printing   10 9 8 7 6 5 4 3 2 1

CONTENTS

FOREWORD

When Robert Graham and Randall Englund asked me to write the Foreword for the second edition of this book, it provided me an opportunity to revisit where Chevron was in 1997, when the first edition was published, and assess where ChevronTexaco is today in our post-merger environment (Chevron Corporation and Texaco Corporation merged to form ChevronTexaco Corporation in 2001). I would like to start by setting the context for my first reading of *Creating an Environment for Successful Projects*.

In the early 1990s, the oil industry had embarked on the development of project processes along with the supporting tools and techniques. We had found an inconsistency in how our projects were being managed and the associated outcomes. As a result, many companies, including Chevron, adopted standard project management processes during this time period. With the endorsement of our senior management, we were able to deploy a standard process that has been recognized as a best practice within our industry. In the first edition of this book, Graham and Englund refer to this as "designing a project management system that is known and trusted."

In 1997, Chevron had been deploying our project process for four years and had just created a new organization primarily responsible for project management. As part of the dedicated project organization, we were particularly interested in the work being done by Graham and Englund and others about the environment for project management.

One of the big issues we were debating was how well our project process was being accepted and deployed within the company. We found the issues that Graham and Englund were raising were some of the same ones we were seeing within Chevron. It helped us decide to embark on a more detailed assessment of our internal culture and look for opportunities to expand deployment of our project process and practices.

One of the early steps was our participation in the Project Environment Assessment Tool (PEAT). This study came out after the book was published and is now covered in this second edition. The results provided key insights into what the issues are. We also found that many of the items the assessments revealed and the conclusions reached in this book were the same ones we had reached independently at Chevron and within the oil and gas industry.

One area where we strongly agree with Graham and Englund is the importance of project management process and techniques in running a business at all levels. As an industry, we also recognized the importance of well-managed projects to nurture our business and manage our capital expenditures. There is strong alignment of our projects and business outcomes across our industry. It is a common practice throughout our business to screen and manage our project portfolio on business drivers such as net present value, rate of return, return on investment, and strategic alignment. At the end of the day, the projects are all about improving or increasing our business. The key is getting both management and the project teams to understand this. I also appreciate the work Graham subsequently did with Dennis Cohen to write *The Project Manager's MBA*, another seminal book that added more financial tools to the project management toolkit.

Much of the drive to make these changes came out of efforts by the major oil and gas companies to benchmark our project performance. The results have been a focus on the importance of managing projects effectively and alignment between line management and project teams. In addition, it provides the ability to see if we are improving, how fast we are changing, and, most important, whether we are getting better than the competition. If we do not measure it, how do we know if we are getting better?

With this background and context for the situation in 1997, I saw several key messages in the first edition of *Creating an Environment for Successful Projects*. The first and foremost is the importance of a project-based organization. The understanding of this from top to bottom of the organization is critical. Everyone involved needs to understand that projects are the growth engine within any company.

One problem we encountered early in our deployment of the new project management process was well described in Chapter Three. Graham and Englund wrote, "In many organizations, there is a general lack of appreciation of the importance of project planning. Upper managers do not seem to understand its necessity and thus do not usually allow enough time for proper planning." As we set out to examine our process deployment, we found this exact issue within our company.

An action resulting from this study included increased focus on educating management at all levels on the importance of project planning, thus allowing project teams the time and resources to do proper planning before launching into implementation. This effort continues today at ChevronTexaco.

Another area that Chevron aligned with Graham and Englund is the importance of having a clear plan for selecting and developing project managers. Chevron and, today, ChevronTexaco believe this is a key to being successful in project management. We have a separate organization and career ladder for professional project managers within our organization. It has allowed us to identify, train, and reward the true project professionals within our company without having to promote them out of project management. It also provides a mechanism to mentor new project managers within our system.

In this second edition of *Creating an Environment for Successful Projects*, Graham and Englund continue to emphasize the importance of project portfolio management and alignment with strategy. This is an area where I think a large number of people can gain benefit. I believe that one of the keys to picking the right projects is that everyone associated with the project should be able to explain why the project is being done. The explanation should be not just that management told us to do it, but what the business benefit of the project is. If we cannot explain how it adds value, we should reconsider whether it should be done.

Another new area of focus is the importance of full-time team members to a project. We have the luxury on most of our large projects of having full-time project teams that are collocated. For many other industries and smaller projects, however, this may not be the case. Diluting the efforts of those project teams by making them work on a large number of projects can reduce the probability of success for all their projects.

Think of it as doing a collection of projects at home. Do you try to focus on one project until it is done and then do the next project? Or do you try to do all projects at once? The same is true for projects at work. You can focus on the critical few and get them done successfully with full-time project teams or have them try all projects at once and risk not being successful. Graham and Englund provide additional arguments in Chapter Three of this second edition to help focus on this crucial topic.

Graham and Englund address a number of key issues in this book that will help anyone involved in managing projects, supporting projects, or managing an organization that does projects. From my view, that covers most businesses today. If you are not doing projects, your business is not growing or changing, and your competition is likely leaving you behind.

I thank Graham and Englund for letting me comment on their book and provide my views on the subject. I hope everyone who reads this book comes away with the same sense of urgency to improve their own project environment that I did.

September 2003   Judd Kuehn
San Ramon, California   ChevronTexaco Corporation

PREFACE TO THE SECOND EDITION

Since this book first appeared in print in 1997, we continue our quest to improve project management. Bob went on to address project management business skills, together with Dennis Cohen, and coauthored *The Project Manager's MBA: How to Translate Project Decisions into Business Success* (2001). They also developed multimedia computer simulations: *Project Leadership* and *Business Skills for Project Managers* (see www.englundpmc.com for on-line links to these products). Paul Dinsmore (1998) joined Randy and Bob to extend *Creating an Environment for Successful Projects* into *Creating the Project Office: A Manager's Guide to Leading Organizational Change* (2003). We now come back to update current thinking about the impact of organizational environments on project success.

Much has changed in the world that we comment on, yet little has changed in terms of key principles for managers to address. This second edition validates many of our original findings, includes more arguments about why these approaches are important, and provides additional examples of how people implement the concepts.

We are pleased to be part of this movement. It has brought us many new friends. Colonel Gary LaGassey, Project Office program manager for the U.S. Air Force base in Aviano, Italy, became a devotee: "At the program level, a considerable part of our approach was derived from the writings and teachings of Robert J. Graham and Randall L. Englund. Their 1997 book, *Creating an Environment for*

Successful Projects: The Quest to Manage Project Management, became our Bible for program leadership during Program Management Office (PMO) startup and continues to be a fundamental part of our thinking as we work to attain recognition as a truly project-based organization."

An information technology manager at a pharmaceutical company says, "I think you'll find our [portfolio management] approach right in line with your philosophy. . . . The team has bought into the process and is willing to implement it. Our management here truly understands what it means to sponsor such an effort and is not afraid to convey their beliefs to the rest of the organization and champion the process."

John D. Trudel (1998) notes that "the authors describe what others have achieved, and they tell how to get started. Yet, I find the book's best content not in what or how, but in why. The book is rich with examples of why typical management behavior interferes with new product development. It clearly explains why upper managers are fearful, why corporate communications are so often poor, and, yes, how to fix such things. The goal is to give project managers the freedom, training, and support to run rather autonomous and effective new product development programs."

A review on Amazon.com notes, "Amazing how a book written in 1997 seems like it was written for current times." Some things do not change, and everything changes. So what is new?

A question often arose about how the pieces of the puzzle interact and what happens if some remain undone. We have added a section about creating an environment for successful organizations to Chapter One to answer this question. We also describe an assessment tool we developed, called the Project Environment Assessment Tool (PEAT).

We are thrilled about how the Revitalization Model in Chapter One helps many people. A project management professional (PMP) in information technology service delivery, Al Gardiner, shared the following experiences:

> I attended the "Creating an Environment for Successful Projects" seminar at the PMI Symposium in Nashville (2001). One of the concepts I remember is the revitalization process. For years, I've been fighting an uphill battle to establish formal, disciplined Project Management in my organization. I ran into all of the typical barriers that I read about from lack of executive sponsorship to educational constraints. Every time I hit one, my team and I would work through it and come out the other side better and stronger.
>
> The one challenge that I have not yet been able to overcome is that of a dysfunctional company. We have recently gone through what you referred to as

"Cultural Distortion." [The company] is in bankruptcy and has a new leader poised to bring us out. While I am hopeful that we will emerge as a strong force in the market, I am prepared to deal with the alternative.

The point of this is to highlight in hindsight the lesson I learned. You cannot change an organization that is going through Cultural Distortion phase. The natural process of Revitalization must occur. You can influence individuals and the outcome of revitalization, but you must allow the organization to develop into its new form before real change can be realized.

This is not to say that you should stop all efforts. To the contrary, you should re-energize your efforts so as to positively influence the revitalization process. The more the company "knows" when it comes out the other side, the less chance that your efforts will disrupt it through "Steady State."

The problem I had to deal with was the frustration of not realizing the organization's cultural limitations. I was constantly complaining about how I was making no headway. In hindsight, I see that we made tremendous headway. We were able to get people to recognize the Project Management profession. We were able to demonstrate many of the benefits of a well-managed project. We encouraged people to embrace and pursue professional development (I sent you the outline of our Friday Learning and Sharing concept shortly after the seminar). My perspective and enthusiasm would have been much different had I recognized the state of the company (in terms of cultural change). I am now resolved to watch and learn from the company as it emerges from its disaster.

Patience seems to be a winning trait just as in most of life's endeavors.

We note that more project selection teams are beginning to appear using the process described in Chapter Two. We added information about how upper management teams may sabotage this process. We also added a section in Chapter Three about the perils of multitasking.

PMP Alfonso Bucero, formerly a senior project manager for HP Consulting in Spain and now a director for the International Institute for Learning, shared what he learned about understanding the need for planning:

I really like the explanation of Chapter Three about the need for planning. I worked for HP in Spain during thirteen years as a project manager. During the first project I managed, I was seen as "*estrange* person" in the organization because I tried to involve all the team in project planning from the beginning. Complaints like "please do it and do not lose your time planning" were very common. The benefits of those practices helped me get respect as a professional who organized tasks and activities before doing them. Understanding the need of planning became more tangible when we had more and more projects.

Why do rational people do irrational acts? We offer our perspective using a net present value approach to bring core teams into better alignment in Chapter Four.

Always in search of the holy grail (also known as organizational structure), we add a new model to Chapter Five that includes a chief project officer. We also note that no one structure is going to solve all problems.

The information system (Chapter Six) gets updated with more on-line capabilities, project manager competencies (Chapter Seven) get a boost, and the learning organization (Chapter Eight) gets energized by organic metaphors. Chapter Nine still shares the HP Project Management Initiative story, but with an increased shift toward the project office concept. The emphasis is on how following best project management practices, rather than a particular approach, is the important focus. Newer project-aware organizations can learn to accelerate their approach to projects based on these learnings.

Alfonso Bucero in Spain again offers these perspectives:

> Developing a Project Management Information System: This chapter helped me a lot. It became one method for me to convince my upper managers about the need for answering questions regarding the project portfolio. In many organizations, upper managers make the decision to buy a software tool before analyzing the needs of project information. Finding the right information about a particular project and being able to answer questions regarding those projects are key for managing successful projects.
>
> Project manager development: I like this approach very much to assist the selection process of project managers. I ran some "transition to PM" sessions and they were very productive. Many times people are promoted to project manager without explaining to them what is the meaning and the implications. The results of these sessions produced wonderful results for the company. Because people assume facts and thoughts without asking for more information, these sessions clarify expectations and are very valuable for individual contributors and also for management people.

Chapter Ten includes a few more ideas on assessment and implementation of a project-based organization. We also draw from architectural evolution to help readers visualize a pervasive project management culture. We added an Epilogue on leadership and the change process. Many new references also appear.

The following example, of upper managers working with a program management office, updates and previews the concepts presented in this book. A program office guided the HP and Compaq merger to exceed savings by greater than $1 billion and one year ahead of schedule. Jim Arena, director of integration effectiveness, benchmarked more than twenty companies about how to do a tech merger on this scale. "Structure follows strategy" and "adopt and go" became guiding principles for a rigorous, shared program management discipline. They established core program teams covering the businesses, functions, horizontal processes, and regions. The whole company was represented in weekly "clean room" meetings; these high-level managers worked full time on the merger with no other line duties, from the announcement at the beginning through legal close. These upper management teams served as a guiding coalition to drive change, provide guidance, review decisions, and make tradeoffs.

The program office set a cadence to get people into a new operating mode. They had clear strategic goals and senior management support to focus on one solution to each issue, not optimized or merged but "perfect enough." They suspended operating reality to cover major buckets of customers and business processes with rules, not exceptions. Instead of slipping into paralysis over the immense amount of work to accomplish, the right people quickly got expert proposals, decided courses for action, and moved on. They used techniques like decision accelerator meetings, which brought cross-functional leaders together to resolve a set of key issues in one day via planned facilitated discussions. They accelerated lessons learned at the highest levels by seeing whole pictures and applying structured rigorous processes—project portfolio management. They created clear product road maps. Fast start workshops served as an information system to share with every employee how the new company would operate and for managers to engage up front with their employees.

What lessons were learned? Jim Arena says, "Start it earlier. The program office was behind and spent two months racing to catch up." He also says, "Reporting was used too extensively to force discipline and behavior changes. This appeared necessary at the time but created a bad taste in the mouth for many people. We learned to drop nuisance factors and focus more visibility on top-level choices." The learnings from intense efforts on completing core integration steps can now be applied truly to exploit the strengths that the two companies brought to the merger.

The environment created by implementing a project-based approach can also be seen in HP Services' commitment to project management. Ron Kempf, director of PM competency and certification for the HP Services worldwide engagement PMO, shared this statement: "HP Services considers strong project management a key ingredient to providing successful solutions to our customers. Our project managers are seasoned professionals with broad and deep experience in solutions, as well as managing projects. Our rigorous business processes make sure you are satisfied. A program road map provides an overall architecture of the project lifecycle while senior HP Services management conduct regular progress reviews to ensure quality. Our world-class project management methodology combines industry best practices with HP's experience to help keep everything on track. Our knowledge management program enables project managers and technology consultants to put our experience around the globe to work for you."

These examples illustrate the possibilities, commitment, and thoroughness required to create an environment for greater project success.

Most heartening is to receive comments like this one: "Ten months ago I started a new company and I am practicing all the principles explained in your book in order to create the right environment for success." We hope this edition continues and expands those practices and friendships.

September 2003

Randall L. Englund
Burlingame, California
englundr@pacbell.net

Robert J. Graham
Mendocino, California
otto@mcn.org

PREFACE TO THE FIRST EDITION

This book is for managers concerned about getting better results from the projects under way in their organizations. New projects that generate new products or services are the principal means of future organizational growth. Projects are the means to implement organizational strategy and organizational change. Projects and project managers create new products, new procedures, new reward systems, new features for old products, and new businesses. The key feature of projects is that they represent something new.

Project management complements but is different from reengineering. Reengineering involves reexamining what the organization is currently doing and striving to do it better. Project management is about what the organization is going to do; it thus represents the future, not the present. Managers concerned about how their organization can develop or maintain steady growth should read this book.

Many organizations are finding it necessary to implement better project management practices. This realization often comes as a result of failed projects. New products that never make it to market or new software releases that do not meet customer needs represent money spent with no return. Today, organizational survival may be at stake when results from projects do not succeed technically, in the market, or within the organization. This book helps managers learn how to create an environment that can help avoid these failures.

When project failures create a focus on the need to change the way projects are managed, people soon learn that this change profoundly affects the entire organization. Successful projects require participation from many parts of the organization; the development of successful project management practices cannot be accomplished in one or two departments alone. Skills in managing across organizations must be developed. The implementation of successful practices requires a coordinated effort involving all departments in an organization. The change must be systematic and systemwide.

Although project managers are most closely responsible for the success of projects, upper managers ultimately create an environment for project success. The way that the directors of divisions, departments, functions, and sections define, structure, and act toward projects has an important effect on the success or failure of those projects and, consequently, the success or failure of the organization. This book is designed to help upper managers create an environment in which projects can be more successful. In line with the vision of virtual corporations for the twenty-first century—edgeless, adapting in real time to customers' changing needs, interacting among multiple, often unrelated processes (Davidow and Malone, 1992)—we believe the true audience for this book is the burgeoning cadre of virtual managers who are or will be responsible for creating new results in cross-organizational environments.

Upper management roles and practices will necessarily change in the move to a project-based organization. It is important to implement changes that support successful project management practices. Upper managers also need to recognize how their behavior can hinder project success and to understand and change those management practices that do so. This book contains valuable insight into such practices and illustrates proven methods that help managers support project success.

Leading the charge for something new are customers, who want more for less. They are finding competitors who are learning how to satisfy their demands. This book shows what managers need to do to keep the new products coming from their organization rather than a competitor's.

Management changes rarely work unless the upper management of the organization is heavily involved. Nor are management changes typically successful unless the people affected by the change understand the reasons for the change and participate in its design. This book helps all managers understand the need for project management changes, whether or not they directly manage project managers.

Although there are many books on how to manage projects, this book fills the void on how to develop project management as an organizational practice. Other books create intense awareness about what to do; this book also describes how some organizations implement the concepts. A "first-level anecdote" is a story about what others have done that often motivates a reader to adopt the concept being described; we go further to provide "second-order anecdotes" that describe how to get started and illustrate creative ways to adapt and apply potent practices. We share details of an organizational process of support for project management as practiced by leading companies.

This book illustrates proven practices by using Hewlett-Packard (HP) and other top companies as examples. Hewlett-Packard is well known for its excellence in project practices. Its high growth rate attests to its ability to manage new-product projects successfully. At the core of HP's successful project management was its Project Management Initiative program, which many other organizations now emulate. Many of the lessons we have learned about the quest to manage project management within HP, as well as a description of the initiative program, are contained in this book.

Outline of Topics

Chapter One examines the need for project management in business organizations and the development of new, project-based organizations. We examine the future postbureaucratic or organic organization, the type of organization where projects are most successful. We then outline the steps necessary to revitalize organizations and change them to project-based organizations.

Chapter Two examines one of the components of a successful environment: linking projects to organizational strategy. It begins by describing what happens to projects without a strategic emphasis. With a strategic emphasis, everyone on the project team understands how their actions affect the success of the project and, ultimately, the success of the organization. Discussion continues on how strategic emphasis eliminates the need for project budgets. Finally, we discuss the role of upper management in multiple project management.

The next two chapters examine upper-management practices that thwart the successful development of project management. Topics include setting the project deadline, allowing time for planning and creativity, the folly of adding people when a project is perceived to be late, the problems of changing project scope because of anxiety, the need for motivating project work, and the importance of developing a core team system. We embrace an organizational learning process that starts where people come from and takes them along paths other than those that would lead them astray.

Chapter Five addresses the problem of organizing the project management effort. We review the problems of running projects in a traditional functional or matrix organization. One solution offered is the internal market type of organization. The chapter closes with a discussion of the functions of upper management in defining and operating a project organization.

Chapter Six covers the importance of information in the successful project management environment. A novel approach is suggested of basing the information system on answering the questions of major project stakeholders. We discuss the problems of developing such an information system and its function in organizational learning.

Chapter Seven discusses project manager selection and development. The chapter begins by outlining the problems with the "accidental project manager," currently favored in many organizations. We then review various studies of project manager selection criteria, a project manager selection process, and a process for transition to the project manager's role.

Chapter Eight covers the basic principles of the learning organization. We stress the importance of learning from projects for developing skill at leading projects. We describe a project retrospective process as a formalized means to learn from projects and provide a project retrospective form for this process.

Finally, we give examples of how to implement the needed changes. Chapter Nine reviews the project management initiative process at HP. This process helped both upper managers and project managers create an environment for successful projects. The chapter covers the components of the initiative process and the functions of the initiative team. These include consulting, training, and information resources as well as the project management conference. Chapter Ten covers similar project management programs in other organizations and outlines what needs to be done to implement such a program in organizations where cultural differences exist that differ from those forming the basis for this book.

We, the authors, consider this book to be a work in progress, the final goal being the development of a set of best practices for creating an environment for successful projects. However, we also know that you, the readers, will probably be following some very good practices that are not mentioned in this book. Those of you who are wrestling with organizational change and implementing new practices are the ones who know best what works and what does not. If you would like to share your experiences for possible inclusion in future editions of this book or if you want to comment on anything included in this edition, feel free to contact us through the e-mail addresses provided.

May 1997   Bob Graham
                                                   Mendocino, California
                                                   otto@mcn.org

                                                   Randy Englund
                                                   Burlingame, California
                                                   englundr@pacbell.net

THE AUTHORS

The authors of this book represent two complementary approaches to the study of project management processes.

Robert J. Graham, PMP, is an independent project management consultant and was a senior associate to the Strategic Management Group. Previously, he taught at the Wharton School of the University of Pennsylvania. He is the author of the highly successful project management simulation "The Complete Project Manager" and of a previous book, *Project Management As If People Mattered*. In 2001, he coauthored with Dennis Cohen *The Project Manager's MBA: How to Translate Project Decisions into Business Success*. In addition to his master's and Ph.D. degrees in business administration, Graham earned an M.S. in cultural anthropology. As an anthropologist, he is trained to observe human behavior in organizational settings. He writes from the point of view of one who has observed, taught, and studied project management in a variety of organizations. When Graham and Englund were asked to speak at a Project Leadership conference in Chicago, the event coordinator said: "Bob Graham . . . has seen it all over the past twenty years of his project management consulting career."

Randall L. Englund, NPDP, CBM, was a senior project manager at Hewlett-Packard and a member of its corporate Project Management Initiative team. Drawing on many years in program management for high-tech new product development, R&D, marketing, field service, and manufacturing, he now serves as an independent executive consultant to guide managers and teams to implement an organic approach to project management. He speaks, trains, and consults on project management with product developers across industries. Although Englund completed an M.B.A. in management at San Francisco State University and a B.S. in electrical engineering at the University of California at Santa Barbara, his real education came while managing large projects at HP and General Electric. He adds the practical slant to this book—the point of view of one who has been there.

A workshop participant noted that Graham and Englund "bring the concepts from way up there, to right down here, equip you with the tools, and empower you to act." They continue to collaborate; along with Paul Dinsmore, they coauthored *Creating the Project Office: A Manager's Guide to Leading Organizational Change* in 2003.

CREATING AN ENVIRONMENT
FOR SUCCESSFUL PROJECTS

The change to project-based organizations

Creating an Environment for Successful Projects

Creating an Environment for Successful Projects

Creating an Environment for Successful Projects

Creating an Environment for Successful Projects

Creating an Environment for Successful Projects

Creating an Environment for Successful Projects

This chapter begins with a typical scenario, a story of project failure, that leads to an outline of the components required to create an environment for successful projects. It examines the need for project management in business organizations and includes examples of successful organizational responses to that need. It then looks at project-based organizations as a basis for the future and the move toward that organizational style. Leading the change to project-based organic organizations requires understanding organizational change processes, so the revitalization process is examined as a model of organizational change. Leading a revitalization requires a strong change agent, so the behaviors necessary to be a successful change agent are reviewed. Finally, the important points of the chapter are summarized as a quick reference guide for the successful complete upper manager.

CHAPTER ONE

LEADING THE CHANGE TO A
PROJECT-BASED ORGANIZATION

When all the conditions of an event are present, it comes to pass.

HEGEL, *PHILOSOPHY OF HISTORY*

M̲ost future growth in organizations will result from successful development projects that generate new products, services, or procedures. Such projects are also a principal way of creating organizational change; implementing change and growth strategies is usually entrusted to project managers. However, project success is often as much a result of the organizational environment as of the skills of the project manager. As the size and importance of projects increase, the project manager becomes the head of a complex development operation with an organizational dimension that can make important contributions to project success or failure. That this organizational dimension may help explain project performance has been strangely neglected in the literature, a problem we address here by examining the role of upper management in creating an environment that promotes project success.

All too commonly, people become project managers by accident. One way to become a project manager is to ask a question at a meeting and then be told, "That's a good question. Why don't you take on the project of dealing with that problem?" Or somebody comes up with an idea and is tapped to make it happen, or the generator of the idea looks around for the first person in sight to whom it can be assigned for implementation. Experience indicates that in the process of developing projects, upper managers often appoint inexperienced or accidental project managers (APMs), give them a project to manage, and then systematically undermine their ability to achieve success. Upper managers do not usually undermine APMs on purpose, but too often they apply assumptions and methods to project management that are more appropriate to regular departmental management. Projects are a totally different beast in many ways. Everyday management generally is a matter of repeating various standard processes; projects, in contrast, create something new.

In addition, upper managers are often unaware how their behavior influences project success or failure. Because previous examinations of project success focus almost exclusively on the functions of the project manager, there is an understandable lack of awareness of the importance of the project environment and the behavior of middle and higher managers in organizations—those managers of project managers whom we refer to as upper managers. It is important to understand the impact of their behavior on the future survival of organizations. Roles and responsibilities are changing as organizations become organic and project based—that is, driven by internal markets and team accountability for specific results. Any lapses by upper managers in the authenticity and integrity of their dealings with project managers and with managers in other departments are likely to have a severe impact on the achievement of project goals.

A Scenario

Many upper managers voice increasing frustration with the results of projects undertaken in their areas of responsibility. They lament that despite sending people out for training and buying project management software, projects seem to take too long, cost too much, and produce less than the desired results. Why is that? To help understand the problem, consider the following scenario.

An upper manager gets an idea, perhaps from reading a book or attending a conference, and has a vision of a product or service that the organization can offer. This vision may differ from what the company normally provides, so creating the product becomes a special project. Talking it over with associates, the manager is delighted when one of the best engineers becomes interested. To get the concept rolling, the manager asks this engineer to manage the project. They both figure the project can be done quickly because the engineer has achieved good results on past work. The new project manager talks to a few colleagues, and soon a team of engineers begins working on the design. After a while, the team comes back to the upper manager with good news and bad news. The good news is that one needed technology is available inside the organization; it was developed in another division, however, so the team needs to borrow a few people from there to get it. The bad news is that another needed technology is not available in the organization, so new people will have to be hired. The upper manager arranges to borrow people from the other division and authorizes hiring the needed employees from the outside.

Delay begins about here. The new employees must be approved by the executive committee and then must have job descriptions defined and developed by the personnel department. Because these new people know the latest technology, they are expensive; even so, it takes them longer than expected to become productive once they are on board because they are not used to the ways of their new employer. Eventually, however, the whole group gets working—until a manager from the other division, for which this special project is *not* a priority, takes back the borrowed engineers. Work slows again as the upper manager tries to negotiate their return. Some engineers are finally freed for the project, but not the same ones as before, so there are more delays until they are brought up to speed.

When work finally resumes, questions arise about marketing the new product and about using patented technology to create it. The upper manager must therefore add people from the marketing and legal departments to the project. Sure enough, the lawyers ascertain that the new employees inadvertently used a technology patented by another company; the upper manager must decide if it is cheaper to pay for its use or develop an alternative technology. The new project team members from marketing are difficult to communicate with because marketing uses a different e-mail system from that of the engineering and legal departments. Decision making is further delayed as upper managers argue over a number of manufacturing issues that had come up on previous projects but were never resolved.

The team grows disgruntled as it becomes clear that the great engineer is not skilled in planning and conflict management; the situation is not improved when the engineer disappears for several weeks to fix problems that have arisen from a previous project. Elsewhere in the organization, people begin to grumble that the project is costing lots and accomplishing little. The upper manager spends time justifying the project to other department managers but cannot avoid finally being called before the executive committee to explain why it is taking so long and costing so much.

If this scenario seems at all far-fetched, consider this letter that one of us received:

> I work in a planning and distribution organization. My duties include leading efforts that are called projects and generally I'm fixing a problem with a process or system. Rarely do I get due dates or objectives . . . and when I press my sponsor[s] on this point they tell me essentially that they just want it done. Coupled with this the department has difficulty achieving the full intent of the

objectives, and we are pretty unproductive (we don't get many projects completed in a year). We are putting together a proposal including development of dedicated project managers in the organization whose entire job is to lead the projects of the organization (as opposed to the current method of choosing people whose work is closely aligned to the project).

Unfortunately some managers feel strongly that they do not want their resources utilized by the project managers (and subject to the project manager's discretion). Plus they want to have access to their people to pursue their own objectives (this includes assigning one of their people as project lead[er] regardless of skill). At this point we need help in convincing these managers to support the process of project management . . .

You can almost hear the voice trailing off in a sigh of frustration.

Another problem is the assumption that project work should take about as long as traditional work. This sets expectations that can never be met, so projects always seem slower and more costly than other activities. Actually, they *should* take longer; project work represents something new and different, so the inevitable unknowns, such as those in the scenario, need to be factored into the expected length. It is also a false assumption that project work can be handled in the same way and using the same organization and the same people as other work. In reality, because project work is different, it requires a project-based organization. The project in the scenario failed because upper management had not created an environment for project success.

Creating an Environment for Successful Projects

What environmental components foster successful projects? Many misconceptions develop into folklore over time, such as the Humpty Dumpty nursery rhyme (see Box 1.1). The king's men may not have been able to put Humpty's pieces together, but the key pieces needed to create a picture of a supportive project environment (see Figure 1.1) can be readily assembled with this book as a guide.

A word of caution: the pieces we are assembling will not stay together without glue, and the glue has two vital ingredients: authenticity and integrity. *Authenticity* means that upper managers really mean what they say. *Integrity* means that they really do what they say they will do, and for the reasons they stated initially. It is a recurring theme in this book that authenticity and integrity link the head and the heart, the words and the action; they separate belief from disbelief and often make the difference between success and failure.

FIGURE 1.1. THE COMPONENTS OF AN ENVIRONMENT FOR SUCCESSFUL PROJECTS.

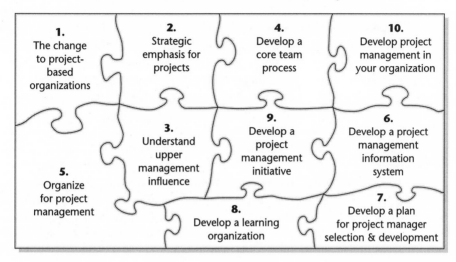

BOX 1.1. A Challenge.

Humpty Dumpty sat on a wall
Humpty Dumpty had a great fall
All the King's Horses
And all the King's Men
Couldn't put Humpty together again.

The character in this nursery rhyme is usually represented as an egg that falls and breaks. In reality, a humpty dumpty was a type of military cannon. During a battle, it was put up on a wall. When the cannon was fired, the recoil sent it off the wall to the ground, where it came apart. The king's horses were the cavalry, and the king's men were the army. They were there to win the battle, but they couldn't put Humpty the cannon together again: they were not able to put together all the pieces required for success.

Each of the following ten pieces of the successful-project picture is the subject of a chapter in this book.

1. Change to Project-Based Organizations. The balance of this chapter examines a process for changing organizations and discusses the requirements of change agents. Changing to a project-based organization requires changes in the behavior of upper managers and project managers. For example, a project-based organization must also be team based; to create such an organization, upper managers and project managers must themselves work as a team.

2. Emphasize the Link Between Strategy and Projects. It is important to link projects to strategy. Upper managers need to work together to develop a strategic emphasis for projects. One factor in motivating project team members is to show them that the project they are working on has been selected as a result of a strategic plan. If they instead feel that the project was selected on a whim, that nobody wants it or supports it, and that it will most likely be canceled, they will probably (and understandably) not do their best work. Upper managers can help avoid this problem by linking the project to the strategic plan and developing a portfolio of projects that implements the plan. Many organizations use upper management teams to manage the project portfolio; this approach would certainly have reduced the problems and delays depicted in the previous scenario.

Chevron, for example, developed the Chevron Project Development and Execution Process (CPDEP), which provides a formalized discipline for managing projects (Cohen and Kuehn, 1996). A key element of CPDEP is the involvement of all stakeholders at the appropriate time. In the initial process phase to identify and assess opportunities, a multifunctional team of upper managers meets to test the opportunity for strategic fit and to develop a preliminary overall plan. The project does not proceed from this phase unless there is a good fit with the overall strategy. Developing a process for selecting and managing a portfolio of projects is the subject of Chapter Two.

3. Understand Upper Management Influence. Many of the best practices of project management often fail to get upper management support. Many upper managers are unaware of how their behavior influences project success. To help ensure success, they are advised to develop a project support system that incorporates such practices as negotiating the project deadline, supporting the creative process, allowing time for and supporting the concept of project planning, choosing not to interfere in project execution, demanding no useless scope changes, and changing the reward system to motivate project work. These topics are considered in Chapter Three.

4. Develop a Core Team Process. A core team consists of people who represent the various departments necessary to complete a project. This team needs to be developed at the beginning of the project, and its members should perform most effectively when they stay with the project from beginning to end. Developing a core team process and making it work are essential to minimizing project cycle time and avoiding unnecessary delays. Important as they are, however, core teams are rarely implemented well without the implicit and explicit support of upper management. Firms that have used core teams, however, often report dramatic results. Cadillac, for example, found that core teams can accomplish styling changes that previously took 175 weeks in 90 to 150 weeks (Cadillac, 1991). Developing a core team is the subject of Chapter Four.

5. Organize for Project Management. The revitalization process described in Chapter One provides the impetus in Chapter Five for determining how an organization may be changed to support proper project management. In the scenario earlier in this chapter, much of the delay can be attributed to the lack of an organizational design that supports project management. In contrast, the decentralized corporate culture of Hewlett-Packard (HP), as one example, gives business managers a great deal of freedom in tackling new challenges. Upper managers have a responsibility to set up organizational structures that support successful projects. Because structure influences behavior, Chapter Five reviews the characteristics of alternative organizational structures and examines what can be done to alleviate some of the problems caused by certain structures.

6. Develop a Project Management Information System. In the past, organizational policies, procedures, and authority relationships held things together. The project-based organization lacks much of that structural framework; instead, the project organization is kept intact by an information system. For example, former HP executive vice president Rick Belluzzo (1996b) envisioned a "people-centric information environment that provides access to information any time, anywhere . . . and that spurs the development of a wide range of specialized devices and services that people can use to enrich their personal and professional lives." Upper managers need to work in concert to develop information systems that support successful projects and provide information across the organization. In this regard, on-line technological capabilities are increasingly attractive and important but do not replace the need for upper management to determine what information is necessary and develop systems to provide it. Chapter Six covers this in depth.

7. Develop a Plan for Project Manager Selection and Development. Future organizations will see the end of the accidental project manager. Project management must be seen as a viable position, not just a temporary annoyance, and project management skill must become a core organizational competence. This requires a conscious, planned program for project manager selection and training. HP, Computer Science Corporation, Keane, and 3M are among the companies that have spent large amounts on project manager training and development, as discussed in Chapter Seven. The development emphasis of these organizations seems justified because the project managers of today will become the leaders of the project-based organization of tomorrow. This is such an important topic that Bowen, Clark, Halloway, and Wheelwright (1994a) advise organizations to "make projects the school for leaders."

8. Develop a Learning Organization.   Chapter Eight summarizes the concepts of organizational learning as they apply to project-based organizations. One key to organizational learning is the postproject review, which helps project participants and the rest of the organization learn from project experiences. Although its value may be priceless and its cost nil, this learning process takes place only if upper managers set up a formal program and require the reviews. When they do, many tools for project improvement can be developed that can help eliminate frustrating delays. For example, British Petroleum (BP) has operated a postproject appraisal unit since 1977 (Gulliver, 1987), and BP managers attribute dramatic results to it. By learning from past projects, they say that they are much more on target in developing new project proposals, have a much better idea of how long projects take, and thus experience less frustration at perceived project delays. Learning from project experience becomes a major emphasis in project-based organizations and can be seen as a competitive advantage.

9. Develop a Project Management Initiative.   HP had an ongoing initiative to continually improve its project management practices. Dubbed the Project Management Initiative, it was part of senior management's breakthrough objective to get the right products to market quickly and effectively. An initiative group works with upper managers and project managers to increase project management knowledge and practice throughout the organization. Project management became very important to HP's success because more than half of customer orders typically came from products it introduced within the previous two years. Shorter product life cycles mean more new projects are needed to maintain growth. Marvin Patterson, a former director of corporate engineering at HP, says, "Due to my experience since I left HP, I would say that HP probably has the best project managers in the world, or at least in this hemisphere. The Project Management Initiative made a huge contribution to this success." The details of an initiative process are presented in Chapter Nine.

10. *Develop Project Management in Your Organization.* Chapter Ten provides suggestions for adapting and applying the concepts in this book to cultural environments that differ from those described in it. For example, Honeywell developed a global information technology project management initiative based on its chief information officer's desire to have modern project management disciplines throughout Honeywell Information Systems be "the way of doing business" and a "core competency." To accomplish this, the initiative group developed a project management focus group of fifteen people from different departments to discuss the basis of good project management. With input from this group, the initiative team developed a project management model, a project management process, and a supporting training and education curriculum; it also promotes a professional project manager certification process. The team's vision was for Honeywell Information Systems to be recognized "as a world-class leader in modern Information Technology Project Management principles, processes, and practices" (Koroknay, 1996, p. x).

3M developed the Project Management Professional Development Center, which consisted of people and services from three information technology organizations. A center offers consulting help for project teams, research on the latest best practices and help in applying them, and a project management competency model supported by a project leader curriculum. It also sponsors a project leader forum, where project leaders can meet in person to share stories and problems. Communication is enhanced by an "electronic post office," a communications network linking all project managers (Storeygard, 1995). These and other company efforts are detailed in Chapter Ten as a guide to developing better project management.

All these examples represent significant efforts on the part of major corporations to meet the challenge of developing project management expertise. Such major effort is needed because the change to project management means changing deeply ingrained habits of organizational behavior. Many cherished and highly rewarded practices need to be replaced by new practices, and this often requires major upheaval.

Major upheaval requires authenticity and integrity on the part of upper managers. Most change efforts do not fail from lack of concepts or from lack of a description of how to do it right. Most change programs fail when upper managers are hoist on their own petard of inauthenticity and lack of integrity. This failure happens because people involved in the situations where managers violate authenticity and integrity sense the lack of resolve, feel the lack of leadership, and despair of the situation. When upper managers speak without authenticity, they stand like the naked emperor: they think they are clothed, but everyone else sees the truth. When upper managers lack integrity they do not "walk the walk," they only "talk the talk," and people sense the disconnection and become cynical. Management cannot ask others to change without first changing themselves. Implementing the concepts in this book depends on upper management's resolve to approach the needed changes with authenticity and integrity.

The Need for Project Management

Forces outside the organization are pushing the need for project management. An important shift in the marketplace is that customers who were formerly content with products now demand total solutions to problems. In the past, customers bought an array of products to solve their problems; the functional or bureaucratic organization provided standard products, each of which was a partial solution to problems. Thus, bureaucratic organizations put out products, and the consumers moved across organizations to put together solutions to their problems.

To provide today's customers with total solutions, project-based rather than product-based organizations are best. The new organization uses multidisciplinary project teams that move across the organization on the customer's behalf to provide a total solution. This continuing trend means that project management is the future of organizational management.

The project management concept is based on cross-functional teams that are assembled to achieve a specific purpose, usually in a specific time and within a limited budget. These teams are temporary; once they achieve their objective, they are disbanded, and the team members assume traditional work or are assigned to yet another project. Because project teams cut across traditional functional lines, they are best suited to provide total customer solutions. Typically, one person is in charge of the team: the project manager or project leader.

Project management is fairly new in organizations. In the past, new products were developed by the staff of the functional organization. But with increasing pressure to get products to market, special project teams were formed; they also proved useful in developing systems solutions for customers. People in organizations suddenly found themselves working on many projects.

There seems to be general agreement that project management is a trend that will continue to accelerate. During workshops and consulting engagements with numerous participants, we find that more and more people, from administrative assistants up to CEOs, are doing project-based work.

The role of upper management is of paramount importance in developing a project-based organization. Such development involves a lot more than moving lines and boxes on an organization chart, sending a few managers out to training, and telling them to "do project management." The process of developing a project-based organization mirrors the desired new organization because the process is itself a project. It requires a vision of how the organization will function and what it will achieve. It requires that upper managers act as a team among themselves and with project managers to change the organization. It requires a change in behavior, as an organization is not a chart but rather the sum total of the behavior of the people who work in it. It also requires a plan and the participation of important stakeholders, such as customers.

A shift to projects cannot be accomplished simply by adding projects to department work because there are substantial differences between department and project work. For one, departments do not foster change; the hallmark of a good department is repeat processes or products, and good department management involves establishing procedures that allow the repeat work to be done as efficiently as possible. This is not conducive to doing something new because departments support the status quo—in fact, they *are* the status quo. Projects, in contrast, foster change and thus disturb the status quo.

Furthermore, departments normally are not cross-functional, whereas projects require a cross-functional view of the entire organization because the target of projects is often a system (such as payroll, customer profiles, customer interface, or a set of products) that is itself part of a larger system, or at least connected to some other system. For a project to be successful, its effects on all other systems must be considered. People skills in departments are more often focused on production rather than on developing processes to achieve unique new results. Tales of failures caused by unexpected consequences are legend in any new operation. It takes a total view of the organization to ensure successful projects, and this requires a cross-functional team. This wide view is normally not found in departments.

Also, departments are assumed to last forever, whereas projects have a limited life. Because projects are temporary, they are not seen as the department's "real work" and so are given low priority and not assigned the best people. This is a recipe for project failure.

Departments are also level conscious. Much of the power and leadership in departments depends on the level in the hierarchy. Projects require multilevel participation. The power should flow to the person who can get the job done, and this may often require that people work for someone below their level. This could be difficult to achieve in departments.

Organizations have found cross-functional project teams to be very effective for project work. For example, when Chrysler went to a platform team for its cab-forward design, it cut the new model development time from three and a half or four years down to only two years. In addition, the number of people necessary went from fifteen hundred to seven hundred. When PECO Energy attempted to refuel nuclear reactors using a departmental approach, it took 120 days. With a cross-functional team approach, PECO set a company, U.S., and world record for refueling time of just under 23 days in February 1995 ("Company Sets Industry Standard . . . ," 1996). Refining the team approach, they set another world record in October 1996, completing the refueling in 19 days and 10 hours. PECO officials attribute this achievement to two years of planning, superb coordination, and great teamwork. Examples like this are commonplace when organizations begin to take the project management approach seriously. Clearly the payoff is well worth the effort.

Toward the Project-Based Organization

In initial attempts to respond to the need for project management, many organizations attempted to integrate projects into a functional organization by using the matrix approach, in which functional managers (designated as FMs in Figure 1.2) control departments such as engineering and marketing while project managers (PMs) coordinate the work across functions.

But in general, the matrix organization tended to cause more problems than it solved. The major fault was that it was a marginal change—a mere modifica-

FIGURE 1.2. MATRIX ORGANIZATION.

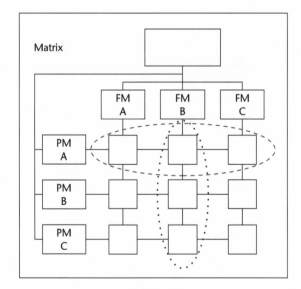

tion to the old hierarchical organization. This meant that many of upper management's assumptions were based on the functional organization or mechanistic model. As a result, many of the behaviors that were rewarded by upper management were actually counterproductive to successful projects. Project team members felt that organizational rewards favored departmental work and that working on projects was actually bad for their careers. Many people working in a matrix complained of being caught in a web of conflicting orders, conflicting priorities, and reward systems that did not match the stated organizational goals (see Figure 1.3). Effective behavioral change requires a change in the reward system, and this did not occur in many matrix organizations.

The use of a matrix for project management is a classic case of rewarding one behavior while hoping for another, that is, rewarding departmental work while hoping for project work. Although people were told that working for two bosses would be beneficial to their careers, experience proved to them that doing project work decreased their chances for promotion. Because they did not see project work as compatible with their personal interests, the project work suffered. The rewarded behaviors were those the organization wanted to discourage, and the desired behaviors were those that went unrewarded. Such organizational perversity is an example of the type described in Kerr's classic article, "On the Folly of Rewarding A While Hoping for B" ([1975] 1995; see Box 1.2).

Because the matrix approach represented only a marginal change, the typical problems of bureaucracy often appeared. In many cases, the money continued to reside in the departments, with projects having limited budgets. Project

FIGURE 1.3. CAUGHT IN A WEB.

BOX 1.2. Organizational Perversity.

Steven Kerr realized that individuals seek to know what activities will be rewarded by the organization and then carry them out, "often to the virtual exclusion of activities not rewarded." However, he found numerous organizations where the types of behavior rewarded are those that the rewarder is actually trying to discourage, even as the desired behavior is not being rewarded at all.

Kerr cites examples such as universities, where "society hopes that professors will not neglect their teaching responsibilities, but rewards them almost entirely for research and publications," as well as "sports teams [that] hope for teamwork but usually reward based on individual performance" and "business organizations [that] hope for performance but reward attendance." We have experienced organizations that say they want upper managers to oversee and mentor projects but reward them based on the number of people in their department. They are, in other words, organizationally perverse: their organization members say they want one behavior but reward activity that will ensure that it cannot be accomplished.

---

members were treated as second-class citizens. In addition, individual positions and promotions continued to reside in the departments, making those groups much more important for long-term career success. Even if projects were given budget authority, conflicts over priorities continued to arise. Rules were then needed to resolve conflicts, and these rules tended to accumulate. Whenever a mistake was made or a conflict noticed, a rule was made to prevent its recurrence. As a result, operational responsibility tended to drift upward, and conflict resolution required top management involvement. Finally, the rules began to guide behavior and became a concern in themselves. People acted with concern for the rules, not with concern for the success of the whole. This is classic bureaucracy in action.

The weakness of bureaucracy brings the tenets of the organic organization into focus. The organic organization is one in which everyone takes responsibility for the success of the whole. When this happens, the basic notion of regulating relations among people by separating them into specific predefined functions is abandoned. The challenge is to create a system where people enter into relations that are determined by problems rather than by structure (see Figure 1.4). In essence, people market their services to those projects inside the organization that need them and are capable of paying for those services.

FIGURE 1.4. ORGANIC ORGANIZATION:
A MARKET-BASED APPROACH TO PROJECTS.

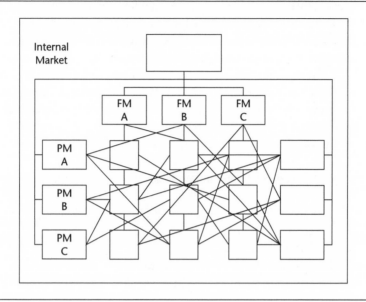

The tenets of such an organization are described in *The Post-Bureaucratic Organization* (Heckscher and Donnellon, 1994), in which the basic building block is considered to be the team. Consensus on action is reached not by positional power but by influence—the ability to persuade rather than to command. The ability to persuade is based on knowledge of the issues, commitment to shared goals, and proven past effectiveness. Each person in the group understands how his or her performance affects the overall strategy.

Ability to influence is based on trust, and trust is based on interdependence—an understanding that the fortunes of the whole depend on the performance of all participants. The empowered manager assesses the level of trust and agreement that exists with another person (Block, 1987) and plans an approach to that person that leverages the strengths of that relationship.

Highly effective people in this organization can influence without authority by using reciprocity as the basis for influence. People need to learn to exchange "currencies" (Cohen and Bradford, 1989) based on respective needs, leading to win-win situations. Communications need to be explicit and out in the open.

A strong emphasis on interdependence and strategy leads to a strong emphasis on organizational mission. In order to link individual contributions to the mission, there is increased emphasis on information about the organizational strategy and an attempt to clarify the relationship between individual jobs and the mission. This calls for a new type of information system where information linking individuals to the strategic plan is readily available.

Guidelines for action take the form of principles rather than rules. Principles are based on the reasons that certain behaviors contribute to the accomplishment of strategy. One important principle is a relatively open system of peer evaluation, so that people get a relatively detailed view of each other's strengths and weaknesses. This calls for a change in the evaluations and reward system. In addition, the organization of the future has no boundaries. There is far more tolerance for outsiders coming in and insiders going out. The boundary between the organization and its customers blurs and the boundaries between levels and departments within the organization disappear. In addition, the postbureaucratic organization eliminates the idea of permanence, where decisions are final. The emphasis is now on decision processes.

Because this type of structure is currently embodied in project teams, the organization of the future will be project based. Customers want to buy solutions, not standard products, and the organizational unit that can respond to this market is the customer-oriented project team. The team works to understand the customer's problems and what the team should achieve. With this understanding, the team can develop new solutions, perhaps ones that the customer had not even imagined. This requires a new relationship between the company and the customer: the customer becomes a vital part of the team.

Customer-driven teams abandon the level-consciousness prevalent in many functional organizations. Project leaders are appointed because of their expertise in running projects, not because they have attained a particular level in the organization. Because the ability to influence is not based on position, level-consciousness decreases. In addition, as there are fewer levels, position becomes less important. A team member may be one or two levels above the project manager on the organization chart but still report to the project manager for that project (as in Figure 1.4). Team members no longer think of themselves as members of a particular function but as members of a team that is doing something for the good of the entire organization. Several customers may become members of the team, as was the case on the Boeing 777 airliner project (King, 1992). Many team members may be from outside the organization, doing work on contract for that particular project. The project manager thus assembles the project team based on what is best for the project, not on what people the organization can spare.

Becton-Dickinson, an organization that embodies this trend, provides innovative technology and advanced solutions in flow cytometry systems (Stoy, 1996). In designing an organization to be more responsive to the needs of development programs, this company found that embedded functional management was delaying the cycle time. To help reduce cycle time, it eliminated functional managers and their departments. The important tasks of functional managers were put into focused groups, and a project management office was established to develop direction for project management in the new organization.

In the future, most organizations will consist of a smaller group of full-time employees and a large contractual fringe of individual contractors or strategic alliances that provide goods or services for given projects. In other words, the customer-based team properly comprises a small core of employees plus relationships with outside experts who work contractually for all or part of a project.

The new internal market organizations are based on areas of expertise and have profit and loss responsibility. Each area provides services to other areas in exchange for a fee. Rather than having their performance measured by how well they stick to a budget, these areas are measured according to how well they complete an internal project that helps the rest of the organization achieve its mission. In this way, everyone knows how their actions affect both profitability and the attainment of a mission that is stated in a strategic plan.

Moving to a project-based organization presents unique challenges to upper managers, as outlined by Wilson and others (1994):

• *The leader has little or no "position power."* The position power inherent in functional organizations has to change as the project-based organization is introduced. The team leader has little direct control over the career path of team members. Instead, team members require an independent career path over which they themselves have control and to which the project work can contribute. Developing such a scheme is similar to the development of individual retirement accounts, where the employer makes contributions but the individual has control of the fund. This type of scheme has been used in universities for years; it allows professors to move easily from place to place, taking their retirement account with them. Organizations need to make it easy for team members to move from project to project, taking their career path progress with them.

Asked by a gathering of project managers whether the project management skill set was transferable to other functions in HP, CEO Lew Platt (1994) replied, "I think if you learn the skills of project management that you can manage a project in manufacturing, or a project in IT, or a project in marketing just as easily as you can manage a project in development. The issues are different, but I think the basic skills are pretty much the same. . . . In these times, it is quite important that you actually do think about moving around from one function to another as a way of getting a fresh set of experiences, reigniting your interest in the job. . . . It's a tremendous growth experience."

Upper managers need to develop project managers and project management so that the project managers can lead based on influence rather than positional authority. Developing project managers and career paths is discussed in Chapter Seven.

• *Conflicts arise over team member time and resource requirements.* Thus, upper managers must have a good plan and work out priorities. Alternatively, internal market pricing may be used to allocate scarce resources—individuals or organizations pay with internal charge accounts, sometimes called location code dollars, for services they find valuable. Value-based pricing mechanisms are a feature of internal market-based organizations. Ideas for allocating resources are covered in Chapter Two.

• *Organizational boundaries are unclear.* Project management often requires quantum leaps in the level of cooperation among organizational units. If people see evidence that cooperation is not valued, then achieving cooperation is almost impossible. The alternatives to cooperation are turf wars and as-needed appeals to higher authorities, neither of which is beneficial in the long run. Upper management needs to create a structure where cooperation is rewarded. This is discussed in Chapters Two and Five.

• *Time and organizational pressures abound.* Upper management must be ready to support the best practices that allow reduction in cycle time. This includes developing a core team system, developing project goal statements, allowing time for project planning, not interfering with project operations, facilitating communication with customers, and supplying necessary resources. In addition, an adequate project time frame must be negotiated so that the team has a chance for a win. These topics are covered in more detail in Chapters Three and Four.

• *Team members do not know one another.* Effective project teams require unprecedented levels of trust and openness. The climate of trust and openness starts at the top. If upper managers are not trustworthy, truthful, and open with each other, there is little chance that project team members will be so with one another. Trust and openness are the antithesis of most bureaucratic organizations. Upper managers coming from a less trusting organization may have difficulty developing high levels of trust.

• *Team members are independent and self-motivated.* Because team members may not even work for the organization, project managers need to develop influence skills, and upper management must support that process.

All these challenges require that upper managers work together to develop a process aimed at encouraging new types of behavior. Members of the organization look to the upper managers for guidance in both strategy and behavior, and if there is a lack of integrity between what is said and what is done, skepticism rises and morale falls. How can upper managers expect good teamwork when they are fighting among themselves? Organizational change requires not just a concept of a new organization but the resolve to create it. If upper managers expect team members to change their behavior, they should be ready to change their own behavior as well. Sending people to project manager training is not enough. The shift to a project-based organization requires a concerted effort from all upper managers.

A Model of Organizational Change

The revitalization process model described by Wallace (1970) considers the time and processes necessary to change behavior. He uses this model to describe a society moving through a series of temporally overlapping but functionally distinct phases of change. Any group of people may be said to have a culture: a set of beliefs, values, norms, and practices that help the group solve its problems. Business organizations are groups of people and thus have a culture too; because this is so, the revitalization model can be used to describe the phases of change in organizational cultures. For changes in organizational culture to occur, behavioral changes in the people who make up the culture need to occur.

The steps to achieve actual change in behavior are difficult indeed. Few believe in the benefits of change until they actually experience them. Change agents often feel like the person described by Plato (see Box 1.3), particularly when their

---

BOX 1.3. Response to Change Agents.

[According to Plato's *Republic*] "human beings are like prisoners chained to the wall of a dark subterranean cave, where they can never turn around to see the light of a fire that is higher up and at a distance behind them. When objects outside the cave pass in front of the light, the prisoners mistake as real what are really shadows created on the wall. Only one who is freed from his chains and leaves the cave to enter the real world beyond can glimpse true reality. . . . Once he habituates himself to the light and comes to recognize the true cause of things, he would hold precious the clarity of this new understanding. . . . Were he be required to return to the cave and contend with the others in their usual activity of 'understanding' the shadows, he would likely only provoke their ridicule and be unable to persuade them that what they were perceiving was only a dim reflection of reality."

Source: Tarnus, 1991, p. 42.

visions of the future provoke ridicule. When new ideas provoke ridicule in an organization, it usually means that the people in it are not ready for change because they do not yet see the need. If upper managers start a change process before they really believe change is necessary, others will sense this lack of authenticity, and the process will fail. A change process is effective when the change leaders believe it is necessary and show the way to others. The revitalization process acknowledges this fact and describes the stages an organization goes through until the majority of its members are ready for change.

The stages of the revitalization process are shown in Figure 1.5. The basically successful organizations develop procedures that allow them to achieve a steady state such that the organizational system handles any problems that arise. But as the environment changes, continued use of the old procedures causes people to enter a period of individual stress. If this is allowed to continue, the organization falls into a period of cultural distortion, where the procedures cause many problems. However, enlightened upper managers can bypass that state and go directly to a period of revitalization, in which new procedures are adopted to match the problems in the new environment.

FIGURE 1.5. STAGES OF THE REVITALIZATION MODEL.

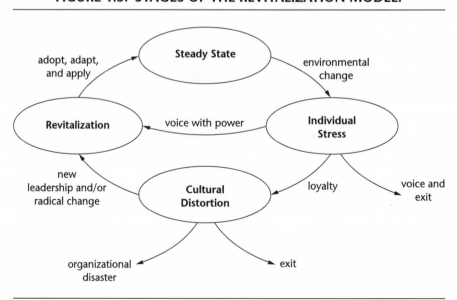

The Steady State

Every organization begins with a set of problems that need to be solved in order to carry on its business. (The case of early AT&T is a good example; see Box 1.4.) Successful organizations develop a culture—a set of beliefs, values, norms, and practices—that help the members of the organization solve these problems. This culture is embodied in a set of organizational rules that are passed on from one generation to the next. Application of these rules keeps the organization in a state of equilibrium. Each year looks much like the last, as the organization produces similar products through repeatable processes. The members of the organization become more and more efficient at applying the rules, and the organization thrives. This is the steady state, which we could equate to the mechanistic or functional model of organizations.

To keep an organization in the steady state, a control system is developed. Whenever outside disturbances threaten the equilibrium of the organization, the control system is capable of detecting and interpreting them and setting in motion practices that counteract them.

BOX 1.4. Procedures at AT&T.

Functional organizations were a necessary step in the evolution of organization design. Consider the American Telephone and Telegraph Company, a forerunner of today's AT&T, which was established on February 28, 1885. It was formed to operate long-distance telephone lines to interconnect local exchange areas of the Bell companies. Although it must have seemed incomprehensible in 1885, the plan was to extend those lines to connect "each and every city, town and place in the State of New York with one or more points in each and every other city, town or place in said state, and each and every other of the United States, and in Canada and Mexico . . . and by cable and other appropriate means with the rest of the known world" (Shooshan, 1984, p. 9).

Such a lofty goal required massive generation of and attention to standard procedures. Without each and every city, town, and place following the same procedures, there is no way the AT&T network could have been completed. The procedures helped to solve problems. After all, there was no way to call to discuss and fix connection problems until the phone was actually connected. So bureaucracy was created by necessity, allowing the next generation of organizations to emerge from it.

Control systems are both internal and external. The external control system attempts to regulate the environment in a way favorable to the organization, such as by gaining patents, monopolies, or other favorable government rulings. The internal control system regulates members' behavior and works to eliminate any threat to the smooth functioning of the organization. Organizations in the steady state are characterized by large and onerous control systems that, as we shall see, become their undoing.

During the steady state, the organization is usually successful and often able to affect its environment more than the environment is able to affect it. This is often due to some patent, monopoly, or new process the organization has developed that is not yet general knowledge. When this is so, there is little time pressure on projects; the control system acts to fend off the need for change. As a result, project management is not really necessary. Projects wend their way through the bureaucracy in due course.

For example, AT&T reached its steady state in the period 1934 through 1960 (Graham, 1985). By 1934, the Bell system had operating companies in most major American cities, and AT&T could proceed to tie them together and provide the dream of universal service. To provide this service, AT&T was given a telephone monopoly in the United States. Given the lack of competition, AT&T developed a steady, stable, predictable, and military-like culture that allowed the efficient realization of the goal. The antitrust cases brought against AT&T during this period were defeated.

The Period of Increased Individual Stress

Over time, the environment of an organization changes such that the existing culture is no longer appropriate to the problems it faces. When, for example, customers begin to demand new and different products and solutions, the assumptions on which the organizational culture was built become increasingly invalid. Following old procedures at such times begins to cause problems rather than solve them. Some individuals in the organization begin to realize that major changes are necessary, but they often go unheeded as others continue to find success using the old ways. During this phase, the organization continues to be successful—it may even experience its most successful period—so it is not surprising that many members of the firm do not see the need for change.

The problems are exacerbated because those who see the need for change and sound the alarm are often forced out of the organization (as Dagwood learns in Figure 1.6). In the process of exit, voice, or loyalty described by Hirschman (1970), people who see the need for change often leave the firm (exit) and join

FIGURE 1.6. EXITS.

Blondie

THERE ARE THOSE WHO SAID I SHOULD RETIRE

AND THOSE WHO SAID I'VE LOST TOUCH WITH TODAY'S TRENDS

AND HAVE YOU NOTICED?

HEH, HEH... *THOSE* AREN'T HERE ANYMORE

© Vic Lee. Reprinted with special permission of King Features Syndicate.

other organizations where the change has already been made or is being implemented—firms that are already in their period of revitalization.

An alternative to exiting is to voice strong opinions about the needed changes. This is often followed by exiting; as other members of the firm do not see the need for change, the advocate of it is likely to be accused of not being a team player. If the individual still does not want to exit, the final alternative is loyalty—succumbing to pressure and going along with the others. No change takes place; the fate of potential change agents during the period of increased individual stress is that they leave the organization or join the majority.

During this period, individual managers may see the need to improve project management in order to cut cycle time. The usual response is to send some engineers to training so they can learn the latest best practices. But when they return, they find they cannot practice the new ideas because others in the organization still see no need for it. They know that best practices require cooperation from all parts of the organization, and because they cannot practice what they know is best, they leave the organization (exit) or decide to ignore the practices (loyalty).

For example, in 1961, AT&T set up a school to teach customized sales. Managers who finished the course returned to find that noncustomized, mass sales were still what really counted in the organization. The frustration level was such that 85 percent of the graduates quit, and AT&T disbanded the school ("Corporate Culture," 1980). As a result, the best practices were never implemented. This is why sending individuals out for training but not supporting the new practices they bring back is so ineffective.

During the time of increased individual stress, the organization continues to decline as its practices become increasingly outmoded. If the leaders realize the need for change at this point and are ready to make them, they can skip directly to the period of revitalization and direct the change process themselves. This path is shown as "voice with power" in Figure 1.5. It is possible even for individuals to invoke the voice-with-power path if they are willing, have skill as change agents, learn how to communicate with upper management, and are able to "speak truth to power" (Graham and Englund, 1995; Englund, Graham, and Dinsmore, 2003). However, the leaders should realize that organizational forces are working against them, which is why organizations often fall into the next phase, cultural distortion, before meaningful changes occur.

AT&T experienced its period of increased individual stress from 1960 to 1974. By 1960, the goal of universal telephone service had been reached, so the AT&T monopoly was no longer necessary. Many competitors wanted to enter the telephone business, but AT&T fought them off in the courts. Between 1960 and 1970, however, it lost a number of legal battles, culminating in the "Above 890" decision—allowing telephone companies to use frequencies above 890 mega-hertz— that opened the way for microwave communication and competition in long-distance service (and brought us MCI). During this period, several attempts were made to make AT&T a marketing organization, but because the company's marketing organizations were structured in typical AT&T mode, they were never elevated above the operations department and thus were never effective. The process of using old structures for new applications is typical of the period of in-creased individual stress and is typically ineffective.

The Period of Cultural Distortion

In this period, old practices begin to cause more problems than they solve. The number of organizational inconsistencies becomes so great that people begin to suffer marked decreases in productivity. The organization may begin to lose money for the first time in its history.

During this phase, there may be a concerted and systematic effort to teach and implement best practices for project management. However, it is usually done only at the lower levels of the organization; upper managers do not change their behavior or do so only ever so slightly. In addition, typically no change in the re-ward system is made to support the new practices—indeed, the system usually continues to reward and support the old practices, and the people in the organi-zation experience the perversity of Kerr's folly ([1975] 1995). In effect, upper managers are systematically undermining the efforts of project managers. The project managers quickly discover that their efforts are not rewarded, so they leave, and things get worse in the organization.

The period of cultural distortion is usually accompanied by the failure of one or two large and highly visible projects. The response is often to find and fire one person, usually the project manager, who is thought to be obviously responsible for the failure. As indicated by Cohen and Gooch (1994; also see Box 1.5), however, this usually merely demonstrates a lack of understanding of the real causes of misfortune. In complex situations, such as large projects with many players, many conflicting stakeholders, and many different departments involved, failure is rarely due to one person's poor judgment. Firing a scapegoat may make upper managers feel good, but because it reflects no understanding of the true causes of failure, it certainly will be woefully inadequate in preventing future failure. So as heads roll, morale sinks and problems continue to get worse.

At this point, the members of the organization face a crisis. Things are so bad that they now realize radical changes must be made. Perhaps this phase is necessary to increase the upper managers' level of authenticity, for now when they say change is needed, they really mean it. Sometimes the needed changes are so radical that upper managers are unable to make them and the organization dies, or the organization installs new leadership. New leadership, if needed, will be most effective if it is brought in from outside the organization.

AT&T experienced its period of cultural distortion from 1974 to 1983. In 1974, the U.S. Justice Department filed suit, seeking to break the company up. The AT&T response was to fight it in the courts, a tried and true method. However, some AT&T employees saw the futility of fighting and began to establish some new patterns aimed at developing a competitive organization. To accomplish this, the marketing department was expanded, and many people were brought in from other organizations. By design, these people had different assumptions, values, and practices that often clashed with those of traditional Bell system managers. As the process continued, it became increasingly clear that the culture was internally distorted and the elements not harmoniously related. The group that wanted the monopoly maintained could not continue to exist alongside the group that wanted competition. Something had to give.

The Period of Revitalization

During this period, leaders are able to eliminate old practices and behaviors. When the organization gets to this point, things are so bad that its members usually bring in a new leader to make changes. The new leader installs a new behavioral code to bring company practices in line with today's problems. There are two phases to this period: establishing a new code for behavior and then adopting the code as the new organizational norm.

BOX 1.5. Causes of Misfortune.

Cohen and Gooch (1994) studied military misfortunes in an attempt to avoid them in the future. Much of the interest in similar studies of project management comes after a disaster on one or more projects. Part of the solution to a disastrous project is understanding what caused the disaster so it can be avoided in the future.

When military disaster happens, how can it be understood and explained? The "man on the dock" approach is common, which is the notion that disaster occurs because one person, typically the commander, commits unpardonable errors of judgment. But this assumes that the person in charge has control over all pertinent variables, which is not usually true. The modern commander is much more akin to the managing director of a large conglomerate; he is the head of a complex military operation, and as its size has increased, the business of war has developed an organizational dimension that can make mighty contributions to triumph or tragedy. In project management, not all failure can be laid at the project manager's feet. Often an organizational component is also important.

The "man on the couch" view says that failure is due to some collective way of thinking that blinds people to the correct actions. Cohen and Gooch argue, however, that if this were true, disaster would be much more common than it is, and the problem would be to explain the reasons for success. Because this is not the case, any collective way of thinking of military leaders is of limited use in explaining misfortune.

The "collective incompetence and the military mind" explanation says that simply living in and serving a hierarchical institution such as an army encourages and intensifies potentially disastrous habits of mind. However, analysis indicates that supposed collective incompetence is more a result of the reward system than of supposed deficiencies of the military mind. Cohen and Gooch recommend looking instead to the organizational systems within which such minds have to operate.

"Institutional failure" is another possible explanation. When the blame cannot be put on one person, it is often given to an entire institution, such as the U.S. Navy. However, knowing what the navy is does not explain how it works, and explaining failures requires knowing how it works. Thus, Cohen and Gooch say we must think of the armed forces not as institutions but as organizations.

They point to the interaction of people, systems, and organizations to explain failure. People cannot be put aside in explaining failure, but they respond to the organization and the characteristics of it that determine how tasks are approached, that shape decisions, and that affect the management of disaster. In addition, organizations have systems that sometimes go awry when failures in two or more components interact in unexpected ways. When this happens, people lose control of the system, and their response is often dictated by the organizational procedures. Examining this interaction of people, organizations, and systems is most fruitful in explaining misfortune.

The first phase begins with a new leader, often from outside the organization, who paints a picture of the new process that the organization must adopt in order to survive. This new code normally includes an increased emphasis on projects and satisfaction of customer expectations. The new code for behavior must then be communicated to all members of the organization. This communication is typically accompanied by a change in the organization's structure to help accomplish the objectives of the new code.

The second phase is directing the process of adapting the new code. People need to learn to discard old behavior patterns and adopt new ones. This phase involves training people in the new behavior and then directing the process of cultural transformation so that the new code becomes natural and routine.

The period of revitalization is often traumatic to members of the organization. If the process has followed its normal course through the period of cultural distortion, the organization is near collapse. Typically, the new leader brings in new upper managers, who trumpet a behavior code that is so radical that 30 to 50 percent of the organization members leave, in one way or another.

AT&T entered its period of revitalization in 1983 with the consent decree that separated the competitive aspects of the business from the remaining aspects of the Bell system. As of January 1, 1984, those who wanted free market competition could go with AT&T, and those who wanted monopoly could remain with the local Bell operating companies. This change was traumatic for those who went with AT&T, for it required implementation of entirely new ways of looking at the business. During the next ten years, AT&T laid off many employees and hired many new people who had never been exposed to the old Bell ways. The transformation continues.

Part of the reason for the turmoil at AT&T was that its managers did not make the necessary changes in 1970, during the period of individual stress. If they had, members of the organization could have spent time getting ready for the change rather than fighting it. When upper managers see the need for change during the period of individual stress, it can be accomplished more rationally and with much less upheaval. We feel that for most organizations, the time for the change to project-based organizations is now. This book is concerned with the rational process of developing an environment for successful projects.

The New Steady State

Here, the organization is again in harmony with its environment. This stage continues until new changes in the environment force the revitalization process to begin again.

The Successful Change Agent

Any successful change requires a successful change agent. History is replete with agents of change who were killed by the very individuals they were trying to help. As shown in the last section, part of a change agent's success is timing. People who offer advice during the period of individual stress are often unheeded, but those who offer the same advice during the period of revitalization are seen as heroes. This occurs because during the period of cultural distortion, more people begin to vividly see the need for change and to seek the very advice they previously shunned. To skip the period of cultural distortion, upper managers must act together as change agents and direct the change before distortion begins. According to Rogers (1983), successful change agents fill seven critical roles:

1. *They develop the need for change.* Change agents show others what the problems are and convince them that they can and must grapple with these problems in order to improve. The successful change agent leads the organization around the period of cultural distortion. After one or two project failures, the change agent argues that this is not just an aberration or the fault of a single project manager. Change agents take the lesson of Cohen and Gooch that failure is not usually caused by just one person but is the result of a combination of problems. Repeated failure is a systemic problem that needs to be tackled by the entire organization.

2. *They make others accept them as trustworthy and competent.* People must accept the messenger before they will accept the message. Upper managers must act with integrity and authenticity, or they will be seen as incompetent; if they "talk the talk" but do not "walk the walk," they will not be seen as trustworthy, and their attempts to bring about change will most likely fail. This has been the fate of many change processes.

3. *They diagnose problems from the perspective of their audience.* Successful change agents see problems from the project manager's point of view. If they regard the project manager as the culprit, the upper manager will never see the project manager's point of view. This indicates that the best project managers in the organization should be involved in the change process.

4. *They create the intent to change through motivation.* Lasting change cannot be dictated from a position of power; it comes from motivating people to solve their problems. Change that is seen as helping to solve the project manager's problems while contributing to the organization's welfare will be enthusiastically applied because the participants are motivated. Change that is seen as benefiting only upper management, however, will be resisted. The change agent motivates the entire

community by showing that the change benefits everyone. People readily adopt practices that are in their best interest.

5. *They work through others in translating intent into action.* A team of project managers who can translate the intent of the change into action is necessary. This is similar to the Project Management Initiative team at HP, discussed in Chapter Nine.

6. *They stabilize the adoption of innovation.* All too often, change leaves with the change agent. Upper managers may put in a set of procedures to help make project management more effective, but then their attention gets directed to other matters, and the changes often fade. An initiative team can outlast the change initiators and help stabilize the adoption of the innovation throughout the organization.

7. *They go out of business as change agents.* If all the previous steps have been successful, the need for the initial change agents vanishes. So should they.

The successful complete upper manager understands the influences that shape organizations, embraces the changes that are required for continued vitality, takes on the role and responsibilities of change agent, and works to develop the postbureaucratic organization through the project management function. If done right, the project management function of today will become the postbureaucratic organization of tomorrow.

Creating an Environment for Successful Organizations

Up to this point, we have outlined the components of an environment for successful projects. Now we need to look at a process for developing those components. Organizations attempting to change their environment in order to support projects report difficulty with the process. We find that the principal cause of the difficulty is that creating an environment for successful projects is not done in a vacuum. Rather, it is usually done within an existing organization. Normally, the existing organization is not a project organization, so creating an environment for projects within such an alien organization can be very difficult, and for several good reasons:

1. Concentrating on the environment is often seen as superfluous. The push is just to get the job done, and the environment is often ignored.
2. Projects are done differently from repeat process work, so the new environment that is created will seem strange to long-term organizational members. This indicates that all members of the organization need to be attuned to the new project environment.

3. Organizations do not install all the components that are suggested, so the resulting environment is not as supportive as it could be. It looks as if the pieces of the puzzle are put together in a dark room, and when the light comes on, they see that pieces are misshaped or missing. Nothing fits together as it should. This "book of reality" describes the current state, sometimes so depressingly that energy to change it is in short supply.

Let us look at how the components support one another to create a stronger environment.

For the first problem, it seems that concentrating on the environment for projects is seen as a rather nebulous and dubious endeavor. If the organization needs better projects, then it seems to be common sense to concentrate on project managers because they are the ones who make the project work. However, it was just such a concentration only on developing project managers that led to the realization of the need to concentrate first on the environment. Many organizations report that they began the change to a project-based organization by first sending project managers out for training. This led to frustration all around as the trained managers returned to find that they could not practice their skills in the current organizational environment. One common example is that project managers are trained that planning is important. However, they experience attitudes like "we don't have time for that planning stuff around here; we've got real work to do." It seems that many older organizational environments could not let the project management processes grow and develop. This experience is similar to a farmer who spends a lot of money for top-quality seed corn and throws it on ground that is hard and dry. Because the environment is not ready, the seed does not develop, and the corn does not grow, no matter how much money is invested in the seed. In this case, only changing the environment will lead to success. Thus, best organizational experiences indicate that concentrating on the environment is a necessary endeavor.

For the second problem, since projects will be done within an existing organization, concentrating on the change to project-based organizations means that everyone in the organization needs to be attuned and trained to support projects. This does not mean that everyone in the organization must be working on projects but rather that everyone must be knowledgeable in the way that projects work so that they can support projects when they can, or at least not hinder them. If this is not done, then project management develops as an island, remote and mysterious to other organizational members. This results in decreased trust and increased jealousy, attributes not conducive to project success. Other organizational members may inadvertently delay projects when in fact think they are supporting them. A successful environment encompasses the entire organization, not just the organization of project management.

For the third problem, a system of interlinking solutions is proposed to help develop the environment for project success. For the complete environment, all the components must be developed as each one affects the other, some in very subtle ways. Some people ask what happens if they do not do one or two pieces of the puzzle. To answer this, let us identify important links among the components.

The first component of a successful environment suggests that upper management teams work to develop strategic emphasis for projects. This upper management team represents the entire organization and reinforces the idea that the participation of the entire organization is necessary to create project success. If this is not done, there is a tendency for the organization to attempt too many projects, a well-known killer of project success. Another tendency will be for projects to be associated with departments and for the project portfolio to be heavily weighted toward the most powerful departments instead of being developed based on total organizational needs. When this happens, project teamwork suffers as team members align more closely with departmental goals than with project goals. When teamwork suffers, project success suffers. Not doing this component can scuttle the entire endeavor.

The second component of project success involves changing some behaviors of upper managers. We continually find upper managers who feel that project management is a thing apart from them, and so they believe that their behavior has little to do with project failure. Organizational reality is quite different. Sometimes even a casual remark by an upper manager negates much good work developed in the first component. For example, the entire organization can be behind project management and the project can be well selected, but if one manager tells the people in this department that project work is unimportant and that departmental work is all that counts, this attitude has serious detrimental effects on the project team and on project success. In addition, upper managers inadvertently scuttle projects while they practice what was considered to be good management behavior in preproject organizations, such as an overemphasis on budget while value-adding aspects of the project get lost. This often overlooked but important component affects project team behavior immensely. Since projects are done differently, upper managers need to manage differently.

The next component of the successful environment considers support of the all-important project core team. The experience in most organizations is that project teams are essential for successful projects, particularly those that endeavor to produce a system solution. Given this experience, the idea of supporting project teams has become nearly universally accepted. The idea of a core team is to have a small group of people represent the most important departments that will stick with the project from the beginning to the end. The idea of supporting a core team is also gaining in management acceptance. However, many organizations that began their quest for project management by installing core teams experience frustration unless they developed the previous two components first. The success of this component is dependent on the previous ones. Unless organizational members are fully behind the project team idea and receive training about project management, they may find it difficult working as members of project teams. Unless the project has been chosen by an upper management team, the right departments may not be represented on the core team. Unless upper managers are properly aware of their influence on project success, they may resort to inappropriate behaviors such as pulling people off the core team to handle other departmental emergencies. Any one of these behaviors can kill the success of the core team, and the lack of a core team can kill the success of the project. This is a key component in the environment for successful projects and is highly dependent on others mentioned so far.

The fourth component involves creating an organization to support the project management endeavor. The usual mistake here is to try to implant a project management system into a functional organization. Of course successful projects require cross-departmental teams. The need for these teams to work well together indicates that a functional organization is the antithesis of what is needed for project organization. The essay on the causes of misfortune in Box 1.5 points to the interaction among people, systems, and organization. The wrong organization helps cause failure and can negate the successes of the first three components. Thus, this component is essential to support and solidify the benefits gained from the first three components.

The fifth component involves creating a project management information system, which is absolutely essential to support the previous four components. Many organizational information systems build on the standards of the accounting system, which is ordinarily defined for a functional organization. In such organizations, information flows up and down the hierarchy and not across and among those hierarchical components. In a project management organization, information flow across components becomes just as important as, if not more important than, the flow up and down the hierarchy. Reporting progress to a diverse set of project stakeholders is extremely important. Since all organizational members will now be involved with or at least be aware of project management, they all need to know the status of the projects. The project management information system informs members of the organization on progress, the upper management team on how their selected projects are doing, upper managers individually on how their projects are doing (an important aspect to relieve their anxiety and help stop them from making mistakes), and project team members of progress and problems. Information generally helps hold a project-based organization together. This component thus reinforces and solidifies the previous four.

The sixth component deals with project manager selection and development. Only now do we come to the activity that caused all the problems in the first place: focusing effort only on training project managers. Many organizations began their quest for project management by sending some people out for training. They found that unless many of the previous components were in place in the organization, the newly trained project managers were not able to practice what they were taught. With the previous components in place, the organization becomes hungry for project manager skills and is ready to support rather than thwart the practice of these skills. Developing project managers is currently far different from when project management first began. At that time, the main emphasis was on technical skills. However, given the developments around the first five components of a successful environment, it becomes clear that modern project managers need to master behavioral, business, and organizational skills along with technical skills. This component now takes its place as of paramount importance in a project-based organization because the first five components require a cadre of trained project managers in order to fulfill its mission.

The seventh component deals with a learning organization, which is necessary to proceed into the future. Without adaptive and generative learning, a project-based organization cannot build on its strengths, streamline its processes, and innovate new ways to be competitive. Taking the time to reflect on what is happening in the organization and asking true inquiry questions provide the nutrients or fuel to adopt, adapt, and apply the other components. A cycle of knowledge creation enables a project-based organization to put ideas, theories, and best practices into methods and tools. The results and practical knowledge that evolve are recycled into modified theories and practices, and so on and so forth. This flow is the lifeblood for the processes, structures, and behaviors that feed and change all other components. The *new story* that gets experienced by all members, partners, and customers is about vitality and flexibility. It replaces the *old story*, where information is hoarded, negative politics abound, and projects do not meet expectations.

The eighth component is a home base where a concerted effort exists to drive the continuous improvement of project management across the organization. This is typically a project office, which many organizations find necessary in order to help create a successful environment and help guide the organizational change necessary to sustain that environment. That a project or program management office is the best vehicle to lead and implement organizational change follows from the premise that:

- projects create the means to generate profits and shareholder value,
- projects change how organizations work,
- each project manager becomes a change agent,
- effective change agents focus on human factors and follow proven processes,
- theory, best practices, and case studies support these factors, and
- these elements require a driving force to make them happen.

With a project office, the other pieces in our puzzle or components now have a clearly visible head and body that guide all efforts to optimize project success.

The Compleat Upper Manager

The successful complete upper manager:

- Understands the need for better project management in organizations of the future.
- Understands that the role of upper management is critical in developing successful project management practices throughout the organization.
- Understands that past organizational forms, such as the functional or matrix organization, may be detrimental to developing good project practices.
- Embraces the tenets of the postbureaucratic organization that emphasize teams, consensus action, empowerment, trust, and open communication.
- Believes in and behaves with integrity and authenticity as a requirement for leading others.
- Leads an organization through the revitalization process.
- Acts with other upper managers as a team of change agents to develop an environment that supports project management.
- Fits together all pieces of the puzzle required to create an environment for a successful organization.

Strategic emphasis for projects

Creating an Environment for Successful Projects

Creating an Environment for Successful Projects

Creating an Environment for Successful Projects

Creating an Environment for Successful Projects

Creating an Environment for Successful Projects

Creating an Environment for Successful Projects

The first section of this chapter, on project management without strategic emphasis, outlines how organizations get into such a circumstance, why projects are often not aligned with strategy, and what problems this nonalignment causes.

Next, a section on linking projects to strategy suggests a process in which upper management is advised to operate as a team to review and select projects that best support organizational strategy. Given that programs should support strategy, a process for project selection and prioritization and an example of a process tool for prioritizing projects are given, including the notions that upper management must understand their possible roles in the process and also limit the number of projects undertaken in order to focus on those with the best payoffs.

To help the chosen projects succeed, the upper management team needs to develop a system that supports multiple project management; various such systems include motivating interdepartmental cooperation and developing project sponsorship.

CHAPTER TWO

GIVING PROJECTS A STRATEGIC EMPHASIS

Where there is no vision, the people perish.

PROVERBS 29:18

O ne of the most vocal complaints of project managers is that projects seem to appear almost randomly. They are often concerned that the projects they work on seem unlinked to a coherent strategy and that upper managers are unaware of the total number and scope of projects being undertaken. As a result, some people feel they are working at cross purposes, on too many unneeded projects, and on too many projects generally. Giving projects a strategic emphasis helps resolve such feelings and is the first move toward creating an environment for successful projects. This chapter covers the steps necessary for giving projects a strategic emphasis.

The Importance of Strategic Emphasis

Raychem, DuPont, Pacific Bell, and many other companies use a product-and-cycle-time excellence process for redesigning their new product development processes (McGrath, 1996). Within this process is a structure that enables the management team to manage the set of projects as well as individual projects. The structure includes a cross-functional management team known as the product action committee. This team sets up the criteria for getting projects into the product life cycle and for passing each gate in the cycle. The team makes decisions during monthly meetings about which projects to continue to sponsor, which to add, and which to discontinue based on information about promised milestones, ongoing costs, and resources. A particular strength of this process is its provision for prioritizing and consciously choosing which projects to keep on the list based on ongoing realistic assessment of available resources.

A council concept is one mechanism used at Hewlett-Packard (HP) to establish a strategic direction for projects spanning organizational boundaries. A council may be permanent or temporary, assembled to solve strategic issues. As a result, a council will typically involve upper managers. Usually its role is to set direction, manage multiple projects or a set of projects, and aid in cross-organizational issue resolution.

Getting upper managers to work together is often a challenge. In trying to get a computer system into the commercial market using a new generation of computer architecture, HP project and upper managers once found themselves running a large number of design teams that had no clear process for coordinating the many pieces into the whole system. Engineers were working at full speed on pieces they understood well, but it was not clear what the complete system would include. Managers of individual projects had little accountability for specifications or schedules, so it was difficult to predict when the system would be ready for market release; yet the CEO was personally overseeing much of the activity and was often touted in the outside press as betting the company on this new computer architecture.

A key defining event helped turn this situation around. One upper manager declared, "I want a system specification and schedule. Each project needs to provide this data to program management. You will then be held accountable to meet these specifications and schedules." Until then, the labs had provided limited or questionable data to program management; when requests came in, the response to make the questioner go away was often to simply "give the kid a number" (see the discussion in Chapter Eight and in Graham, 1989) without much effort at detail or accuracy. But after that upper manager's defining statement, behaviors abruptly changed. Held accountable to make and meet their commitments to specifications and schedules, managers knew they had to provide accurate and realistic data. More cooperation occurred across the organization as people nailed down dependencies and deliverables in order to plan their work, the program management office became empowered to implement project management because it had upper management support, and the program achieved notable progress.

The initial problem in this scenario need not have happened, but bureaucratic structures often get in the way of developing solutions. Departmental turf wars come about from a win-lose mentality where winning budget in one department means losing budget in another. When this is so, departmental cooperation is not rewarded and projects suffer accordingly. The members of such organizations need to shift from the win-lose mentality to one of cooperation.

Developing cooperation requires that upper managers take a systems approach to projects: this means look at projects as a system of interrelated activities that combine to achieve a common goal. The common goal usually is to fulfill the overall strategy of the organization. The interrelationship of projects normally comes from the set of people working on them; usually all projects draw from one resource pool, so they interrelate as they share the same resources. Thus, the system of projects is itself a project, with the smaller projects being the activities that lead to the larger project (organizational) goal. Accomplishing this goal is the aim of enterprise project management (Dinsmore, 1998). Failure means a haphazard organization that drifts with each opportunity or individual desires. It also leads to organizations that violate business fundamentals and mimic the dot.bomb crash.

Project Management Without Strategic Emphasis

One would think that rational people could avoid problems. After all, don't you usually act rationally? Why is it that actions by others often appear irrational? The problem may be with group interactions where each person's behavior is rational but the collective interaction is not. (See Box 2.1 for a mathematical example.)

BOX 2.1. Rationality and Groups.

How might teams of rational individuals produce irrational results? Because they sometimes do, it seems that the team approach may cause more problems than it solves. But before abandoning the approach, we should first understand how rational groups can produce irrational results.

One of the tenets of rationality is that if a person must choose between A, B, and C, and prefers A over B ($A > B$) and B over C ($B > C$), then A is also assumed to be preferred over C ($A > C$ and $A > B > C$).

Suppose that each member of a three-person team—X, Y, and Z—has rationally ranked A, B, and C, with these results:

$$X: A > B > C$$
$$Y: B > C > A$$
$$Z: C > A > B$$

Now assume the team makes pairwise comparisons to determine the final choice. The vote between A and B yields $A > B$ by a two-thirds majority of X and Z. The vote between B and C yields $B > C$ by a two-thirds majority of X and Y. With $A > B$ and $B > C$, one assumes $A > C$. But the vote comparing A and C yields $C > A$ by a two-thirds majority of Y and Z. Thus, the vote of rational people yields the irrational result $A > B > C > A$.

Managing projects, formerly the specialty of a few people, has grown into a central part of the upper management role. Today it seems that just about everybody is working on projects. However, the growth of projects has not been well planned in most organizations; indeed, in many cases, it seems to have been a random process. Projects in organizations that do not emphasize strategic project management have a typical growth sequence (see Figure 2.1).

First, project creep sets in. Today, projects emerge as the standard organizational response to change. In the past, staff functions existed to deal with new products and procedures, but organizational downsizing has eliminated or altered many of these. New ideas are now embodied in projects and staffed by people from the affected departments. Without even realizing it, everyone seems to be doing more and more projects—and in addition to their normal departmental work. This is a piecemeal response to the changes in the environment that were outlined in Chapter One. A full analysis of the situation is usually not considered at this time. People begin to experience stress as a result of the change in procedures and increased workload. Because there is no process in place for project selection, far too many projects are initiated; people find themselves working on a variety of unrelated projects, often far too many at one time. The projects are usually not successful, adding to the strain.

Second, project leaders are appointed by accident. Ad hoc project teams find it difficult to achieve anything new without a project leader, so management finds a victim—someone to appoint as leader who can be blamed for failure—and the problem is considered solved. This person is often the one with the most technical knowledge about the problems facing the team; if, for example, the project is to develop a computer system, the best computer systems analyst most likely becomes the project leader.

This is a well-known source of problems, akin to making the best schoolteacher the school principal. It often ends in disaster. Just as teaching skills are not the same as administrative skills, technical problem-solving skills do not necessarily translate to project management skills. Projects run by those with none but technical skills will often be technical marvels that do not solve organizational

FIGURE 2.1. PROJECTS WITHOUT STRATEGIC EMPHASIS.

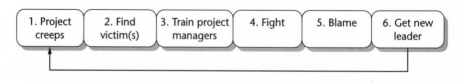

problems, and thus they fail. More failures mean increased organizational and individual stress.

Third, upper management recognizes the problem of accidental project leaders and sends them all out for training. Training people in the skills of project management is one step toward solving the project management problem. However, it is only a first step and by itself may cause more problems than it solves. Often, freshly trained project leaders find it difficult to implement what they have learned because their training goes against organizational norms of behavior. They may struggle to explain the terminology and trade-offs of project management to upper managers who are not versed in these topics. Upper managers become frustrated because they think the training was not successful; the project leaders become frustrated because they cannot do the things that will lead to success. All concerned experience increased stress. The organization is bordering on the period of cultural distortion, where the culture begins to cause more problems than it solves.

This is not a systems approach to the problem, and it does not address the strategic aspects of projects. A big mistake after the training decision is concentrating first on project managers themselves. There is often a rush to obtain people with good project management skills or to train them in the art, but having good project managers does not guarantee good projects. Certainly it is difficult to have good projects without good project managers, but many more factors must combine to yield successful projects (as illustrated by the "man on the dock" example in Box 1.5).

Fourth, with a lack of upper management support and direction, project leaders begin to fight among themselves. At this point, the accidental project managers probably have little knowledge of how their projects fit the organizational strategy. They often lack priorities, access to needed people, cooperation from department directors, and the ability to keep members on their project teams. Projects are working at cross purposes.

Partly this is because projects cross departmental lines (see Box 2.2). Project X may be top priority in department A but low priority in department B. Thus, X's manager may find it difficult to get people from department B to work on the project; they will tend to heed directions more from their department manager than from the project manager. Unless an organization has some mechanism for facilitating interdepartmental cooperation, there is little chance that the project manager will solve such a problem.

This is cultural distortion in full bloom. People begin to retreat into their departments, as they do not want to be associated with losing projects. The usual departmental defenses are mounted. Old animosities resurface as accusations and finger pointing mount. The power of the bureaucracy reasserts itself.

Fifth, frustration mounts, and the project management process is blamed for the failure. Upper management often decides that it should reorganize to solve

---

BOX 2.2. An Example of Uncoordinated Projects.

For the project priority process to be effective across an organization, the priorities must be the same in all departments involved. All too often, it seems that upper managers identify an entire list of projects as "top priority." In a typical example, I (Robert Graham) was consulting for a financial services firm where three departments—marketing, systems, and operations—were involved in issuing credit cards. The upper managers created a list of ten important projects but did not set overall priorities. Each department then created its own prioritized list, but the priorities were not uniform across departments. It became difficult for project teams to function when a particular project was first priority in marketing, fifth priority in systems, and last priority in operations. Animosities developed in the project team when some members did not give that project the attention that other members expected. To solve this problem, a process was developed to coordinate priorities across departments. Upper managers can avoid such problems and help project teams be effective by setting priorities that are uniform across the organization.

---

the problem, but this favored response rarely works. The project management problems are put on hold while everyone attends to the reorganization. Projects languish, and people are reorganized into new groups.

Sixth is the point of revitalization, where a new leader could step in and install a new code of behavior that supports project management. It is possible for a champion to take the lead, using voice with power (as described in Chapter One); however, it is more likely that the upper managers need to become fully involved. They need to act as a team to select projects based on organizational strategy, make certain all departments support prioritizing the projects at the same levels, ensure that people do not work on too many projects, allocate adequate resources to each project, and provide upper management sponsorship for all projects. That is the ideal; unfortunately, the reality is often a return to step 1.

A systems approach is just good project management. It requires that the upper management team act like a project team. The members of the team need to devote some of their departmental resources toward the achievement of overall organizational goals. The systems approach begins by linking projects to strategy.

Linking Projects to Organizational Strategy

There are many reasons to develop a strong link between projects and organization strategy. People on projects are looking for direction, particularly when setting project goals. What is the project to accomplish? To answer, it helps to know what the organization as a whole is trying to accomplish. When project leaders understand organizational strategy, they have a guide for action. It helps them define the goals of the project.

This is where the upper management team can best exert strong leadership—leadership based not on coercion or control but on values, which involves articulating a vision of the organizational strategy, linking the project to the vision, and then serving the values of the project managers by helping them achieve the project goals. Value-based leadership serves the needs of the followers—in this case, the project managers.

Understanding the strategy is also motivational. A typical question at the beginning of a project is, "Why are we doing this?" The project manager needs a solid and motivational answer. "We're doing it to achieve return on investment" does not normally stir people's souls into action. People are more motivated by opportunities to learn, develop new products, use new tools or technologies, open new markets, or help others in new ways. Understanding how their project is a part of a total system to achieve these types of goals will help motivate them.

A clear link to strategy helps develop interproject cooperation. Projects do not normally have dedicated resources; they must share them with other projects and with the departments. To make intelligent choices about the use of the resource pool, project managers must know what other projects exist, what resources they require, what the relative priority of all other projects is, and how all the projects add up to a coherent strategy.

Project managers need to know that they are not alone—that others require resources too. They should understand that their requests for resources are evaluated in the light of a greater vision to achieve organizational goals. Similarly, their performance is evaluated in the light of the contribution they make in achieving the overall organizational vision, not just their performance on a single project. This spirit of cooperation is more likely to be achieved if they feel they are part of a larger project—part of a project team that is implementing a strategy. They will be more cooperative with other projects when they see the needs of their project in the light of the needs of the entire organization.

The Problem of Suboptimization

The basic reason for wanting cooperation and communication is to avoid the problem of suboptimization, which occurs when individual project managers try to optimize their own projects by hoarding resources and otherwise acting independently of all other projects. Such behavior may make one project more successful, but usually at the expense of others: one part of the system is optimized, but the total system is suboptimized. Box 2.3 contains a historical example of the phenomenon.

> ## BOX 2.3. The Tragedy of the Commons.
>
> The "tragedy of the commons," first identified by ecologist Garrett Hardin (1968), describes a situation where people make decisions that maximize their individual benefit but in so doing collectively destroy the whole.
>
> In many parts of the world, common grazing areas existed historically in small towns. Originally, all people could bring their sheep to graze on these commons, as they were called. But as farmers increased the size of their herds, less and less grazing area was available to others, whose herds were also growing. Eventually the commons were overgrazed. Each individual made decisions in his or her best personal interest, but the commons, and the common interest, were destroyed.
>
> The tragedy of the commons shows what happens when participants of a common system do not take into consideration the effect of their individual decisions on the system as a whole.

The first step in the fight against suboptimization and for the implementation of strategic emphasis is for all participants to understand the total system. They need to know the total number of projects in the system, the goal of each project, the goal of the system, and the other participants. The upper management team needs to take the lead in defining the project management system for all participants.

The next step is for participants to understand that the common resource pool will be managed by the upper management committee or program management office. This means that upper managers allocate resources based on a rational assessment of what is best for the entire organization—a major change for organizations where the "squeaky wheel" allocation system formerly predominated. The combination of individual knowledge of the system and the existence of a body to manage the common resource pool should eliminate the resource allocation problem.

To make all this work, there needs to be a means of communication among system participants, one that allows open and rapid communication between and within all levels of the project management system. All project managers need to know what other project managers are doing so they can know what effect their decisions have on others and on the system as a whole. Upper managers need to know the current resource allocations across all projects, and the projects' status, so they can make rational resource decisions. (This is addressed in more detail in Chapter Six.)

Any lack of upper management teamwork reverberates throughout the organization. If upper managers cannot act in unison, there is little hope that the rest of the organization can do it for them. Any lack of upper management cooperation will surely be reflected in the behavior of project teams, and there is little chance that project managers alone can resolve the problems that arise.

Examples of Upper Management Teamwork

Box 2.4 presents one example of how upper managers worked together to support a project. Another example, also at HP, is a cross-organizational council that was pulled together expressly for resolving issues concerning the input/output (I/O) architecture for a new line of computer systems. The processor architecture was solid, but portions of the I/O were either vague, broken, or undefined. Hundreds of technical issues were logged against the system architecture by developers who encountered problems. Individual project teams were optimizing solutions to fit their objectives (organizational suboptimization). Meanwhile, the overall architecture was at risk of becoming a mess.

One project manager (a champion) took the initiative to convene an upper managerial council to do something about the growing problems. The council accepted ownership of the task of resolving the problems. It authorized groups of engineers to study, propose, review, and accept solutions to the problems, first establishing a set of priorities and constraints to guide the groups. The council of managers met at least once a month to review progress and make changes. When several issues bogged down, the council authorized an escalation path to two of the managers who would listen to the arguments and make decisions. Because of the tremendous impact on time to market of projects dependent on the outcome of the study groups, the council kept appropriate pressure on making progress. At the end of the resolution phase, it enthusiastically supported a celebration party for the hard work contributed by hundreds of engineers. The group manager wrote personal letters of appreciation to all participants. They listened to recommendations from a retrospective analysis of the issue resolution activities and took action on suggested improvements, applying them to subsequent projects that were initiated to resolve additional issues. Over time, the process improved dramatically, and the anxiety of this group lessened.

These examples indicate how upper management teamwork has a vast and important influence on project success. We strongly suggest that organizations begin by developing councils to work with project managers and implement strategy. These councils or boards exercise leadership by articulating a vision, discussing it with the project managers, asking them their concerns about and needs for implementing the strategy, listening carefully to them, and showing them respect so

---

BOX 2.4. Upper Managers Working as a Team.

As a program manager at HP, I (Randall Englund) was asked to head a task force updating a hardware system product life cycle for a computer division. The life cycle defines a structured framework of checkpoints and checklists for all functional areas from "lust to dust"—from the inception of a new product idea, through development, out to the market, and on to final discontinuance. The division manager wanted only one life cycle to be used by all participants on all projects. This was to be linked to the phase review process that coordinated the development of complex computer systems among multiple divisions and provided a reporting path to senior management. Common terminology and consistent expectations had to be developed and agreed on.

The organizational structure at the time consisted of five R&D managers within the division who worked on different hardware platforms for different market segments. There were two marketing departments in separate divisions, manufacturing in a separate division, and support in a separate division.

Each organization provided a person to work on the task force. Early drafts received ample feedback from people whom the upper managers asked to review the document. To get support for the life cycle proposal we developed, I went to all the R&D managers to personally elicit their concerns and support. I then went before the R&D council that meets regularly to decide issues of common concern. After working through a large number of issues voiced by each member, the council agreed to adopt the modified life cycle. Other task force members similarly got explicit support from their managers to support the life cycle. I then went before the division manager and his staff for a "ribbon cutting" and launching of the new life cycle. The division manager asked, "Are you sure you got the full support of all R&D managers?" I could answer in the affirmative because there was upper management support for the project, all managers cooperated in the development process, thorough reviews were conducted, and adjustments were made based on the feedback. This process, which culminated in explicit commitment by the whole management team, led to full adoption of this life cycle for all projects. It continues to work well today.

---

that they become engaged in the process. In this way, upper managers and project managers develop the joint vision so necessary for implementation of strategy.

A Process for Project Selection and Prioritization

Once the upper management team is established, they can develop a process to select projects that will achieve organizational strategy. In addition, these projects need to have a consistent priority across the departments. This involves several steps, as shown in Figure 2.2 and elaborated on next.

FIGURE 2.2. AN APPROACH TO SELECTING PROJECTS.

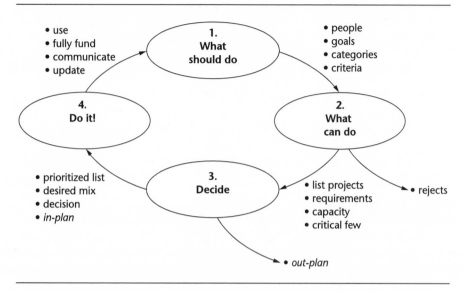

What to Do and How to Know When You Are Doing It

First, identify who is leading the management team for project selection. A bit of time spent here to put together a strong team can pay dividends later by getting the up-front involvement of the people who will be affected by the decisions that will be made. Take care not to overlook any key but not so visible players who later may speak up and jeopardize the plan. This team may consist solely of upper managers or may include project managers, a general manager, and possibly a customer. Include representation of those who can best address the key opportunities and risks facing the organization. The leader needs to get explicit commitment from all these people to participate actively in the process and to use the resulting plan when making decisions.

The team begins by listing all projects proposed and under way in the organization. Many times this step is a revelation in itself—"I didn't realize we had so many projects going on" is a common comment. The intent is to survey the field of work and begin the organizing effort, so avoid going into detailed discussion about specific projects at this point. Put all projects on one master list (with sublists if necessary) so there is visibility across the organization.

Group the projects into "buckets" that will later make it easier to facilitate a decision-making process. Wheelwright and Clark (1992b; also see Box 2.5) suggest using grids where the axes are the extent of product change and the extent of process change. Some organizations use market segments. The benefit to this is that seeing all projects and possible projects on a continuum allows checking for completeness, gaps, opportunities, and compliance with strategy. This might also be a good time to encourage creative thinking about new ways to organize the work. Use creative discussion sessions to capture ideas about core competences, competitive advantage, and the like to determine a set of buckets most effective for the organization. For example, the buckets might be the following:

- Evolutionary or derivative—sustaining, incremental, enhancing
- Platform—next generation, highly leveraged
- Revolutionary or breakthrough—new core product, process, or business

The team needs to clarify or develop the goals that the set of projects should reach with regard to organizational strategy. Then start aligning each project with its contribution to the strategy. Elaborate scoring methods are often devised that later provide a means to compare projects. Some organizations use narratives to describe how each project contributes to the vision; others use numerical scores based on predefined descriptions. The discussions at this stage center around the organization's purpose, vision, and mission. It is also helpful to set thresholds or limits for projects that help to screen out projects so that later prioritization efforts

---

BOX 2.5. A Case Study at HP.

Wheelwright and Clark's model (1995) provides a means for mapping a product family into platform classifications by their degree of product and process change. An after-the-fact evaluation shows the evolution of products from a computer peripherals division at Hewlett-Packard (see Figure 2.3). The original product from the first platform, A, and later an entirely new platform, L, were breakthrough developments. The original platform spawned four derivative products, B to E. Economic success from these products, especially E, fueled subsequent platform and enhancement projects F to I. K replaced F and G while J was still under development; its commercial success drove the need for major changes in marketing. When J reached the market, it made all preceding products obsolete. L targeted a new high-end marketplace and serves as a base platform for other extensions (Benton, 1995). Although the upper managers did not have access to this complete map when they initiated product development, the mapping process is nevertheless valuable as a means to study successful strategies and to plan future strategies.

FIGURE 2.3. SEQUENCE OF NEW PRODUCT INTRODUCTIONS AT HP.

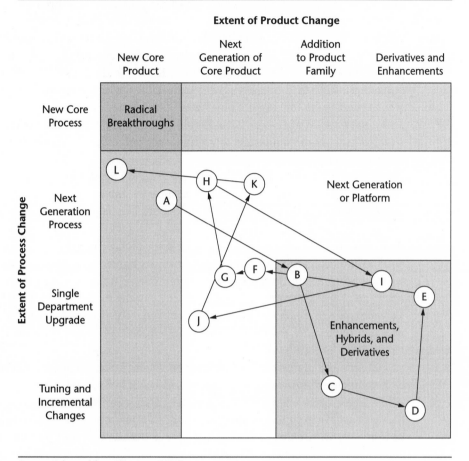

Source: Adapted from Benton, 1995.

can focus on fewer projects. Cooper, Edgett, and Kleinschmidt (2001) provide additional approaches to maximize the value of a portfolio, achieve a balanced portfolio, and develop a strong link to strategy.

Within each bucket, determine what criteria will be used to assess the "goodness"—quality or best fit—of choices for the plan. Teams often discuss projects before agreeing on criteria; reversing the order is much more effective. Several books on R&D project selection (Martino, 1995; Turtle, 1994; Westney, 1992) provide a robust set of criteria for consideration. Most important is to identify the criteria that are of greatest significance to the organization. The role of each criterion is to help compare projects, not specify them. Select criteria that can measurably compare how projects support the organizational strategy with ratings such as High, Medium, and Low.

It is not necessary to constrain the process by using the same criteria across all buckets of projects. Consider using different criteria for different buckets and possibly for different stages in the life cycle. Kumar and others (1996) document research showing that the most significant variable for initial screening of projects is the extent to which "project objectives fit the organization's global corporate philosophy and strategy" (p. 279). Other factors, such as available science and technology, become significant only during the commercial evaluation stage of the product life cycle.

Writing a thorough description of each criterion helps ensure understanding of the intent and expectations of data that must be supplied to fulfill it. One team of three or four people reported spending a full five days working solely on the criteria they were to use for decision making. And this was only the beginning; they next involved customers in the same discussion before reaching consensus and beginning to evaluate choices. An "aha!" occurred when people found they were wrong to assume that everyone meant the same thing by such terms as *packaging;* some used wider definitions than others, and the misunderstanding surfaced only through group discussion. Asked if the selection process ever failed the team, its leader replied, "If the results didn't make sense, it was usually because the criteria weren't well defined."

Criteria that deserve to be singled out for more attention are those related to core competences. A core competence is the collective know-how of an organization that gives it a competitive advantage. This know-how represents learning that is driven by business strategy and built through a process of continual improvement and enhancement that may span a decade or longer. Usually a core competence is thought of as an organizational ability. For example, a medical systems business may have the core competence to build software that is reliable enough to use in applications critical to life. Core competences may also integrate a number of components and skills, such as when a professional services business integrates its abilities to identify customer needs and create specialized software into a package for one customer's environment. Because a core competence provides potential access to a wide variety of markets and is difficult for competitors to imitate, a project selection process benefits greatly from identifying a clear set of competences and having the means to assess how potential projects use them.

Before moving to the next step, the team should establish the relative importance of all buckets and criteria. Assign weighting factors for each bucket and for each criterion within each bucket. This is a matter of "weighting, not gating"; all criteria are important but some more so than others. Examples of these criteria and weightings appear in Englund and Graham (1999) and Englund, Graham, and Dinsmore (2003). Weighting factors become extremely important when adjusting the portfolio to match new strategic imperatives. Criteria may stay the same but weightings are adjusted up or down to match their revised importance.

What the Organization Can Do

The next step for the team is to gather data on all projects. Use similar factors when possible to describe each project to help the comparison process. Engage people in dialogue to get agreement on the major characteristics for each project. This is a time to ask basic questions about product and project types and how they contribute to a diversified set of projects. The person consolidating the data as well as each member of the team should challenge the data instead of accepting assumptions that may have been put together casually. When putting cost figures together, consider using activity-based costing models instead of traditional models based only on parts, direct labor, and overhead. Activity-based costing includes the communications, relationship-building, and indirect labor costs that are usually required to make a project successful.

Using a funnel concept (see Figure 2.4), the team can constantly apply screening criteria to reduce the number of projects that will be analyzed in detail. Identify existing projects that can be canceled because their resource consumption exceeds initial expectations, costs of materials are higher than expected, or a competitive entry to the market has changed the rules of the game. The screening process should help eliminate projects that were conceived based on old paradigms about the business. The team can save discussion time by identifying projects that must be done or that require simple go/no-go decisions, such as legal, personnel, or environmental projects that should fall right through the screens and into the allocation process. Can project deliverables be obtained from a supplier or subcontractor rather than internally? The team needs to constantly test project proposals for alignment with organizational goals.

The next part of gathering data is to estimate the time and resources required for each potential and existing project. Then the team identifies the resource capacity both within and outside the organization that will be available to do projects. Use realistic numbers for resource availability, taking into account other demands on people's time. This step is often overlooked, resulting in massive overbooking of resources with a whole host of attendant problems.

All the actions in this step of the process are intended to screen many possible projects to find the critical few. The team may take a path through multiple screens or take multiple passes through screens with different criteria to come up with a short list of viable projects.

FIGURE 2.4. FUNNEL FOR SCREENING CHOICES.

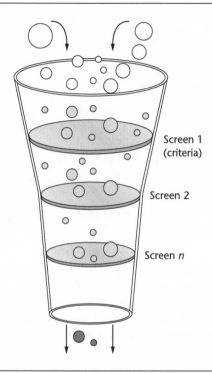

Note: Bubble size corresponds to project size.

Source: Drawn by Randall Englund.

Decide on Projects

The next step is to compare estimated resource requirements with available resources. A spreadsheet is useful to depict allocation of resources according to project priority (see Figure 2.5). Document all supportive data using terms that can be compared across projects.

The team can now prioritize remaining projects. Focus on project benefits before costs so that the merits of each project get full consideration. Later, include costs to determine the greatest value for the money. Compute overall return from the set of projects, not from individual projects, because some projects may have greater strategic value than monetary value. Requiring every project to promise a high financial return is a sure-fire way to diminish cooperation across an organization. For example, a computer system division may depend on an interface card from the networks division to produce a whole product. But if the networks

FIGURE 2.5. SAMPLE RESOURCE ALLOCATION PLAN.

FMY R&D FY Resource Allocation Plan

Project Description	Skill	Resource Requirements FY				Skill	Resource Capacity FY			
		Q1	Q2	Q3	Q4		Q1	Q2	Q3	Q4
						A Initial Resources				
						Design	8	8	7	7
						Electrical	15	14	13	13
						Thermo	10	10	11	11
						Mechanic	6	6	6	6
						TOTAL	39	38	37	37
		B				C Remaining Resources				
1 Dynamic Adding	Design	3	3	3	3	Design	5	5	4	4
Device (DAD)	Electrical	9	9	9	9	Electrical	6	5	4	4
	Thermo	5	5	6	6	Thermo	5	5	5	5
	Mechanic	4	4	4	4	Mechanic	2	2	2	2
	TOTAL	21	21	22	22	TOTAL	18	17	15	15
2 Mini Optical	Design	4	4	3	3	Design	1	1	1	1
Model (MOM)	Electrical	4	4	4	4	Electrical	2	1	0	0
	Thermo	3	3	3	3	Thermo	2	2	2	2
	Mechanic	1	1	2	2	Mechanic	1	1	0	0
	TOTAL	12	12	12	12	TOTAL	6	5	3	3
3 Supersaturated	Design	1	1	1	1	Design	0	0	0	0
Observation	Electrical	2	1	0	0	Electrical	0	0	0	0
Node (SON)	Thermo	2	2	2	2	Thermo	0	0	0	0

Note: Allocation of resources comparing capacity (starting top right) with requirements (middle), leaving the remaining resources (right): $A - B = C$.

division has other priorities, it may not commit to developing the card. Such situations require the prioritization process to happen higher in the organization. Also recognize that some future projects must be funded early in order to ensure a revenue stream when current projects taper off.

Using previously agreed-on criteria and weighting factors, the team can compare each project with every other one and repeat the process for each criterion. (See the discussion and example later in this chapter about using an analytic hierarchy process to facilitate this step.) Consider using software to compute results. The objective is to come up with an ordered list of projects.

Finally, the team is ready to decide which projects to pursue. Ask what the organization should do, not what you can do. Especially in high-tech industries, people are often tempted to include a new technology without being sure that customers are interested or will get value from the investment. Some people lack the stamina to deal with the details of implementation and so are ready to jump to a new solution at the slightest glimmer of hope from the latest technology. This is a recipe for disaster. Also, be careful to balance the important projects rather than giving in to urgent but not so important demands.

Be prepared to do fewer projects and to commit complete resources required by projects that are selected. Decide on a mix of projects consistent with business strategy, such as 50 percent platform projects, 20 percent derivative projects, 10 percent breakthrough projects, and 10 percent partnerships. Note that these total only 90 percent; taking a lesson from financial portfolio management, diversify the set of projects by investing in some speculative projects. The team may not be sure which markets or technologies will grow, so buy an "option" and make a small investment to investigate the possibilities. It is also important to leave a small percentage of development capacity uncommitted to take advantage of unexpected opportunities and to deal with crises when they arise (see the discussion later in this chapter on queuing theory).

After completing this process, record projects that are fully funded in an aggregate project plan (in-plan). In a separate section or another document, list projects for future consideration (out-plan). The plan of record (POR) is both a process and a tool that many organizations use to keep track of the total list of projects. It lists all projects under way or under consideration by the entity. If a project is funded and has resources assigned, it has achieved in-plan status. Projects below the cut-off line of available resources or that have not yet achieved priority status are on the out-plan. Project managers describe one benefit of the POR process as identifying gaps between required and actual resources. For flexible changes, the process gets all people into the communications loop. If people want to add something, management has to decide what should be deleted. The process helps two divisions that have to work together to agree on one prioritized list instead of two. The process uses direct electronic connections for bottom-up entry of projects and resources by all project managers into a centralized administration point.

One tool used to communicate and keep track of programs offered by a corporate internal market program is program sheets. One page per optional program provides a high-level summary of what the program is, the results expected, and when results will be available. The customers for the programs are internal operating divisions. The program sheets are distributed to them during targeting cycles, or during "road shows" at which programs are presented and discussed. The divisions can then choose to participate in funding the programs if they find value in them.

Do It! Complete the Process

No job is complete until it is acted on. The team needs to evangelize all others in the organization to use the aggregate project plan to guide people who plan work, make decisions, and execute projects.

The team or the responsible upper managers need to enforce the plan by staffing projects according to it. Match people skills to project categories to tap their strengths and areas for contribution. With a process in place that lays out all possible projects, the organization is in a position to use staffing assignments to motivate and train people on big-picture business needs. It is helpful for a list of projects to be made available such that individuals can indicate their interest in participating in one or more.

The same people who develop the plan are also the ones who can best update it periodically, perhaps quarterly or as changes occur. View the plan as a living document that accurately reflects current realities. An on-line shared database is especially effective to gather data directly from project managers about resources needed for each project. This system can be used both to gather data when developing the plan and to update it.

Analytic Hierarchy Process as a Decision-Making Tool

One tool that can assist in the decision-making process is the analytic hierarchy process (AHP; Saaty, 1990). Because of the interactions among the multitude of factors affecting a complex decision, it is essential to identify the important factors and determine the degree to which they affect each other before a clear decision can be made. The AHP helps structure a complex situation, identify its criteria and other intangible or concrete factors, measure the interactions among them, and synthesize all the information to obtain priorities. The priorities can then be used in a benefit-to-cost determination to decide which projects to select. The method offers a test of the consistency of judgments and helps test the compatibility of potential projects with established ones. The AHP organizes feelings and intuition alongside logic in a structured approach to decision making—helpful in complex situations where it is difficult to comprehend multiple variables together. An individual or team focuses on one criterion at a time and applies it step by step across alternatives.

The British Columbia Ferry Corporation of Canada, a provincial crown corporation that provides passenger and vehicle ferry service to forty-two ports of call throughout coastal British Columbia, uses AHP and software in the selection of products, suppliers, and consultants. AHP helps in determining the best source for fuel; contracting professional services such as banking, insurance brokers, and ship designers; evaluating major computer systems; selecting service providers such as grocery suppliers and vending and video game companies; hiring consultants; and evaluating various product offerings. Using the tool with interdepartmental teams makes decisions more readily accepted, as each member of the team participates in the decision-making process.

The U.S. Navy uses AHP to determine factors driving the selection of electronic equipment for submarines. By using AHP to analyze factors critical to submarine missions along with alternative solutions, the navy highlights critical issues and reduces the time needed to make equipment selections. Rockwell International Space Systems uses AHP for criteria weighting, utility functions, and sensitivity analysis on projects including development of new space launch vehicles, surveillance satellites, and architecture studies. The closed-loop process allows teams to understand what is most important to the client (Expert Choice, 1996).

The heart of AHP is a pairwise comparison of each element with every other, repeating the process at each level of a hierarchy. For our purposes, the elements are either criteria or projects. The process is as follows:

1. Define the goal desired for the organization's set of projects.
2. Structure a hierarchy listing criteria under the goal and possible projects under the criteria (see Figure 2.6). A criterion may have subcriteria. Determine the weighting for each criterion.
3. Construct a matrix comparing the relative contribution of each project with each other project for each criterion in the next higher level. Use a scale such as that in Table 2.1 to indicate relative contribution. If a project does not contribute more than the one it is being compared against for that criterion, enter a reciprocal number (see Figure 2.7).
4. Obtain all judgments required to develop the matrix in step 3. Multiple judgments can be synthesized by using their geometric mean.
5. Repeat these steps for all levels in the hierarchy.
6. Compute the priorities for the projects, possibly using a computer and matrix algebra (see Saaty, 1990).

For example, say a group of upper managers get together to choose the best new projects for the product family. More choices are available than the organization has the capacity to support. The first task is to identify which criteria to enter into the decision-making process. After give-and-take discussion, it is decided that the criteria are price, key specifications, channel of distribution, and technology risk.

FIGURE 2.6. A HIERARCHY OF GOAL, WEIGHTED CRITERIA, AND PROJECTS.

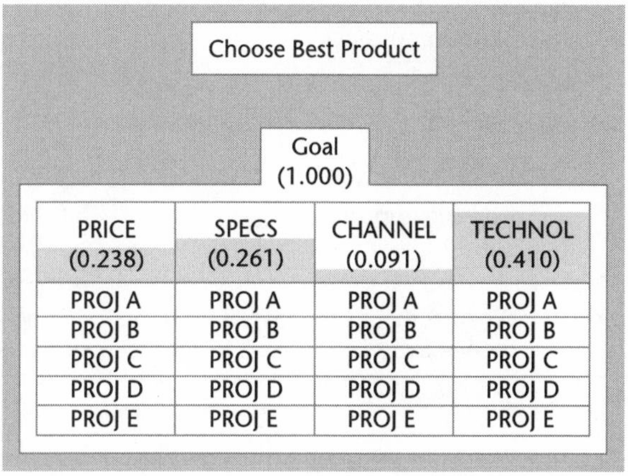

| | Choose Best Product | | |

| | Goal (1.000) | | |

PRICE (0.238)	SPECS (0.261)	CHANNEL (0.091)	TECHNOL (0.410)
PROJ A	PROJ A	PROJ A	PROJ A
PROJ B	PROJ B	PROJ B	PROJ B
PROJ C	PROJ C	PROJ C	PROJ C
PROJ D	PROJ D	PROJ D	PROJ D
PROJ E	PROJ E	PROJ E	PROJ E

Next, the criteria are ranked according to priority by making pairwise comparisons between them. Which is the more desirable criterion and by how much: A price range or key specifications? Channel of distribution or key specifications? Technology risk or price range? These questions are asked about all possible pairs.

If five projects (A to E) are contending for the top new product slots as in Figure 2.7, compare project A with each of the others on the first criterion, price. In the row for project C, for example, the team determines that project A is strongly preferred to C, so the cell gets a 1/6. However, project C contributes moderately more than project B, so that cell gets a 2. Project C compared to itself gets a 1. Log the answers in a grid similar to Figure 2.7 using the scale from Table 2.1. Rate the project along the side compared to the project across the top; if the side project is preferred over the top project, put a number in the appropriate cell depending on the degree of preference. If the top project is preferred to the side project, invert the number.

Complete the comparison of each project with each other one for the price criterion (see Figure 2.8). The priority value for each project is obtained by multiplying its priority score from Figure 2.7 with the weighting factor for the criterion (0.238 for price). Then move to the next criterion (specification) and repeat the process. Do the same for the other two criteria. The result is a series of four boxes. The priority scores within each box are compared to the other boxes using

TABLE 2.1. A Scale for Pairwise Comparisons.

Intensity of Importance	Definition	Explanation
1	Equal importance	Two elements contribute equally to the property
5	Essential or strong importance	Experience and judgment strongly favor one element over another
9	Extreme importance	The evidence favoring one element over another is of the highest possible order of affirmation
Reciprocals	When activity *I* compared to *j* is assigned one of the above numbers, then activity *j* compared to *I* is assigned its reciprocal	

FIGURE 2.7. MATRIX OF PAIRWISE COMPARISONS.

Project	A	B	C	D	E	Priority
A	1	7	6	4	2	.45
B	$\frac{1}{7}$	1	$\frac{1}{2}$	$\frac{1}{3}$	$\frac{1}{5}$	.05
C	$\frac{1}{6}$	2	1	$\frac{1}{3}$	$\frac{1}{4}$	.07
D	$\frac{1}{4}$	3	3	1	$\frac{1}{3}$	.14
E	$\frac{1}{2}$	5	4	3	1	.28

Note: Rows A through E represent a comparison of each project with each other project for one criterion. The "Priority" column is a calculated result of the comparisons; a higher number represents a higher priority for that project.

the rank-order scoring decided on initially for the criterion. The outcome is one ordered list inclusive of all projects and all criteria. The team then reviews the list for consistency and decides how to proceed.

A detailed explanation for computing the priority scores and the final rank-ordering list according to Saaty is quite complex, involving eigenvalues and eigenvectors, so it is much easier to get a software package that does the computations. As an alternative, a spreadsheet could be constructed to normalize the numbers.

FIGURE 2.8. A HIERARCHY SHOWING
PRIORITIZED RESULTS FOR ONE CRITERION.

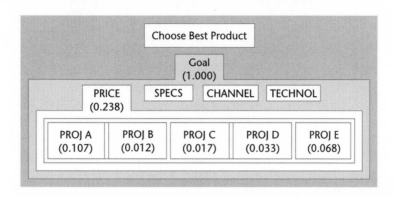

This process appears complex and analytical but is easy when a software tool handles the computations and the management team concentrates on the comparisons. It is thorough in guiding the team to consider all criteria, both emotional and logical, and to apply them to all projects. The software tool ("Expert Choice," 2000) also pinpoints the inconsistencies recorded by the team and prompts further discussion to justify the scoring, make adjustments, or correct data entry errors.

Frame (1994) offers an alternative "poor man's hierarchy." He puts selection criteria along the side as well as across the top of a grid. If the criterion on the side is preferred to the one on the top, put a 1 in the cell. If the criterion on top is preferred, put a 0 in the cell. Diagonals are blanked out where criteria would be compared to themselves. Below the diagonal, put the opposite value from corresponding cells above the diagonal. Then add up the numbers across the rows to get total scores, which provide a rank order. One team modified this process to replace the 1s and 0s with an actual count of how people voted in each pairwise comparison of alternatives. Again, they added up the rows and normalized the results for a priority order.

One of us has used a simple version of the pairwise comparison process to select a speaker for a conference. A colleague recommended three speakers very highly, but there was a slot for only one. Asked to compare speaker A with B, the colleague chose A. Comparing A with C, he again chose A. Comparing B with C, he chose B. His answers clearly revealed that A was the preference and B was the preferred alternative.

Now for a reality check. The previous process is thorough and integrates objective and subjective data, but when all is said and done, people often throw out the results and make a different decision. Sometimes the reason is a hunch, an instinct, or simply a desire to try something different. Sometimes people have a pet project and use the process to justify its existence, or another hidden agenda may be at play—perhaps the need to maneuver among colleagues, trading projects for favors. Politics at this stage cannot be ignored and are not likely to just disappear. It is imperative for individuals to become skilled in the political process. Over the long run, however, organizations that follow a process similar to the one described will increase their odds of success because teams of people following a systematic process and using convincing data to support their arguments will produce better results than individuals. Their projects will have more visibility, and the quality of dialogue and decision making will improve.

Pipeline Management

The previous discussion focuses on determining the best mix of projects in the portfolio. It does not address how projects progress and interact throughout their development. A typical problem is overcommitted resources, which results in fewer projects getting completed or achieving their goals. John Harris and Jonathan McKay (McGrath, 1996) ask, "What specifically needs to be done to get the desired mix of projects to market?" (p. 136). They offer a pipeline management framework (see Figure 2.9).

All three of these activities need to be in place and synchronized continually as projects progress through their life cycles:

- Strategic balancing sets priorities among opportunities and adjusts organizational capabilities to deliver new products.
- Pipeline loading adds visibility and fine-tunes resource deployment throughout both the plan of record decision-making process and the project execution stages.
- Aligning functional delivery ensures that functional managers maximize rather than suboptimize the flow of projects.

Especially during pipeline loading, projects are reviewed in consideration with other projects, not in isolation. The objective is to actively manage the entry and exit of projects from the plan of record into the pipeline and seamlessly handle midcourse corrections. Data-handling tools are necessary (but do not replace management responsibility) to analyze project priorities, understand resource and skill set loads, and perform pipeline analysis. This holistic view continually strives to balance realistic project requirements and ongoing development capacity. Effective

FIGURE 2.9. A PIPELINE MANAGEMENT FRAMEWORK.

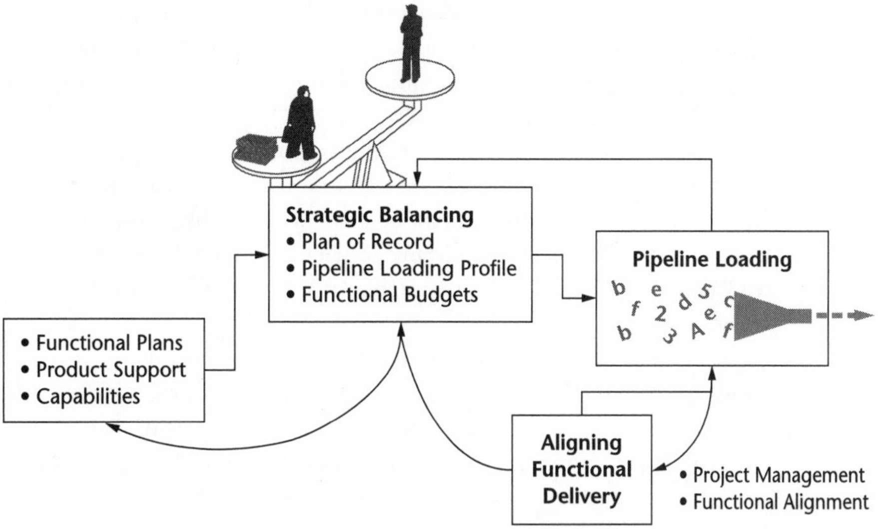

Strategic Balancing
- Plan of Record
- Pipeline Loading Profile
- Functional Budgets

Pipeline Loading

- Functional Plans
- Product Support
- Capabilities

Aligning Functional Delivery

- Project Management
- Functional Alignment

Source: Adapted from Harris and McKay in McGrath (1996).

project management performance contributes heavily to the predictability of project schedules and resource requirements and, thus, the success of the portfolio.

The Importance of Upper Management Teams in Creating a Project Environment

It is easy to underestimate the importance of the role of upper management teamwork in choosing projects that are aligned with organizational strategy. If this is not done well, it affects all other components of the project environment.

The upper management team represents the entire organization. For projects to be successful, they need to be supported by everyone in the organization. There was a time when projects were done mainly in departments—usually a group of engineers doing something who probably did not, and probably did not want to, interact with other members of the organization. Unfortunately, the days of the clandestine project team are over, as other members of the organization are usually necessary to make a project outcome successful. The first step in gaining overall organizational support is to have the project selected by a team of upper managers who represent the entire organization. When this happens, no one feels left out and no one feels that he or she was not consulted, so there is a better chance that people will support the projects selected. When upper managers can say, "I was there; I know why this project was selected, I know how it links to overall strategy, so I know why we should support it," the chances for overall organizational support increase drastically.

Having an upper management team decreases the chances that the project will be seen as aligned with any particular department. When projects are aligned with a particular department, one hears expressions like, "Oh, that's the systems project," or, "That's an engineering project." Support begins to wane as people say, "We're in the marketing department! Why should we work on that systems project?"

Having an upper management team also decreases the chances that subsequent upper management decisions will work against project success. In a sense, the upper management team works as a check on upper management behavior. Individual upper managers will be less likely to make changes unilaterally when they know the result will be reviewed by the upper management team.

The workings of an upper management team can have enormous beneficial effects on the project team itself. The basic rule is "as above so below." That is, much of the dissension on project management teams is actually caused by disagreements in the upper management area. If project team members feel that their managers do not think the project is important, then there is little chance that they will give their best effort. This means that for optimal team functioning, the project manager has to spend time motivating recalcitrant project members. This takes time and potentially contributes to project failure. Team motivation and development is strengthened when the upper managers of all team members agree on the importance of the project.

Organizing for project management will probably require some sort of reorganization. An upper management team closely involved with selecting and monitoring project success could well be more supportive of making organizational changes, such as appointing a chief project officer, as a part of creating a successful project management environment. One manager involved in creating a successful environment observed that "implementing resource management/ pipeline management and portfolio management engages the functional managers, thus causing them to be more tightly integrated into the change."

Upper management project teams that span the organization will better understand and support the need for a project management information system that spans the entire organization. The team could also realize that project management skills are uniquely different and support the effort necessary to choose and develop effective project managers. They will also understand the benefits of becoming a learning organization and then perhaps call for a project office to lead the change and develop the environment for a project-based organization. Thus, we see that the project management team is critically important to help develop all other components of the environment for project success.

Potential Problems in the Project Selection Process

In Homer's epic Greek poem *The Odyssey*, after Odysseus and his sailors recover from her spell and transformation process, goddess Circe (daughter of the sun god Helios) warns about the dangers that lie ahead on the journey home from Troy. Men who pass near the island of the Sirens get charmed by the sweet song of the siren creatures and never return. Heeding Circe's instructions, Odysseus saves himself by ropes binding him to his ship. Later, the god and musician Orpheus vanquished the Sirens with a more beautiful and compelling song; the Sirens lost their power and turned to stone.

Organizations operate under the spell of finance. Transformations occur when they reorganize or implement new processes. The lure of numbers or new technology easily leads teams astray. A call to death may occur in the disguise of an alluring promise—the Sirens are not strange creatures of the sea but familiar institutions of the world of money (Korten, 1999). A call to life brings us back to the beauty of natural systems. Recognize that project portfolio management is not just about numbers. Forecasts are inherently fictitious and can be manipulated to suit any scenario. An analytical process presents itself as real. However, the management team cannot relieve itself of the obligation to stay involved, think, and make appropriate adjustments. Developing a statement of shared values and guiding principles early in the process binds the team together and helps balance their approach and outcome.

A recurring observation about organizational life, particularly life in a hierarchy, goes that fame and glory are allocated individually and not collectively. That is, all the trappings of organizational life—bigger office, larger budget, increased power—are based on what individuals do in their departments and not on what they do on teams. Because of this tendency, a fallacy appears in the idea that upper managers will cooperate together to truly choose projects that best benefit the entire organization. There will always be the tendency for individual managers to guide the selection of projects in a way that best benefits their own individual departments. Of course, these projects will be dressed up to look as if they are being promoted for the common good when in fact they are being promoted for the individual good. There are several ways to do this in any organization, so the upper management team should be on the lookout for maneuvers. Successful military commanders never actually want to engage in battle; rather, they want to maneuver their forces in such a way that other sides feel they will be defeated and thus leave the field. In these cases, maneuvers are actually the key to success rather than the reality of the situations. In project prioritization cases, look out for these maneuvers:

1. *Promote your category.* Pick the category that best supports your position, and lobby for that category to be given the highest weight. For example, the engineering department argues that without new product development, the organization will die. Organizational survival is normally the top priority on everyone's list, so the group may unwittingly give new product development a higher weight than necessary.

2. *Promote your criteria.* Argue for evaluation criteria that best support your position. For example, sales often have a greater impact on return on investment than do engineering costs. By pushing return on investment as the top criterion for success, the marketing department makes itself appear more important, and thus worthy of a larger budget.

3. *Cook the books.* We have often been involved in creating data in order to support the cause of one organizational unit or another (see "Getting Reliable Data," Box 8.1). This practice is much more common than was previously thought. As this edition is being written, the newspapers are daily exposing yet another organization that has falsified data in order to look good. An entire auditing firm disappeared due to its involvement in a much-publicized book-cooking scheme. The old adage that "figures don't lie but liars figure" seems particularly applicable in the situation. The upper management team needs to study carefully and validate the sources of data they use.

4. *Maneuver.* Most management decisions are actually made in the hallway, not in the meeting room. People who make it to upper management ranks have demonstrated a high degree of organizational savvy, which typically involves such classic maneuver tactics as lobbying, pulling rank, cutting deals for future votes on another's favorite project, and bait and switch. It is not surprising to see managers resort to these tactics if that means they get to keep their favorite projects.

These tactics happen because people rarely check when the project is done to see if expectations were met. By the time the project is done, the people who made the decision usually no longer occupy the roles they did when the decisions were made. This is why decisions can be made on career management, self-aggrandizement, and ego gratification: they know they will not be there when the final reckoning comes due. Because of this, the final reckoning is seldom made, often because no one calls for it. Thus, installing some sort of reckoning to see if the assumptions were met becomes an essential ingredient to make the system work.

Unfortunately, this task is very difficult to do in most organizations. The project takes too long, or new competitors arrive, or there is a technological breakthrough, or the customer redefines project objectives. Therefore, devise a set of interim measures. One reason that project costs are often measured so diligently is that this is an interim measure with the assumption that when costs are kept in check, future success has increased probability. The same is true for the time the project takes. However, these measures should be seen as only interim, and the organization should work to measure actual benefit of the project outcome. With these data, maneuvering becomes more difficult but certainly not impossible.

Multiple Project Management

Once the strategic projects are chosen, upper managers are advised to support and fully fund them through staffing decisions that make managing multiple projects easier. The main problems with multiple projects are caused by interdependencies—that is, the need to share resources. If one project requires a resource more than expected, it affects other projects requiring that resource. Such problems grow exponentially as the number of projects rises. Decisions made on one project affect the others, a fact often not realized until the projects are near completion.

Axiomatically, projects of high quality and minimum duration involve dedicated full-time people located together and led by a project manager who has full control over the resources needed. When this is the case, the project is independent of others and thus not affected by resource decisions. This ideal is seldom possible in business organizations, but it can serve as a goal. Upper management can institute guidelines to approach the ideal and promote factors that minimize cross-project dependencies. A practical tactic is to create a time-based interface chart of all projects, listing deliverables and dependencies and skill sets required. Update this chart regularly, and use it as a status report and troubleshooting tool. Three other overarching actions that might be taken are decreasing the number of projects, reducing the number of projects per person, and building in extra capacity.

Decreasing the Number of Projects

Fewer projects generally mean less disruption to the resource pool, even if the number of changes per project stays the same. Many upper managers think fewer projects also mean fewer new products, but this is not necessarily the case; projects that do enter the pipeline are more likely to actually get done and in a more timely manner. That leaves more time for other projects. In other words, although fewer projects are being worked on at any given moment, the same number, if not more, are completed over a given longer span.

Wheelwright and Clark (1992a) cite an organization that reduced the number of its development projects from thirty to eleven: "The changes led to some impressive gains . . . as commercial development productivity improved by a factor of three. Fewer products meant more actual work got done, and more work meant more products" (p. 78). Addressing an HP project management conference, executive vice president Rick Belluzzo (1996a) emphasized the need to focus on doing fewer projects, especially those that are large and complex: "We have to be very selective. You can manage cross-organizational complex programs if you don't have very many. If you have a lot of them with our culture, it just won't work. First of all, we need to pick those opportunities very, very selectively. We need to then manage them aggressively across the company. That means have joint teams work together, strong project management and leadership, constant reviews, a framework, a vision, a strong owner—all those things that make a program and project successful."

Reducing the Number of Projects per Person

No one should work on more than three projects at a time; core team members and project managers should work on no more than two at once. Reducing the number helps increase productivity on projects and cuts cycle time. For team members to switch focus to another project and reacquaint themselves with it takes time—perhaps a full day per switch. If people have five projects and must attend to each for one day every week, the likely consequences are obvious. With computer systems, it is called *thrashing:* it occurs when time-sharing systems get so caught up in vigorous context switching between programs that no real work gets done. The same thing happens to people engaged in too many projects.

What single change might best improve project management? Tom DeMarco (1995) states that people are frustrated by too much task switching and recommends that if upper management does only one thing to change its management system, it should act to let people work on one project only, one task at a time.

Reducing the number of projects per person also reduces the number of projects disrupted when someone leaves the organization. When key people leave, the projects they were working on experience delays as new people are brought up to speed; the fewer projects they worked on, the fewer are delayed.

Building in Extra Capacity

It is well known that systems experience problems and delays whenever system utilization approaches 100 percent (see Figure 2.10 and Box 2.6). Highways and airports, for example, can usually handle traffic easily up to about 90 percent of capacity. Above that, they begin to experience massive congestion and delays.

BOX 2.6. System Utilization Formulas.

From queuing theory, the study of waiting in line, come some interesting dynamics of system utilization. Let λ represent the demand on a system, usually specified as the arrival rate to be serviced. Let μ represent the service rate of the system. The system utilization, ρ, is given as λ/μ. When $\rho = 1$, the system is 100 percent utilized—apparently a manager's dream. But a second look says otherwise. The average time waiting for service, W, is one measure of system effectiveness. The higher the average wait, the less effective the system. This measure is given by $W = 1/(1 - \rho)$. Now when $\rho = 1$, W is infinite—a manager's nightmare. It is also interesting to see the behavior of the waiting time as ρ approaches 1.

ρ	W
0.7	3
0.8	5
0.9	10
0.95	20
0.98	50

As system utilization approaches 1, small increases in utilization yield large increases in waiting time and thus large decreases in efficiency. As any system approaches 100 percent utilization, the chances of breakdown increase exponentially.

FIGURE 2.10. INCREASED WAITING TIME AS UTILIZATION INCREASES.

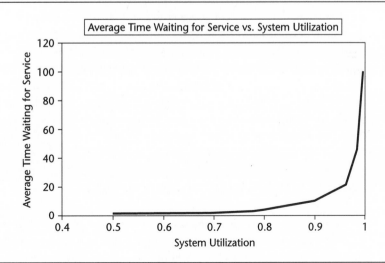

Average Time Waiting for Service vs. System Utilization

Project systems are not immune from this constraint. A small delay in one project may cause resources to be released late to another project, causing a delay in the second project too—probably a substantial one. Thus, upper managers should build in an extra resource capacity of about 10 percent to handle unexpected delays.

Wheelwright and Clark (1992a, p. 78) state that "to improve productivity further, [one] company built a 'capacity cushion' into its plan. It assigned only 75 full-time-equivalent engineers out of a possible 80 to the 8 commercial development projects. This way [the company] was better prepared to take advantage of unexpected opportunities and to deal with crises when they arose."

Upper managers may feel that extra capacity is wasted time. However, whenever the extra capacity proves unneeded, the unassigned time can be used to allow people to be creative and think about the next project or product. Some companies, such as 3M, have an informal guideline for upper managers that 10 to 15 percent of budgets and people's time should be unassigned or discretionary. This gives engineers time to think about what new products the company could be producing in the future. So the "wasted" time is actually quite valuable time.

The combination of reduced project number and extra capacity has dramatic effects on the ability to manage multiple projects and to handle new projects as they arise. If the resource pool is too tightly scheduled or overcommitted, project changes ricochet off one another. Changes to A affect B and C, which eventually ricochets back to A. People delayed on one project are unable to move on to the next; these delays mean others have to replan and refocus. The entire set of projects thus may be affected by a small delay in one project. Furthermore, if too many projects are changed, none gets enough executive attention. This causes even more delays and a possible failure to implement the overall organization strategy.

Reducing the number of projects and building in extra capacity greatly lessens the chance of this happening. Todd Abraham (1995), vice president of strategic technology development at Pillsbury, is a firm believer in the project prioritization process: "In terms of doing the right projects, what we're trying to do with prioritization is create organizational capacity, and what each of you can do by prioritizing projects better is create more capacity for the organization and make each of your lives easier to get those extra resources for nonfunded projects. We do that through focus and alignment."

Motivating Multiple Project Management

Ultimately, there must be some reason for people to work together—some motivation for individuals to see beyond a single project or department toward the organizational whole. A new plan will not readily be adopted merely because it is right, nor will people necessarily cooperate without motivation; they must see the benefits of working together. Following are some of the more effective methods of motivating cooperation:

- *Institute a profit-sharing plan.* A profit-sharing plan based on the overall results of the organization is a good way to focus attention on the benefits of cooperation. HP has used such an approach since early in its existence. It is not unusual to hear individuals refer to profit sharing as a reason to avoid expense and to cooperate in ways not directly related to job descriptions.
- *Appeal to the organization's goals.* When cooperation lags, upper managers may need to remind people of the company's purpose. Striving to reach departmental goals often takes focus off overall goals, so it may be worthwhile to emphasize the company aim of (for example) producing innovative products for customers. One company in the medical equipment field reminds managers that the overall goal is to produce products that save lives, which cannot be accomplished by just one department. Especially for people in organizations that have such critical goals, this type of reminder can refocus them on the need for teamwork.
- *Stress the individual benefits of teamwork.* These benefits may include personal recognition for successful interdepartmental projects, less chance of working on canceled projects, better information for scheduling departmental activities, better potential results for the individual, better feelings within the individual—or even the belief of having simply done the right thing.
- *Develop a better system for scheduling people.* A big problem in multiple project management is scheduling people and allocating their time between project work and departmental work. To handle this, a good project management information system (see Chapter Six) is invaluable. The demands of project work and departmental work often conflict; left to their own devices, department managers and project managers might well schedule more of individuals' time than is available in a reasonable workday. Such individuals are bound to be demotivated by feeling that they cannot do all the work desired from them, that they have lost control over their time, and that upper management has abdicated its responsibilities to them. Because they cannot do all the work, they must decide what parts of it to do—and they will probably defer to department work if that is where their future lies. If so, project work will suffer.

The problem can be eased if people help to schedule their own work. One way to do this is to make everyone responsible for covering their own salary. That is, they "sell" a percentage of their time to various projects. Once they sell 90 percent of their available time, they are covered; the other 10 percent is set aside for emergencies or creativity. This certainly helps their motivation, as they will not overallocate their own time; they gain some control over the allocation and influence it toward their personal skills, desires, and needs; and they feel more confident that upper management knows what it is doing and thus that the organization will be successful. This sort of self-scheduling process was in operation for the professional staff of HP's project management initiative and most consulting organizations. It certainly embodies one of the tenets of the organic organization, and it works in such disciplines as services and advertising as well.

Viable as this is over the long term, it has the potential for dysfunction in the short term. Cooperation could be diminished if the process is measured too tightly; total light is just as blinding as total darkness. People can take the process too far and defeat the very thing they are trying to promote.

Ideally, a project manager's salary is covered by one project and a core team member's by one or two. Other team members could work on three or even four projects at different times—including departments, which become de facto projects that bid for people's time. The percentage of time going to the departments is based on mutual agreement between the department managers and the individuals after considering the needs of the individual, the department, and the system of projects.

No motivation will make multiple project management work unless all the people involved want it to. Upper management can work with all project stakeholders to design a plan and put in place motivators and rewards such that it is in everyone's best interest to make the system work. Department managers must be recognized for contributing people for project work. Project managers must see the benefits of cooperating with other projects to allocate the resource pool—or at least see the folly of not cooperating. Individual team members should be able to allocate their time and must be rewarded for their work on multiple projects.

Developing a Project Sponsor Program

Even after upper management has set priorities and chosen projects, each project needs an upper management sponsor—someone interested in its success and willing to pledge to help it succeed. The sponsor need not fight the battles but must provide air cover for the troops.

It is difficult to overestimate the importance of the project sponsor. As a consultant to a financial services firm, one of us reviewed five systems projects, two of which were considered less than successful. All five had followed the same methodology and had been led by experienced project managers. The difference between them was that the successful projects had visible and vocal project sponsors who helped see them through rough times. The others did not. At least in these cases, where other factors influencing success were relatively equal, sponsorship meant the difference between success and failure. It alone cannot guarantee project success, but sponsorship is a necessary ingredient for success.

The sponsor implements upper management decisions, ensuring that the project delivers as promised while implementing the strategy envisioned by the upper management team. The project sponsor is also responsible for upper management review of the project plan. Thus, the sponsor negotiates with the project team on resources, deadlines, and project scope and helps out on cross-department issues. The sponsor should review the following components in any project proposal:

- *Signed goal statement.* The project manager and the core team develop a goal statement for the project and have it signed by themselves, contributing department managers, and other project stakeholders. It is the responsibility of the sponsor to ensure that the project goal will indeed help implement the top-management strategy. As an example, Figure 2.11 shows the Boeing 777 airliner project statement that involved United Airlines as the customer and Boeing as the supplier. Signed by managers at both companies, it provided directions for the multiple project teams needed to implement the project.
- *Project plan.* The project plan should include a vision statement for the project as well as a statement of the project's purpose, total mission and sub-objectives, milestones, schedules, and resource usage. One form of project plan, the project charter statement, is used by many information technology communities. Prepared for each project, it provides a consistent format that gives upper managers all the information they need to compare projects.
- *Risk analysis.* An analysis of the business and technical risks of the project ensures that some forethought has been given to what could go wrong and how to avoid or react to those events. Former HP colleague Tom Kendrick (2003), in identifying essential tools for failure-proofing projects, says, "Risk management information is critical to the portfolio decisions. It allows you to assess the credibility of the estimates for overall return, and it is often the primary factor that triggers changes in the project objectives. Best-in-class companies reject questionable projects early, before too much investment is made. Best-in-class high-technology companies spend less than 5 percent of their research and development budget on failed projects. In the typical high-tech company, the figure is far higher" (p. 19).
- *Contingency plan.* If things go wrong, this specifies what will be done about it.

The project sponsor should attend the project start-up meeting and the phase review or milestone meetings and participate in go/no-go decisions for funding of future phases. The sponsor is also advised to be involved in negotiation for resources, responsible for the utilization of those resources, and on the escalation

FIGURE 2.11. EXAMPLE OF A SIGNED STATEMENT BETWEEN PROJECT TEAM AND CUSTOMER.

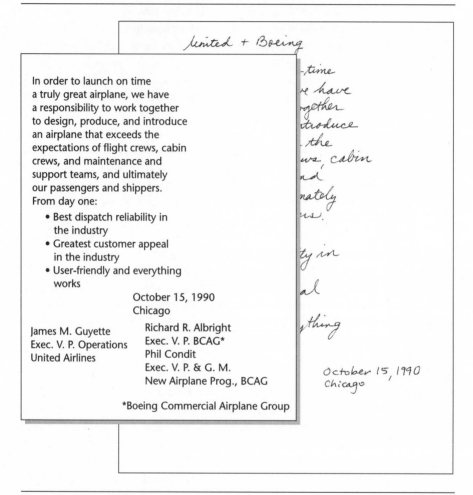

In order to launch on time
a truly great airplane, we have
a responsibility to work together
to design, produce, and introduce
an airplane that exceeds the
expectations of flight crews, cabin
crews, and maintenance and
support teams, and ultimately
our passengers and shippers.
From day one:

- Best dispatch reliability in
  the industry
- Greatest customer appeal
  in the industry
- User-friendly and everything
  works

October 15, 1990
Chicago

James M. Guyette
Exec. V. P. Operations
United Airlines

Richard R. Albright
Exec. V. P. BCAG*
Phil Condit
Exec. V. P. & G. M.
New Airplane Prog., BCAG

*Boeing Commercial Airplane Group

Source: Seattle Post-Intelligencer, Apr. 19, 1994, p. 2.

path to resolve problems should they arise. Without project management processes, Kendrick (2003) says that "all the power in an organization is in the hands of management; all negotiations tend to be resolved using political and emotional tactics. Having little or no data, project teams are fairly easily backed into whatever corners their management chooses. With data, the discussion shifts and negotiations are based more on reality" (p. 24).

Most problems that sponsors have to deal with involve interdepartmental cooperation, emphasizing the need to motivate such cooperation and to help develop a coherent set of projects that aim toward a central strategy. A sponsor needs to be armed with good reasons for cooperation and with a plan of record that lists all projects and their contribution to the central strategy. These communication tools are invaluable in solving interdepartmental problems.

In addition, the information system for projects should have sufficient "what-if?" capability to show the overall effect of changes in staffing levels. The decision to make a change in one project should be made in the light of how it will affect other projects and ultimately the overall strategy.

The sponsor needs to be knowledgeable enough about the project to represent it to senior management. If interest in it wanes in the executive suite, the sponsor needs to become a salesperson, talking it up and ensuring that the benefits of its success are widely known. The sponsor must be able to stress the value-added aspects of the project, the vision behind it, and its fit with overall organizational strategy. This allows others to deal with the chaos of projects, the natural ambiguity of project life.

The sponsor should also be involved in the project deadline-setting process (which indicates that the upper management bonus system should not be tied to project completion); deadlines should be based on competition, product roll-out schedules, available staffing levels, and reasonable implementation times. They should not be tied to management-by-objectives deadlines but to a negotiation process where the sponsor and project manager examine the project plan, scope statement, and staffing levels to determine what is reasonable. Such a process is described in more detail in Chapter Three.

Project sponsors are most effective when they are supportive, not meddlesome. This means they work best as advisers and take direct action only when asked to by, or in consultation with, the project manager. The key difference between advice and meddling is the degree to which advice must be taken. If the advice can be rejected by the project manager, it is support. If it must be followed, it is meddling. Normally upper managers are not accustomed to having their advice go unheeded, so it is often difficult for them to be the best kind of project sponsor. But having advice ignored now and then has advantages: it avoids gaining a reputation as a meddler, and it justifies protecting the team from meddling by others.

From time to time, the project sponsor may need to apply reasonable pressure on the project team to keep it on track. Reasonable pressure is that which is consistent with the goals, schedules, priorities, and project management practices of the organization in general. The most effective sponsors are known for the questions they ask rather than the orders they give. The pressure they exert is in the form of questions: Will the project implement strategy? Will the deadline be met? Where is the contingency plan for newly discovered risks? When was the last time the customers and end users were asked for input? How can I help with team motivation?

Unreasonable pressure is inconsistent with project management practices, usually taking the form of directives and orders rather than questions. Examples of unreasonable pressure include using position power to force results of decisions, arbitrarily moving project deadlines, reassigning team members without project managers' knowledge, and imposing one's will or style on the team. Sponsors need to remember that they are not in charge of the project but are there to serve the project team. Sponsors are often not the customer for the outcome of the project; therefore, they need to be careful not to make decisions that jeopardize usability of the outcome.

Sponsorship training is a best practice among successful organizations. Many sponsors are new in grade or new to projects. They cannot know all that is expected of them, especially in a weak project culture. In *Creating a Project Office* (Englund, Graham, and Dinsmore, 2003), one program manager tirelessly explained and validated his mission and objectives, developed a sales presentation, and kept management in the loop. He developed a comprehensive sponsorship training program that focused on roles, time investment, and key responsibilities. He positioned sponsorship as a question of mind-set, commitment, and competence. Some organizations develop a Web site with complete descriptions of sponsor roles and assignments.

The Compleat Upper Manager

The successful complete upper manager:

- Knows that projects without strategic emphasis often end in failure.
- Works to develop a system of projects and links them to organizational strategy.
- Knows that a system of projects uses a common resource pool and that the pool may be abused without cooperation across the organization.
- Develops a system to manage the resource pool and reward interdepartmental cooperation.
- Develops an upper management team to oversee project selection.
- Selects projects based on comparative priority ranking of contribution to strategy.
- Reduces the total number of projects to minimize possible disruption.
- Reduces the number of projects for all individuals so as to focus their attention.
- Allows extra capacity in a resource pool for emergencies and for creativity.
- Motivates people to make a multiple project management system work.
- Develops a system where individuals have more control over allocation of their time.
- Assigns and trains an upper management sponsor for each project.

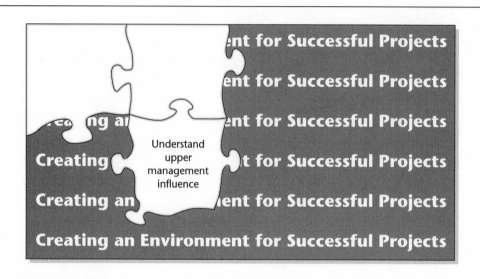

Understand upper management influence

Creating an Environment for Successful Projects

An important aspect of the new project environment—the need to focus on one project at a time—is covered in the beginning of this chapter. The next important theme is understanding the need for planning. Some assume that planning is not necessary and that it increases cost, takes time, and is of no benefit. However, this chapter shows that planning decreases costs, decreases time, and increases quality. It also examines other needs: setting the project deadline, managing on the learning curve, understanding the difference between support and interference, and motivating project work. Finally, it considers the impact of the project manager as hero and suggests that upper managers need to change the way project managers are discussed and rewarded in the organization.

CHAPTER THREE

HOW UPPER MANAGERS INFLUENCE PROJECT SUCCESS

Everyone is bound to bear patiently the results of his own example.

PHAEDRUS, A.D. 8, FABLES 26.12

I n the previous chapter, we held that upper managers set the stage for project success by developing a strategic emphasis for projects. This chapter reviews some of the common mistakes made as the selected projects progress. Setting a strategic direction is an important first step, but the benefit of it may be lost if upper managers continue behavior patterns that were successful in standard department settings but ultimately undermine successful project completion. Many of these patterns are habits that are no longer questioned. However, in the new project environment, many old habits have to be changed. In many ways, dropping old habits is more difficult than learning new ones, but the change is necessary to create a successful project environment.

A Universal Upper Management Problem: Attempting Too Many Projects Simultaneously

One problem that seems almost universal is an attempt by managers to schedule too many projects at one time. Whether projects arise at random or were selected by an upper management committee, everyone wants their project done *now!* Of course, there is never enough capacity in the organization to do all projects simultaneously. Nevertheless, there is usually pressure to run as many projects as possible at the same time, doing them in parallel. The usual management response to this problem is to spread people across many projects and tell them that "multitasking is the way we do things here" and that "everybody knows that is the best way to get the most work done."

Many upper managers pride themselves on being able to do more with less, but the people working on projects realize that multitasking among projects decreases their efficiency on any one project. This means that while there is an army of people working on a large array of projects, constant switching from one project to another means that in reality they do less with more.

If you could solve only one problem, this is it. The solution is to have people concentrate on just one project at a time, finish that project as quickly as possible, and then move onto the next project. The goal is to switch from doing projects in parallel to doing them in series.

The simple fact is that multitasking is counterproductive because it takes time to switch from one project to another. A person working on one project for a few days has to stop thinking about that project, begin remembering details of the new project, and then spend time getting up to speed on what happened on the new project while working on the other project. According to research by Rubenstein, Meyer, and Evans (2001), for all types of tasks, subjects lost time when they had to switch from one task to another. These time costs increased with the complexity of the tasks: it took longer for subjects to switch between more complicated tasks. The researchers say that this costs as much as 20 to 40 percent in terms of potential efficiency lost on the time costs of switching. These are fairly incredible numbers: a 20 percent loss in efficiency translates to one day per week in productivity that is lost due to task switching.

Switching projects is a very complicated task, so the time lost in project switching is probably closer to 40 percent, meaning that two days per week per person are lost on this practice. Switching from one project to another project requires a very complex readjustment of working parameters due to the following attributes of projects:

- *Time line and due date differences.* Shifting from one project to another requires a reset in the mental time horizon. This includes the final due date, time remaining on the project, and a sense of urgency that drives progress on projects.
- *Project goals.* Internalization of project goals drives the behavior of project team members. Switching between projects with radically different goals requires a radical mind reset so that team members can do the right work on the right project.

- *Phase of the project.* As projects progress, the contents of activities are radically different from the beginning to the end of a project. For example, the project planning phase requires much thought and discussion, while the project execution phase requires more action. Switching from a project that is in the planning phase to a project in the execution phase requires totally different types of thinking and action.

- *Disciplines involved.* Project team members become accustomed to working with a certain set of organizational disciplines on the project team. For example, you may be accustomed to working on one project team with a member from marketing. When you switch to the other project team, you may assume a marketing person is on it, but there may not be; in fact, you may be working more with people from finance. This is another change in mind-set requiring a totally different way of thinking, creating difficulty in switching from one to the other.

- *Team members involved.* People on teams get used to working with certain individuals and getting to know their reactions, sore points, agendas, and so forth. Switching from one team to another requires constant adjustment to different personalities and ways of communicating, all the while slowing down progress from forming, storming, and norming to performing.

- *Project manager.* Different project managers have different styles. Switching from one project manager with one style to different style can be disconcerting and disorienting, resulting in a general loss in efficiency.

- *Time passes.* While the team member was away from this project, decisions were made and some progress occurred. Time needs to be spent reviewing these decisions and progress so that the team member understands the situation when he or she rejoins the project.

Because of this complexity, the switching costs move closer to the 40 percent figure cited in the research: two days of productivity per week are lost simply to the process of switching. This means that most organizations could realize a 40 percent increase in productivity simply by having their team members concentrate on one project at a time.

What Can Be Done

The simple answer to this problem is to switch from doing projects in parallel to doing them in series: project team members work on one project only and finish that project before moving to the next one. Although this is a well-known remedy, it is not popular. In fact, the news article announcing the research results on multitasking contained a warning that "your boss may not like this one." The warning note seems incredible because most bosses tell you they are trying to find ways to get projects done faster. Now, there are research results telling them how it is done, and yet it assumes the boss will not like the solution. The reason is that the suggested solution goes against so much received wisdom (see Box 3.1) and organizational lore that most managers find it a threatening suggestion. Thus, the manager has to choose between doing the right thing and doing what is acceptable in the organization. It is only the bold manager who chooses to do the right thing.

We hear it every time we suggest putting people on projects full time. The usual argument is that we do not need people full time on most projects, but that these other projects need to get done too, so it makes no sense to have a person sit idle while other work needs to be done. "I've got a boss, and that boss will not think well of me when he sees people sitting idle while project workloads continue to grow. Other people in the department will get jealous and begin to grumble

---

BOX 3.1. Received Wisdom in Organizations.

Received wisdom is normally considered to be a set of ideas that people in organizations believe are true, or at least act as if they believe they are true. This organizational wisdom is normally passed on from generation to generation and is thus received by newer members in the organization as part of the socialization process. Beliefs that are part of the received wisdom in organizations are usually easy to identify because they are often prefaced with phrases like, "It's just common sense" or the ever popular, "Everybody knows"— for example, "Everybody knows that project planning is a waste of time because nothing ever goes according to plan," or, "It is just common sense that multitasking increases efficiency when it is used to fill everyone's time to 100 percent."

The beliefs in received wisdom are normally held dearly by those at the top of the organization. After all, these people got to that position by following the received wisdom. As others join the organization, they must demonstrate that they too believe the organizational wisdom. If they do not, they will be exited. As a result of this process, the organization fills with true believers. Because these beliefs are so widely held in the organization, any attempt to challenge or change these beliefs will normally be met with ridicule. This is often true even when objective data are presented that show the beliefs to be false. Thus, we see that received wisdom is the organizational equivalent of Plato's cave fable in Box 1.3.

because they're working 110 percent of the time while other people have slack. Besides, if I don't get my favorite project started along with the others, then the organization may lose interest in my project, and it may never happen."

Notice that most of these arguments have very little to do with the project and a lot to do with upper managers' received wisdom and how they think they will be viewed in the organization. To begin, the data on task switching indicate that it often makes sense to have people sit idle while there is work to be done. The math is fairly simple. Suppose you had two 20-week projects, A and B, each requiring a project team to work 4 days per week per project, for a total of 80 days of work on each project, or 160 days of work total. If they were done in series, then project A would be done after 20 weeks' duration, and project B would be completed at the end of 40 weeks. However, 200 days would pass for only 160 days of work. Now suppose you are "in a hurry," and since the team has 1 day per week free, you attempt them in parallel, working 4 days on one project and then 4 days on the other project. This makes it looks as if you save a day a week, or 40 days off the total duration, so that both projects will be completed at the end of 160 days (32 weeks).

This is a type of thinking that makes working in parallel look good. However, even at the low end of a 20 percent switching cost, this means adding 1 day per week duration to the workdays required, or 40 days to the time necessary to complete the projects. This does not mean that 40 days of work are added but rather that only 3 days of work are accomplished for each 4 days that transpire, so 40 days are added to the total duration, not to the days of work. This means that both projects now are completed at the end of 40 weeks. This represents a decrease in efficiency because when done in series, the results from the first project would be available after 20 weeks. If the projects are markedly different, then the switching time will be closer to 40 percent, which means that 80 days' duration are added to the total time. In this case, neither project is ready until 48 weeks out. (See Figure 3.1.)

FIGURE 3.1. SERIES VERSUS PARALLEL SCHEDULE.

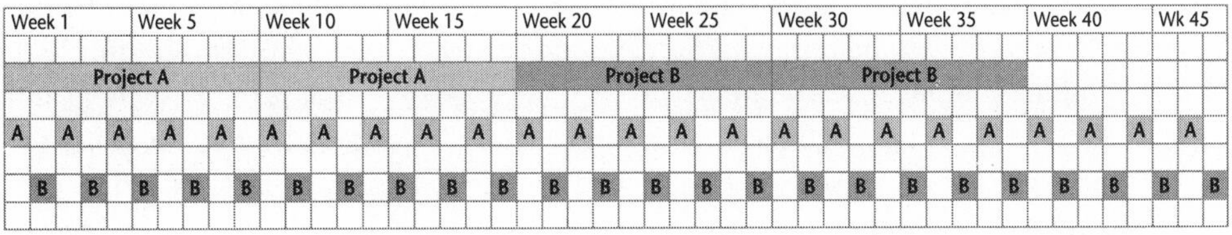

So now we see the choice:

- People sit idle for 1 day per week, and if the projects are done in series, then the results from the first project will be available after 20 weeks and results from the second project will be available after 40 weeks.
- If the received wisdom in the organization is that it makes no sense to have people sit idle, then the results from both projects will not be ready for 40 to 48 weeks.

Sadly, most managers choose the second option due to the demands of the organization. Such is the perversity of organizational life. Normal received wisdom is that efficient organizations have everyone working 110 percent of their time. Reality is quite different. However, if the boss truly believes that all people must be fully assigned for all their time, then the manager has a difficult choice: to make the decision that is right for the projects and potentially irritate the boss or make the decision that pleases the boss and potentially irritates the projects. This decision becomes much more difficult when other managers reporting to that boss make the boss-pleasing decision; in that situation, the enlightened upper manager looks out of step, out of sync, and potentially out of a job. The safer choice is to go along and thus perpetuate the status quo.

The field of concurrent engineering advocates doing many activities in parallel to shorten product life cycles. This is okay if different people do the activities and in different functional areas. The problem arises if the same person or persons try to do tasks in parallel. With different people, it still falls on the program manager to task switch. Keep people doing project work focused as much as possible on a single project.

An Example: The Israeli Aircraft Industries

The Israeli Aircraft Industries (IAI) is a company that services airplanes. Burkhard (2000) found that its troubleshooting engineers averaged fifty jobs on their desk at any one time; consequently, the lead time for these tasks averaged 135 days, and engineers put in a great deal of overtime. The company made a change so that all engineers had no more than three jobs on their desks at any one time. The rest of the jobs were held back and released only when the old ones were finished. Within six months, lead times fell from an average of 135 days to between 25 and 30 days, overtime declined to zero, and slightly fewer people were handling the same volume of work. Since their lead times decreased so drastically, the company now uses this as a competitive advantage: some jobs are quoted in 2 weeks while competitors quote 10 to 12 weeks.

This is an example of the dramatic results they can be achieved when changing from parallel to serial. Burkhard (2000) noted nothing pointing to new training or new technology. The reduction in lead time can be totally attributed to the time costs associated with switching between tasks. With jobs in parallel, there was significant switching time from one job to another. When jobs were then done in series, switching time declined dramatically so that most of the previous switching time could then be used to get the job done. Engineers originally averaged 50 jobs, and lead times averaged 135 days; now they have three jobs, and lead times average only 30 days. This means that before the queue discipline was installed, about 100 days were used up for task switching. At fifty jobs, that is 2 days of switching time per job and answering calls from customers about status—time that can now be used for working rather than waiting.

Understanding the Need for Planning

In many organizations, there is a general lack of appreciation of the importance of project planning. Upper managers do not seem to understand its necessity and thus do not usually allow enough time for proper planning. Some upper managers see planning as something done by the planning department or by managers at an off-site meeting once a year—not as something that affects their daily lives. They do not see or sense much relationship between the company strategic plan and the daily work of the organization. They notice that people tend to do today what they did yesterday, which does not appear to require special planning. They may be accustomed to working in departments that use repeatable processes and products.

A project, however, has few repeat elements; most of it is new. At the beginning, project team members should not do what they did yesterday because that work was done for a different project. Also, one cannot rely entirely on the knowledge gained from previous projects because new projects are different. Nor can one watch others for a guide to behavior, because at the outset of a project, no one is doing project work; rather, they are doing project planning, which is often wrongly interpreted as doing nothing. This apparent lack of activity is often upsetting to upper managers, so project team members may start doing something, usually the wrong thing, based on departmental work or work on some previous project. That pushes planning to a time after activities start. But planning must precede activity; the project plan is the guide to daily project activity.

Upper managers need to understand project management practices and support the project planning process. They should know about the terminology and tooling of project plans—about project objective statements, work breakdown structures, estimates, scheduling, contingency planning, and trade-offs among scope, schedule, and resources. That some upper managers do not know about these things is unsurprising; perhaps their careers did not include training in project management. Whatever the reason, they may be unaware not only of the need for project planning but of the effort it takes to develop the tools. If that is the case, they certainly do not know the benefits that planning can bring. Project managers may come to believe that such upper managers embody Graham's second law: "If they know nothing of what you are doing, they assume you are doing nothing."

Lack of emphasis on planning frequently leads to defining solutions before defining the problem. Unfortunately, this is also a bias of many team members. If the upper manager does not support or allow time for planning, some project teams are happy to begin work on their favorite solution before fully defining the problem. Presented with solutions, wise upper managers ask, "What problem are you solving?"

Figure 3.2 illustrates a classic example of organizational perversity: the rewarding by management of behavior it professes to discourage. It has been noted that upper managers in America have a strong bias for action, which they translate into pushing for, expecting, and rewarding action on the part of their subordinates. When projects are first started and funded, anxiety can cause upper man-

FIGURE 3.2. BIAS TOWARD ACTION BEFORE PLANNING.

"You people start designing while I find out what they want!"

agers to push hard for results: "Get going, and do something! Don't just stand around planning." Too often, project managers respond by making a giant leap toward disaster.

Unenlightened upper managers say that planning is costly, takes time, and decreases quality because the time spent on planning could have been devoted to the product; thus, they view it as expendable. Actually, planning is a critical element that decreases costs and total project time while increasing product quality.

One way of understanding how upper managers influence project success is to look at the activities on which they focus their attention. Hamel and Prahalad (1994) question the issues that preoccupy senior management. What drives improvement and transformation agendas? They report that on average, senior managers devote less than 3 percent of their energy to building a perspective on the future. From Hamel and Prahalad's experience, however, management teams should spend 20 to 50 percent of their time over a period of several months to develop a distinctive point of view about the future and then be willing to continually revisit it, elaborate on it, and adjust it as the future unfolds: "It takes substantial and sustained intellectual energy to develop high-quality, robust answers to questions such as what new core competencies will we need to build, what new product concepts should we pioneer, what new alliances will we need to form, what nascent development programs should we protect, and what long-term regulatory initiatives should we pursue" (Hamel and Prahalad, 1994, p. 4). Instead, they find that most management time is spent on restructuring and reengineering, which have more to do with shoring up today's businesses than creating tomorrow's industries.

On another level, Wheelwright (1996) posits that management's ability to influence product development outcomes is greatest at the beginning of a project, when crucial program decisions are being made. However, he shows an activity profile indicating that most management attention and influence is spent in the latter or back-end stages of a project, solving problems and fixing things. Why? Because back-end efforts are highly visible, current and urgent, comfortable and known, and enjoyable because they give instant results and provide quick feedback. If problems are solved, the rewards are high; if not, no real blame accrues. In contrast, fuzzy front-end efforts tend to be conceptual. Their impacts are vague, attract little feedback, and are hard to quantify and measure; achieving results from them is difficult because fewer data and more options are available. They are risky because they expose decision making to second-guessing, and the skills and processes needed to deal with them are usually ill defined. It is no wonder that project managers emulate upper management involvement preferences. Thus, upper managers need to examine and alter their own time management choices if they are to lead the change to an environment that results in consistently successful projects.

The Benefits of Planning

Project planning brings many benefits. The most important three are project cost reduction, project time reduction, and project quality improvement.

Project Cost Reduction

A large portion of the cost of any project is attributable to changes made to the project plan, the product design, or the final production process. To decrease total project costs, needed changes should be made at the beginning of the project whenever possible; it is usually much cheaper then. Early determination of needed change is a sign of good project planning. A good project plan itemizes time for both expected and unexpected project changes, and it even encourages changes, but only early in the project. Emphasis on quality and planning does not automatically blow the budget; in fact, good-quality planning and scope management actually help reduce costs in the long run.

A key part of quality planning is defining customer expectations and checking the assumptions of product designers against actual customer desires. Here, one could use a technique such as quality function deployment (QFD). Barry Boehm (1981) provides some insights into how much it costs later if quality management is not properly done at the beginning of the project. Assuming that it costs $1 to correct an assumption in the requirements phase, following are the approximate costs of doing so in later project phases:

Design phase	$3–6
Coding phase	$10
Development testing	$15–40
Acceptance testing	$30–70
System operation	$40–1,000

Experience at Hewlett-Packard (HP) shows that hardware development and warranty costs follow a similar cost model. So good planning and quality management are also good budget management.

Another good example (Vidans, 1992) is a joint venture formed between a Japanese automotive supplier and an American seat manufacturer to design, develop, and manufacture automotive seats for an American corporation. Most Japanese engineering changes occur at the beginning of the product development process, whereas most U.S. engineering changes occur at the end, at which point they are estimated to be ten times more expensive. The number of changes is the same in both countries, but the Japanese timing makes theirs much cheaper to accomplish. If other countries are to do the same, the thrust must come from upper management.

Project Time Reduction

The Japanese spend an enormous amount of time (by U.S. standards) on up-front planning. An important aspect of the Japanese project management style is to get all functions and departments, including suppliers, involved as equal partners, even showing them that way on the schedule chart. This stems from the thinking that every member of the team is equally important and that all must buy into the concept of the product being developed. Such a philosophy requires heavy involvement of all partners, including upper managers, in the concept phase of the product feasibility process. At this point, changes are more easily made if objections are raised. Although this process may seem time-consuming (at least to the American mind), it shortens the project cycle time by raising questions and objections early in the project, when changes can be made quickly.

One quality circle demonstrated this approach. A sales development team at the factory debated seemingly forever over what problem should be solved, finally choosing to work on the need for backup support of incoming telephone calls when individual sales engineers were not available. By carefully crafting a statement about the problem being solved and what problems were not being addressed, the team focused in such a way that work and creativity could proceed at a fast pace. Decisions were quickly made on alternatives because they could be measured against the problem statement. Presentation of the proposal to peers and management went smoothly; execution happened almost instantly. The up-front discussion time appeared almost painfully long, but it enabled fast movement on the rest of the project.

Planning can also avert project crises. If some small but important step is forgotten early—for example, getting clearance from the legal department—it will likely cause massive delay later. Having a project plan is no guarantee that mistakes will not be made. But if the entire core team on the project helps develop the plan and upper management reviews it, the chances of missing an important element are greatly diminished. In that case, planning saves time by averting crisis.

Project Quality Improvement

An important part of the definition of project success is customer acceptance. In the language of Total Quality Management (TQM), the final product must meet or exceed customer expectations. Projects fail in this respect if the project team did not fully understand what the customer wanted or what it was trying to achieve with the final product. This is doubly difficult because there is no product to touch at the beginning of the project; often customers do not really know what they want until a prototype is put into their hands. Allowing enough time for customer analysis can help alleviate this problem.

The steps to quality project management come from the definition of successful projects. There are two distinct but interlinked phases: quality planning and quality control (Juran, 1992). Quality planning involves determining who the customers and users of the product are, determining what they need from the product, and then developing features that fulfill those needs. Quality control involves determining statistical tests and procedures to ensure that the product works as intended.

As part of quality planning, the project manager needs to differentiate early on between the customer and the end user. The customer is usually the one paying the bill for the outcome of the project but may not be the end user—the person who actually uses the final product. Often the customer's requirements do not adequately reflect the needs of the end users, so asking them for requirements gives only a partial picture. Thus, project managers need to get both customer and end user input to the project plan, and this involvement often requires upper management support and participation. Upper managers also need to downplay or balance their personal or company goals and influence at the expense of satisfying real customer needs.

The aim of quality planning is to have very few changes to product specifications during project execution and to develop a product that meets both customer and end user expectations. The purpose of planning with the customer is to uncover the end users' hidden expectations, which often do not emerge until they see the product at work. This is an argument for prototyping as a part of quality methodology.

The degree to which prototyping is needed often depends on knowledge of the market and the customer. The other major consideration is the cost of project failure. For a "bet the company" project, knowledge of customer expectations is paramount, and prototyping is essential. For an internal project to help the accounting department, customer expectations are usually better known, and prototyping is not as important.

It helps to compare markets with technologies (see Table 3.1). When working with old technology in an old market, the supplier usually knows more about the product than the customer. The suppliers actually generate expectations by showing the application of the old technology. In addition, the supplier usually knows the customer's applications and so may know more about the customer's hidden expectations than the customer does. This is basically a show-the-benefit type of project.

TABLE 3.1. Comparing Markets and Technology.

	Old Market Customers Known	New Market Customers Unknown
New Technology	Work with known customers to develop application	Work with unknown customers to develop application
	Failure rate high, payoff high (IBM 360)	Failure rate very high, payoff strategic (Xerox)
Old Technology	Show new application to old customers	New application in new market
	Failure rate low	Failure rate medium
	Payoff low	Payoff medium to high

Applying old technology in a new market requires understanding the new customer. Here, suppliers often fail to do a good job; they feel they know the technology well, but what they really need to know is the new customer's new applications. The project manager usually views the applications through the lens of the technology but should work hard to see them through the eyes of the customer and the end users. Luckily a prototype exists—the old technology—so the project manager can consider how it may be used in the new application. This is mainly a modification type of project.

Applying new technology presents special problems. There is no existing prototype; the product does not exist until the project creates it. The project manager works to define the product and customer expectations at the same time, making the creation of a prototype nearly essential. The task is a little easier if the market is known, for then the project manager is working with familiar customers and applications. If the market is not known, the project manager and the rest of the core team need to become familiar with it. In such cases, using focus groups, customer contact groups, and end user groups in addition to prototyping may be valuable; putting end user representatives on the core team is another possibility.

Projects that involve new technology have high failure rates. Most projects do involve new technology, so they should be considered high-failure ventures; project-based organizations must be able to support higher failure rates than traditional organizations.

Zells (1992) advocates end user and core team involvement in a process called Total Employee Involvement (TEI), part of TQM: "TEI deploys the responsibility for quality throughout the organization—by coordinating the skills to design and build products. Using the cross-functional team-building process, all of the people within (and without) the organization who can directly affect the product's outcome collaborate from the product's inception" (p. 32).

Clearly, quality requires a high level of customer and end user involvement from the beginning of the project. It is a state of mind that defines discovering and meeting customer expectations as the top priority of the project. Quality is a journey as well as a destination, so discovering and meeting customer expectations is seen as a process as well as a goal. TQM includes both quality assurance and quality control.

Motorola (Schmidt and Finnigan, 1992, p. 311) says that "one of the fastest ways to improve quality is to focus on reducing cycle time. . . . [With a focus] on cycle time, defects were reduced at a much faster rate than [when focusing] on defect reduction alone." Project planning is a well-known tool for decreasing cycle time and a factor in producing higher quality. Other quality tools include rapid prototyping, QFD, and "making one to throw it away."

Only upper management can establish the supportive roles and structures to make planning a regular part of the project management process. Upper management needs to require a project planning process and ask for the project plan when discussing and reviewing project progress and changes. In this way, the organization gets the benefits mentioned previously. Without this support and encouragement, proper planning will most likely not be done.

Developing a project plan also begins the learning process concerning how projects are best completed in the organization. Comparing project experience to the original project plans is a key part of a project retrospective process, which is an essential part of creating a learning organization (see Chapter Eight) and learning how projects are best managed in the organization. Support from upper management is essential in developing this learning process.

Setting the Project Deadline

Upper managers also affect project success through their involvement in setting the project deadline. It seems that when upper managers begin to develop projects, their first concern is deadlines. When they pass a statement of the project goal and a deadline to a project manager at the same time, the deadline cannot have been set based on the needs of the project. Most likely, it was based on perceived competitor actions, market windows, the bonus system of the organization, the end of the fiscal year, wishful thinking, or other methods of dubious benefit. Such deadlines are often missed, and they cause anxiety, fear, and distrust: anxiety as project team members fret over how to finish impossibly soon, fear as they ponder what will happen if the deadline is missed, distrust as they assume the upper manager may have other unreasonable demands as yet unrevealed. This does not set the groundwork for success. The successful project is based on sharing legitimate information and developing trust, and developing trust begins with setting the project deadline.

The temporary teams developed for projects need trust among their members in order to be successful. Otherwise, everybody completes tasks themselves because they cannot rely on anyone else. On a multidisciplinary team, this is an impossible situation; not every team member is fully versed in all of the disciplines needed to complete the project. Therefore, developing trust is of paramount importance for project success.

Block (1987) approaches relationships in organizations on the basis of two dimensions: agreement and trust. People either agree or disagree about where they are headed, and they either trust or distrust one another's way of pursuing these ends. How to approach another person depends on the existing levels of trust and agreement. Block suggests a three-step approach: exchange visions, purposes, or goals; affirm or negotiate agreement; and affirm or negotiate trust. It is very difficult for many people, especially highly trained professionals, to be comfortable addressing issues that build or destroy projects on the basis of justice and integrity. But left untreated, lack of trust often thwarts the quest for successful projects. Upper managers thus should focus on building and maintaining trust with project members and partners, encourage the openness that allows others to come to them with issues of trust, and coach others to treat issues of trust as high priorities.

Munns (1995) argues that because teams are temporary, the time normally needed to develop long-term trust in interpersonal relationships is not available. He suggests, therefore, that the initial opinions of the individuals entering the project are important in shaping its final outcome. These initial opinions, coupled with the initial actions of the project manager and the upper management of the organization, can send the project into a spiral of increasing or decreasing trust. Once trust begins to spiral downward, it is difficult to change its direction.

Upper managers are important in this situation because they help to develop the initial conditions for building trust. This begins with the process for setting the deadline. Trust can be developed by using an iterative information discovery and deadline negotiation process in which upper managers and project managers work as a team to determine the appropriate project deadline. The appropriate deadline, one that everyone can believe in, is set based on the best information, judgment, and collective wisdom available.

The process may begin with the upper manager's developing an initial deadline to share with the project manager, along with reasons for it and an explanation of how it was determined. The upper management deadline most likely represents the minimum time in which the project might be completed. Upper managers understand that work expands to fill the time allotted to it; they may wish to set the shortest possible deadline so as to hold down that expansion.

The next step is for the project manager to meet with the project core team to determine a schedule based on project requirements and available resources. That deliberation most likely determines the maximum time to project completion. Project managers know that there are many unknowns in a project and that completion dates are estimates at best. However, they also know that once a deadline date slips from their lips, it will be cast in stone by other members of the organization. The project manager's best interest is often served by setting the latest possible deadline date. At this point, the upper manager and project manager have, in effect, set the minimum and maximum possible time boundaries for project completion.

The two managers then meet to negotiate a deadline somewhere between the minimum and the maximum. Base it on the needs of the organization as a whole, experience working on similar projects, and the requirements of this new project. If the upper manager negotiates in good faith, the deadline will be believable, which is important for building trust and motivation. A project deadline can be very tight, but if team members believe it can be done, they will meet it. If they do not believe it, they will scoff at it and most likely not meet it. The best deadline is one that everyone considers believable.

In addition to the final deadline, there must be agreement on milestone deadlines. Milestones are major accomplishments on the path from the present state to the future state of project goal fulfillment (Anderson, Grude, Huag, and Turner, 1987). These milestones are set as a part of the process of developing the project plan or as part of a standard project life cycle. Like the final deadline, milestone deadlines need to be negotiated with upper management. Record all assumptions used in setting the deadline and milestone dates in the project documentation, and review them as part of the normal project process and the project-end retrospective. In this way, upper managers develop a process that will lead to more realistic deadlines for future projects.

Negotiating the project deadline works only if team members trust upper management not to change the deadline without renegotiating. If upper managers change the deadline unilaterally, the team will likely assume that the negotiation was a sham and that the upper managers are not to be trusted. Without trust, the entire project system begins to disintegrate.

This does not mean that upper managers have no flexibility in changing the deadline; they simply need to involve the project team. Most people can deal with change if they understand why it is necessary. Cialdini (1993) reports interesting research supporting the well-known principle of human behavior stating that people are more likely to do something if they are provided a reason: 94 percent of the time people complied with a request when the word *because* was used; when it was omitted, only 60 percent complied. Amazingly, even when no new information followed after the word *because* to justify compliance, 93 percent still agreed. The word apparently carries the power to trigger an automatic compliance response. Trust is increased if upper managers truthfully describe why change is necessary and work with the team to develop a new deadline.

True leadership means involving all affected parties in the deadline decision. Upper managers can easily affect the success of a project by taking a team approach to the setting of project deadlines.

Managing on the Learning Curve

Another area where upper management actions have considerable effect on project success is in managing in a learning, creative situation. By definition, projects attempt to develop something new—something that has not been produced the same way before. Because a new end is sought, the project work that will bring it about is best done in an environment of learning and creativity. The repeatable processes and products of the traditional management environment are rarely appropriate, and they may actually be detrimental. Thus, upper managers need to understand best practices for managing on the learning curve.

What is a learning curve? Figure 3.3 shows several relationships between the amount of time devoted to an activity and the percentage of that activity that is complete at that time. The straight line indicates the normal path of progress when an activity has been repeated many times. Because the work necessary to complete the activity is familiar, it progresses at a fairly steady rate. Not all repeated activities progress along an exactly straight line, but the general pace tends to be more predictable and steady than when work is new and must be learned as it is being done.

The curve in Figure 3.3 shows the path of progress in a learning and creative situation: the learning curve. It is common in project activities. Russell and Evans (1992) list the stages of the creative process as follows:

Preparation:	Analyze the task, gather ideas, question assumptions
Frustration:	Period of inability to solve problem, doubts of one's abilities
Incubation:	Put the issue on hold and hand it over to the unconscious mind
Insight:	Experience the "aha!" moment normally associated with creativity
Working it out:	Finish the creative product

FIGURE 3.3. RELATIONSHIPS BETWEEN TIME AND COMPLETION.

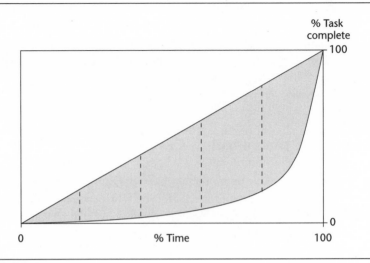

This progress pattern is reflected in the curve on Figure 3.3. Note that in creative situations, the percentage of the task completed is often low at the beginning, and then output builds rapidly as the deadline nears. This is because creative work must incubate. There is much consideration of alternative possibilities at the beginning of the task and then a synthesis of solutions as the deadline draws near. The creative process is done with the activity deadline in mind, but there needs to be enough time for the synthesizing process to take place. This emphasizes again the importance of setting believable deadlines for both project milestones and the final product.

Many upper managers feel it is their prerogative to change deadlines. Perhaps a competitor has taken an unexpected action; maybe the product is needed sooner to boost earnings. Or the upper manager may simply believe that the project is taking too much time. Justifiable reasons for finishing the project faster can always be found, and when they are, upper managers may believe they are taking appropriate action by moving up the deadline or adding people, or both. This may be effective where people are doing repeat work; indeed, it is a tried and true management response to change. However, in creative situations like projects, it is absolutely and demonstrably incorrect and probably will lead to project failure.

The basic reason is that the project constraints of outcome, cost, and schedule are interrelated: a change in one causes changes in the others. An arbitrary change in schedule thus affects the outcome and costs. To understand this relationship, look again at Figure 3.3. If the deadline is arbitrarily moved up, the creative process is short-circuited, and solution synthesis will not take place. Something will be delivered at the new deadline, but not at the quality levels originally desired. Thus, the change in schedule changes the outcome.

The arbitrary change in schedule also has a negative effect on the trust level between upper manager and team members. As discussed, project deadlines should be negotiated between the team and upper management, a process that builds trust. Suddenly moving the deadline without team input destroys that trust. Without trust, team morale plummets, and the project heads for disaster. Thus, taking steps that may be appropriate in repeat process environments can destroy the project that is producing the very outcome upper management seeks. Pity, isn't it?

Another favored action for cutting time is to add people halfway through an activity. Upper managers may do this if they do not understand the project learning curve—if they think the project is late because (for example) less than half the work is done halfway to the deadline. The expectation of straight-line progress instead of learning curve progress creates unwarranted concern. Adding people to solve the nonexistent lateness problem is a well-known folly of project management.

Brooks's Law (see Box 3.2) is taught in many project management seminars. But many project managers say they have difficulty following the advice not to add people to late activities. This is because upper managers often encourage and reward the wrong behavior. Adding people to late activities may work in departments but not in projects. If the team does not ask for more people, upper managers should not force people on them. If the plan was developed with all core team members and if the deadline was negotiated, there is a good probability that the project will not be late.

BOX 3.2. Brooks's Law.

Frederick Brooks was the project manager for the IBM 360 operating system project. Researching why the project was completed a year late, he concluded (1975) that one reason was that he added people when he thought the activities were behind. This added confusion, consumed more time because the new people had to be brought up to speed, and demotivated the team member. From this he formulated Brooks's Law:

> Adding people to late software projects tends to make them later.

Subsequent experience shows that this law holds for all projects with creative parts, not only software projects.

Upper managers often support adding people to projects; such a step does sometimes work in departments. Or perhaps they believe in the "bias for action" promoted in some popular books, or because it gives them the impression of being in control of the situation. This is like making a wide detour rather than sitting in a traffic queue: it may take more time, burn more gas, and put more miles on the car, but it gives a feeling of control and a sense that something—anything!—is happening.

Being in control depends on the definition of control. Upper management does not control a project by directing action or checking actual action against expected action. Control means checking results against expected results, and the expected results are embodied in the plan. Stacey (1992) offers a new mental model for managers concerned about control. The future of organizations, he says, is unknowable but will emerge from the spontaneous, self-organizing interaction between people he calls bounded instability—a state of chaos that exists between stable equilibrium and explosive instability. Thus, businesses must strenuously seek to operate in a chaotic arena in order to achieve success over the long term. This means being highly sensitive to small changes, dependent to some extent on chance, and being ultimately constrained by business control systems. The future, says Stacey, "cannot be intended by its managers; it can only emerge from the chaotic interaction between it and the systems constituting its environment. When managers employ control systems that utilize both negative and positive feedback at the same time, they sustain their organization in a state which makes it possible for innovation to occur" (pp. 78–79).

Upper managers can apply this advice by emulating a modern manufacturing practice: fix the process, not the product. That is, provide clear goals and training for people to work on innovative tasks (but avoid commands), expect work to happen chaotically and autonomously (even if it seems out of control), and design a process that checks progress at crucial decision points (rather than micromanaging work in progress). Manufacturers today often follow a just-in-time concept, recognizing that work happens when it is pulled along by successor activities in small, flexible batches. This allows deviations to be spotted quickly because each task is accountable to assess its inputs and outputs.

In project management, control means monitoring deviation from the plan and then taking steps to return to the planned outcome. Still, all too often a rush is made to add people to projects perceived as being late. To understand this behavior better, refer again to Figure 3.3. Project activity usually proceeds at a rate indicated by the curve on the chart, whereas uninformed upper managers expect to see progress as shown by the straight line. In other words, they expect half of project activities to be completed when half the time allotted for the project has passed. Worse, for much of the project's life, the gap between the straight line and the curve continues to increase. This is also a measure of the increasing anxiety of these managers. Their anxiety is greatest after about 60 percent of the allotted project time has expired. At this point, the managers are wringing their hands wondering what to do, and when the anxiety gets too great, they "run out of hand cream" (see Figure 3.4) and add people to the activity—sometimes even when they know better—in the hope that nothing bad will happen to them this time.

Unfortunately, adding people to perceived late activities, although wrong, is supported in most organizations. Those who do not take action and at least appear to be in control will be chastised if the project is indeed late. Those who do act and thereby cause some of the lateness are seen as having the "right stuff." This is yet another example of organizational perversity that needs to be changed by upper managers if an environment that supports best practices is to be created. The matrix of perceived rewards shown in Figure 3.5 illustrates this particular perversity. It contrasts the rewards given for adding people with the rewards for

FIGURE 3.4. OUT OF HAND CREAM.

FIGURE 3.5. MATRIX OF PERCEIVED REWARDS.

	Activity	
	Late	Not Late
Action	+	++
No Action	−	0

not taking such action. For example, if the project manager takes action but the project is late anyway, the action is still rewarded (the plus sign at upper left) because the upper manager would have acted too. If the project manager takes action and the activity is not late, it is a double plus. If the project manager takes no action and the activity is not late, there is no penalty. However, if the project manager does not act and the activity is late, the evaluation is often negative; the project manager is seen as being "asleep at the switch" and thus not capable.

Notice that the only negative on the matrix is next to the correct action. Where the upper manager grants rewards in this manner, it is in the project manager's best interests to take the incorrect action. A far better situation is for the upper manager to understand the proper behavior and change the rewards to match.

What happens when a manager pulls a person from one team to place him or her on another? The impact of yanking a person off one project is to slow it down. The impact on the other project of adding a person is to slow it down. You make one project late in order to make another project late—another "great moment in management"! This is such a fundamental mistake that you would figure it would never happen. The intent to motivate a team actually has the effect of demotivating it. Knowledge workers are not interchangeable parts.

Managers often ask what to do if they do not add people but an activity is still late. If the activity is truly late and not just perceived to be, the first reaction should be to go to the project plan. Is the activity on the critical path? If not, the lateness will not affect the final date of the project, and there is little problem. If the activity is on the critical path, determine what future activities can be changed to make up for this one. An activity can be expedited by adding people before it begins or scaling back its scope. To do this requires having a plan and believing in it, another benefit of an extensive planning process.

Upper management can help the project manager control the project by asking questions that encourage the desired outcome:

- Do you know the deadline?
- Do you know what is required by that deadline?
- Do you know that you have to deliver it?
- Do you know the consequences of late delivery, not just to the project but to the people waiting for it?

If the project manager can answer yes to these questions, the project will most likely be finished on time. However, for the upper manager to believe in this process requires using it successfully over time. Those who react to perceived lateness by simply adding people never get that chance.

Just as adding people during a task is rarely helpful, neither is the opposite: starving projects of the people they need. Upper managers kid themselves and the organization if they approve a project for execution but do not assign sufficient numbers of people to accomplish the scope of work. One large product development project passed a very thorough up-front planning checkpoint that included a staffing plan from multiple project teams. Month after month, a graph of actual staffing versus the plan showed a severe shortage. These shortages were called to upper management's attention by the program management office, but no corrections were initiated. The project was finally canceled after two years of effort and millions of dollars spent. Many factors contributed to the cancellation, but a key one was insufficient staffing to execute the ambitious set of specifications in the scope of work. Many people were frustrated for a long time, and the work went down the drain because of resource starvation.

A process called pipeline management integrates product strategy, project management, and functional management. John Harris and Jonathan McKay (see Rosenau, 1996) believe effective pipeline management is achieved by fine-tuning resource deployment for projects during ramp up, ramp down, and mid-course adjustments. In this environment, "projects are not added to the pipeline until resources are available to staff them adequately" (p. 69).

For upper managers to manage on the learning curve requires that they understand the resource utilization patterns of project activities. Not all activities on a project will be new; some activities will repeat those undertaken on previous projects, meaning that certain people in the organization know what kind and level of resources were used to implement them in the past. Upper managers should ensure that these activities are staffed at the level already known to be best. About activities that are new and unique, the best source of information is probably the project team itself. Resource allocation should be one consideration in setting the initial project deadline and milestone deadlines. Successful upper managers know that there is no simple way to change the deadline and so take the initial trade-off between project deadline and resource level seriously. They do not change the resource levels or deadlines without the input and participation of the project manager, and they refrain from adding or encouraging more resources for a project unless the project manager asks for more. The upper manager and the project manager need to work together continually to negotiate any changes in schedules or resource levels.

The Difference Between Support and Interference

Upper managers may say they want new and unique products, but project managers sometimes find that if a product is too new, upper managers change its specifications to make the new look like the old. The reason is that a unique product can fall outside the comfort zone of an upper manager, who then prevails on the project manager to force changes in product design. In project management, the problem of "high muckety-mucks mucking it up" is a familiar one.

Of course, upper managers can have opinions and make suggestions. Properly offered, these are welcomed and even sought by team members. It is not that upper management participation and support is undesired, but that the team does not want interference in its job of meeting project goals. The main difference between interference and support is whether the team must make the changes suggested. If not, the suggestions are support. If so, the suggestions are interference.

Project-based organizations should have a "no muckety-muck" rule. This does not mean that upper managers cannot track progress on the project and make suggestions. It means that they are well informed and that their suggestions are solicited, but that the project team does not have to implement the suggestions of individual upper managers. However, if the project team is off track and change is definitely warranted, a suggestion for change may come from the entire upper management committee. Such a change may well be considered mandatory, but the need for it has to be seen by every upper manager, not just one.

HP's 1993 annual report provided a description of seam teams—groups of engineers assembled to work on a particular problem across the organization and make certain nothing falls "through the seams." Engineers rather than managers are chosen to lead seam teams to give the teams more independence and not tie them too closely to specific project groups. Some engineers are intimidated by management presence and thus are more likely to speak freely in the seam team environment. Managers are free to discuss issues with seam team members but must be careful not to overly influence them. The teams enjoyed defining their workplace as a "no manager zone" by posting signs saying, "No managers allowed."

This indicates that people can work faster without management interference, decreasing cycle time. In addition, forcing a change in specification is the opposite of empowerment. Teams feel empowered when they can determine their own way to reach the goal. An empowered project team is usually a more successful project team. Upper managers who interfere and continue to exercise the command-and-control style of management will find it demotivating to well-functioning teams.

When a conference program needed to be downsized due to economic cost constraints, one director unilaterally forced cuts and sent messages suggesting people not attend. He perceived his role as driving cutbacks instead of leading people to be creatively involved. He dictated what the program manager should do when he could have explained the situation and asked for ownership in response. This is a difference between interference and support.

Motivating Project Work

Upper management practices can have a significant impact on project success by motivating project work. There are two facets to the motivation: rewarding project work and setting a general climate that makes good project work the norm for the organization.

Most reward systems were installed before projects became so important to organizational success. Not surprisingly, therefore, these systems actually discourage project work. Project work is often added to people's regular work, making it seem of secondary importance, and it may not be considered in performance appraisals. More work and no recognition provides little motivation; under such circumstances, people do project work when they get a chance. To encourage project work, review the reward system that is in place. People respond to what is measured, so if project work is not measured and rewarded, successful projects in the organization will be rare even if all other best practices are implemented.

Especially important to motivating project work is making it part of team members' regular evaluation. Too often, evaluations and appraisals are done by the department director without input from project managers. If a person contributes a significant amount of time to projects, it should clearly be reflected in the appraisal process; otherwise, project team members get the message that project work is not "real work" by the organization's definition.

Upper managers need to set a climate that makes project work the norm of the organization. HP's seam teams reaped the benefits of a supportive climate: over a few months, they developed and tested three times as many new products as usual and compressed design cycles from months to weeks. "We were really free to have fun and solve a problem," said a team member. "Management was there to help us get the people and resources we needed, but they let us work without distractions."

For any such project team, experience indicates that managers need to provide clear, stable objectives. As team members come from several groups, how managers interact with their peers is important. The entire management team must buy into and support the team concept. Managers need to allow their people sufficient time to participate in team activities and to delegate more technical decisions than they may be used to. Teams need to be given authority as well as responsibility to address team issues.

Another factor in climate setting is expecting project managers to execute the basics. Some project managers claim not to have or take the time for some forms of basic project work—training or planning, for example—because no one in management has demanded it of them. If upper managers do not ask for a project plan, these project managers do not plan. If upper managers do not understand work breakdown structures or metrics reports, these project managers do not provide them and track progress based on them.

Sometimes setting the environment for successful projects requires finding a new hero. What type of person is most talked about in the organization? Upper managers help to define project manager behavior when they talk about former project heroes. Mentioning those who encouraged the right kind of behavior motivates the best practices in others.

In seminars, we posit two potential organizational heroes, A and B. B has good plans and develops good project teams; as a result, this manager's projects usually go well—according to plan, close to the deadline, and without too much hassle. Most problems are foreseen as a result of the planning process and there are few last-minute rushes. The results are well-documented and accepted by the customer.

Potential hero A is somewhat different. This project manager has no plans because this is an action organization: if you want results, start fast. So A's team starts. The flurry of activity pleases upper management. Later, there is a catastrophe that supposedly could not have been foreseen. Legions of people are pulled in at the last minute. Enormous energy is expended; people work late into the night and on weekends to fix the problem. At the last possible moment, someone discovers a fix, and the product is rushed to the customer. Of course, it is not exactly what the customer wanted, and there is little documentation, but these problems are fixed later.

Which type of hero is more discussed in any given organization? Hero A. Which type of hero is most desired? Hero B. Which should be emulated by a new organization member who wants to become a hero? At seminars, the answer is usually A—which is good for seminar presenters but not for organizations. Too many organizations support known detrimental behavior: they are organizationally perverse, rewarding behavior A while hoping for B. Upper management changes this by rewarding and talking about proper behavior.

AT&T's heroes were symbolized by the "Golden Boy." Originally the trademark of Western Electric, "The Genius of Electricity," the mighty Greek godlike twenty-four-foot-high sixteen-ton nude statue entwined in cables was prominently displayed at AT&T headquarters. It was renamed "The Spirit of Communications" by the local Bell operating companies. The statue designer, Evelyn Beatrice Longman, wanted it to symbolize Mercury's speed, the era's continuing sense of mystery about all things "electric," and the modern messenger, the telephone.

AT&T became famous over the years for its ability to pull off miracles in times of natural disaster. The rescuers were often treated as heroes. According to Ono (1990), this mentality carried over to more mundane problems: "Employees who could go in and rescue a botched implementation were often commended, rewarded, and promoted" (p. 14). But when AT&T's Bell System monopoly ended in 1984, the hero approach was incompatible with the project management approach that had become necessary. Says Ono: "The carryover Bell System mentality of admiring heroic rescues of projects had to be replaced with admiration for doing a competent job again and again" (p. 14).

The millennium push to resolve Y2K computer issues provided a stark reminder about the usual heroes. Project managers and teams around the world worked furiously for many months to make the ticking of the clock into the new century a nonevent in terms of computer failures. They were so successful that few hero stories emerged. Companies and the press were poised to document heroic midnight efforts. Being hard pressed to find any, people stopped talking about the true heroes: those who had completed their projects successfully. All computer users, both direct and indirect, however, owe them a great debt of gratitude.

One story by the Project Management Institute ("Y2K Leader Receives Jenett Award," June 2001, p. 1) corrects this injustice. Irene Dec, vice president of International Investments of the Prudential Insurance Co. of America, in response to winning the Eric Jenett Project Management Excellence Award from PMI, says, "My thanks to . . . my companywide Y2K team for their creative out-of-the-box thinking, their commitment and motivation, their desire to overcome obstacles, and the pride they had in performing their work in a world-class fashion. The four attributes represented by the trophy—strength, wisdom, labor, and beauty—accurately describe the Y2K team. We were strong; we never gave up. We had the wisdom to rethink a strategy to try to find a better way to overcome obstacles. We labored late hours and weekends for long periods of time. And we became a beautiful family who believed in each other."

Looking at the issue through pictures, Hero A (Figure 3.6) hurls fire in one direction, creating activity and commotion. Hero A may also be considered a problem solver, but only in the sense that he puts out fires that in some cases are the same ones he created earlier. Hero B (Figure 3.7) plans projects carefully and makes the team the hero when solving problems. B is usually good at avoiding crises; A is good at solving crises. In most organizations, both types of people are needed and should be rewarded at the proper times.

At an internal project management conference, HP CEO Lew Platt (1994) was asked which manager serves the company better: the one who gets the company out of crises or the one who anticipates crises and knows how to prevent them. He answered: "We need both types, and we will continue to value both of those skills. I think a lot of you believe that the people who do crisis management get more recognition and more rewards than those who simply get the job done. I really don't believe that's the case. I look at all of the stock options, all of the star

FIGURE 3.6. HERO A.

FIGURE 3.7. HERO B.

options that we give out, and most of the stars are given for people who get the routine job done very well, not the people who manage their way out of crises. So, we value both."

His point is well taken: upper managers should ensure that both types of behavior are rewarded when appropriate, and that all are aware of such rewards.

The Project Manager as Hero

The story in Box 3.3 is adapted from Joseph Campbell (1990). The text not in parentheses is Campbell's synthesis of the typical hero story as told in many cultures. The text in parentheses is an interpretation that delineates the project manager as hero.

BOX 3.3. The Project Manager as Hero.

The mythological hero (accidental project manager), setting forth from his common day hut or castle (cubicle), is lured, carried away, or else voluntarily proceeds to the threshold of adventure. There he encounters a shadow presence (top manager, department director) that guards the passage. The hero may defeat or conciliate this power and go alive (conciliate through stakeholder management) into the kingdom of the dark, or be slain by the opponent and descend into death (be fired).

Beyond the threshold, then, the hero journeys through a world of unfamiliar yet strangely intimate forces, some of which (the high muckety-mucks) severely threaten him, some of which (the core team) give magical aid. When he arrives at the nadir of the mythological round, he undergoes a supreme ordeal (manages the project to completion) and gains his reward. The triumph may be represented as the hero's sexual union with the goddess-mother of the world (no comment!), his recognition by the father creator (top boss of organization), his own divinitization (becomes a project management consultant), or again—if the powers have remained unfriendly to him—his theft of the boon he came to gain (he goes to another firm and takes project management knowledge with him); intrinsically, it is an expansion of consciousness and therewith of being. The final work is that of the return (to the original department). If the powers have blessed the hero, he now sets forth under their protection (top management approves the move); if not, he flees and is pursued (the project manager runs back to his old department manager and begs for his old job back). At the return threshold, the transcendental powers must remain behind; the hero reemerges from the kingdom of dread (goes back to his original department). The boon that he brings restores the world (he teaches them about project management).

The Compleat Upper Manager

The successful complete upper manager:

- Realizes the need to change some behavior to accommodate the ambiguity inherent in project situations.
- Understands the need for planning on projects and fully supports a project planning process.
- Supports focus on single tasking rather than multitasking to improve efficiency.

- Negotiates reasonable and believable project deadlines based on the project plan and available resources.
- Encourages and rewards desired behavior rather than behavior that may be detrimental to the project.
- Understands that the practices of project management are often different from the practices of departmental management.
- Realizes that projects create something new and does not change project specifications because of anxiety over that newness.
- Does not interfere in project operations.
- Provides adequate staffing.
- Ensures that the organizational reward system properly motivates work on projects.

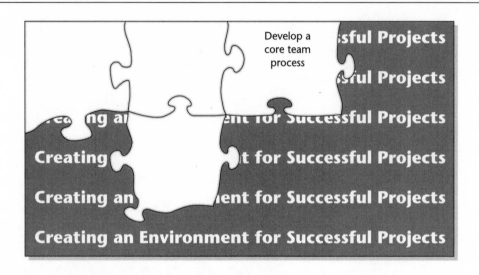

Develop a
core team
process

Creating an Environment for Successful Projects

This chapter begins by defining the concept of core teams, explaining what they are, what they do, and what they can accomplish. This is followed by a discussion of how upper managers can develop a core team process. To help implement the core team process, we describe the benefits of core teams, showing how they help improve product quality, customer orientation, and project speed and how they become a career position for some technical people. The functions of upper managers in staffing and making the core team concept work are also explained. One of the most important functions is developing a team reward system. A description of special team concerns, such as international and cross-organizational team challenges, and rational thinking concludes the chapter.

CHAPTER FOUR

DEVELOPING AND SUPPORTING CORE TEAMS FOR PROJECT SUCCESS

There is no such thing as an accident. What we call by that name is the effect of some cause which we do not see.

VOLTAIRE, *LETTRES DE MEMMIUS III*

Successful projects are completed by project teams, not upper managers. But the background work of upper management teams often leads to project team success. Good project teams may seem to come together by accident. The right people may happen to coalesce on a team, but usually good project teams result from upper managers' setting the stage that allows team success. This chapter reviews the benefits of developing and supporting a core team system for project management.

Project teams represent the cornerstone of the postbureaucratic organization. They confer benefits but also have costs. In particular, upper management flexibility is affected when core teams are in place; upper managers often sense that some of their power is lost to the teams. Upper management teams need to agree that the benefits are worth the costs and support team implementation. Otherwise, the benefits discussed in this chapter will not accrue.

The Concept of Core Teams

Most organizations are segmented into departments that help achieve economies of scale when producing repeat products. However, the department structure is not the best one for producing new products or applications. Developing a new product involves passing it through all the departments until it is ready for market. Along the way, it will undoubtedly encounter the over-the-wall problem (see Figure 4.1), where it is passed back and forth between two departments and often back to a previous department. This causes delay and adds to the project cycle time, and the transit times and numerous handoffs cause information loss that decreases final product quality. The over-the-wall method is not good project management.

One way to eliminate this problem is to establish a core team for each project composed of a person from each affected department. These individuals work on the project from beginning to end. The core team members represent their departments and direct the work of the people in that department on the project. They are empowered to make decisions about the project. Others may come and go on the project as needed, but the core team is the stable group of people who are continuously dedicated to the project (see Figure 4.2).

An example of using core teams to decrease cycle time and focus on customer expectations is the Ingersoll-Rand case (Kleinfield, 1990). Reviewing its cycle time for new tool development, the company found "it was taking three years to make a tool, then three and a half, and heading towards four" (p. 1). It described its development process as a series of walls:

> Marketing would think up a product and throw it over the wall separating it from engineering. Engineering would look at what came flying over and say "Did some lunatic dream this up?" and whip it back to marketing. Later it would thunder back in revised form. Engineering would then work up a design and toss it over the wall to manufacturing, but back it would go. Later

FIGURE 4.1. THE OVER-THE-WALL PROBLEM.

FIGURE 4.2. CORE TEAMS SAVE TIME.

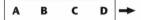

manufacturing would make the product and hurl it over the wall to sales. These people would try to sell it to customers who perhaps did not want it in the first place [p. 1].

Ingersoll-Rand responded by developing a core team of six people that was dedicated to the project. This team cut the design cycle to a year and a half. Attesting to the quality the team was able to produce, the new tool won an award from the Industrial Design Society of America. The project team formation was such a radical departure from standard procedures that it would not have been possible without upper management support for the core team process.

A core team typically comprises representatives from each department involved in developing and implementing the new product or application. To receive the maximum benefit of a core team, assign members to work on the project full time. It is a fundamental management principle that full-time people are more productive than those who divide their time among several projects. Time division diminishes the ability to focus attention on any one project. The learning process necessary on projects requires long periods of concentrated effort in order to arrive at creative solutions. Such effort is impossible if people are spread among several projects that all require the same long concentration, and without concentrated effort, the quality of the final product invariably suffers.

To get the highest quality in the minimum time, projects need full-time core team members—preferably all in one location. Collocated team members can most easily and frequently exchange ideas; many difficult team communication problems are eliminated or reduced when the team members interact on a daily basis. When team members from different departments see each other every day, they also begin to lose some of their departmental identity and begin to identify more with the team. This fosters team cohesiveness while continuing the benefits of the multidisciplinary perspective. Collocation is thus an important impetus to the process of project team building.

For some projects, it may not be feasible to have all team members working full time for the entire duration of the project. Projects typically require different expertise at different phases, so some members may move on and off the team. But while these temporary members are working on the project, they should do so full time. The core team members, however, do not move in and out and should therefore be full time on the project from beginning to end.

When Allen-Bradley adopted this approach, it specified that cross-functional teams would see product development through from "womb-to-tomb" (Heckscher and Donnellon, 1994, p. 225). By staying with the project throughout its lifetime, the core team members are aware of or involved in all major decisions made about the product, and they "own" the product as a team. Each core team member

---

BOX 4.1. Core Team Derivation.

Core teams represent a return to the guild approach to production that was common before the Industrial Revolution. Core teams are also a response to the organizations that were developed as a result of the Industrial Revolution. Note that the bureaucratic organization was a replacement for the guild system. Efficiency came with standardization. Now that we are returning to a modified guild system, we will give up some efficiency but will gain customization. With the guild approach, one craftsman would make customized products to fit the requirements of the customer. The craftsman had to understand the customer, the product, and the customer's use of the product.

Source: Adapted from Graham (1984).

should feel accountability for the whole project, not just one piece of it, and this can be accomplished only when they stay for the duration. Promoting such team ownership is an important aspect of the upper manager's role in creating the environment for successful projects.

The core team helps organizations return to a customer focus. During the Industrial Revolution, organizations were built around repeat processes that made repeat products. While concentrating on the product, they lost sight of the customer. It was then required that the customer understand the product and devise appropriate uses for it. This was certainly the way with early computer products: they were bought and then programmed by the buyer to fit the needed application. But the Industrial Revolution has given way to the customer revolution, and these customers now demand applications and solutions to problems, not just products. Satisfying this demand requires a return to the old guild approach, where one person worked with the product from the beginning through to the customer application (see Box 4.1). However, modern products and applications are too complicated for just one person; they require a team in place of a single craftsman. The new craftsman is thus the core team.

Led by a project manager and responsible for project success, core teams represent the departments involved in bringing a product from concept to customer. The members are people with complementary skills who are committed to the goal of the project and hold themselves mutually accountable for it. Thus, they take the time to render their best judgments on important issues. As team members develop, so does the team; eventually, it is able to apply a collective wisdom that is so important to eventual project success. Developing this collective wisdom may be expensive, but the results can be priceless.

Developing a Core Team Process

For the upper management team to develop a core team process:

- Require that each project have a core team.
- Define core team membership as an important position in the organization. Commitment to the core team should be full time or at least a large percentage of each member's time.
- Support core team involvement in defining the project goal and completing the project plan. Core team members should be heavily involved in the project start-up meeting.
- Resist moving core team members once they are assigned.
- Motivate, evaluate, and reward core team membership.
- Support regular core team meetings.

A common mistake in implementing project management is ignoring the process of developing core teams. Core team process implementation requires a long-run view of projects; often only upper managers have this view. On occasion, the project manager is told to plan the project, or just to get started and then bring people on board as necessary to accomplish the project work. This invites disaster: it propagates another version of the over-the-wall problem, complete with lack of team buy-in and difficult communications problems.

The typical excuse used to justify the "as-needed" approach is that people are busy and it costs money to have them involved when they are not needed. Granted, these people are busy, but often what they are busy doing is putting out the fires lit by the last project, or they may be busy working on projects that should have been done long ago. Most projects take about one-third longer than they should, or one-third longer than they would if they were properly staffed and motivated—and proper staffing includes the use of a core team. Not using core teams because people are too busy is a circular excuse: people are not on core teams because they are too busy, and they are too busy because they were not on core teams.

The circle must be broken. Doing so requires the intervention of upper managers who have a long-term view of the importance of project management. Yes, core teams are expensive and yes, assigning people full time to them may seem extravagant, perhaps even requiring a temporary increase in organizational staffing levels. However, the long-term benefits of core teams, including increased quality and decreased cycle time, can easily pay for the temporary higher expense. Upper managers need to know and believe in the benefits of core teams in order to develop the strength and resolve to implement them.

Core team membership becomes important when people get motivated to participate. The first North American woman to reach the summit of Mount Everest, Sharon Wood (1996), described the process she underwent to get accepted on the team of thirteen Canadian climbers. In front of other potential team members, she responded to three questions: Why do you want to climb Mount Everest? What can you contribute to the team? What do you hope to gain from this experience? In thinking about these questions and answering them in public, she experienced an attitude change at that moment from curiosity to commitment. Taking a lesson from this testimonial, some groups now use a similar process to gain commitment from core team members, especially on large cross-organizational projects. During the project start-up meeting, they describe why they want to be on the team, what they can contribute, and what they hope to gain from the experience. The results are an increase in motivation, a sharing about expectations, and inputs to management about rewards that will motivate team members.

Benefits of Core Teams

People in organizations that do not use core teams may be unaware of the many benefits accruing from their use. Following are some of these benefits.

Core Teams Reduce Cycle Time.   Some may argue that having all departments involved from the beginning of a project wastes money, but it actually saves money in the long run. Core teams cut cycle time and so get the product completed faster. Given the concept of life cycle described next, it is much better to get a quality product to market as fast as possible to maximize its potential.

In the past, people considered a product to have a particular life cycle that would achieve a certain level of sales no matter when it was introduced. The example in Figure 4.3 shows a typical life cycle of slow growth, rapid growth, leveling off, and decline. The shaded area under the curve represents the total sales the product could expect. However, it is now clear that products are examples of a certain concept and that the concept itself has a certain life cycle. Products that represent that concept and are introduced early in the concept life cycle have greater sales than products introduced later in the concept life cycle. For example, consider the IBM Selectric (bouncing ball) typewriters. This was a concept in typing and word processing that used a movable and replaceable typeface ball. At one time, these typewriters were commonplace, but the concept life cycle turned out to be about fifteen years; it was replaced by dot matrix printing (later replaced itself by laser and inkjet printing). The bouncing ball typewriter concept finished its life cycle, and introducing any product based on it now would be folly.

To maximize profit potential, a product must be on the market as early as possible in the concept life cycle. Figure 4.4 shows the sales potential of a product introduced at the beginning of the concept cycle; the darkest portion shows the total sales potential of a product introduced later in the cycle. Potential sales at that later stage are much lower because the concept that the product represents completes its cycle soon after the product is introduced. According to the oft-quoted McKinsey study (Smith and Reinertsen, 1991), if a project is late for an amount of time equal to 10 percent of the projected life of the product, there will be a loss of around 30 percent of the potential profit. If the project goes 50 percent over budget but is delivered on time, there is a loss of about 3 percent of the

FIGURE 4.3. PRODUCT LIFE CYCLE.

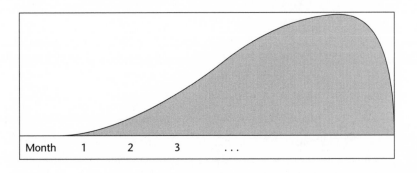

FIGURE 4.4. CONCEPT LIFE CYCLE.

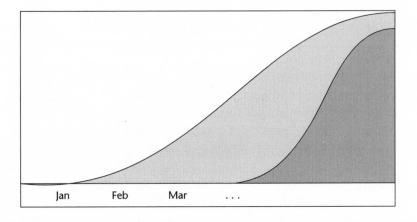

potential profit. Many restrictive assumptions were made in the McKinsey study, so the numbers quoted should not be taken as absolute projections. But they do indicate that a significant amount of additional profit may be gained by being fast to market and that this profit often outweighs by several times the extra costs incurred in speeding to the market. Therefore, the core team that helps deliver a product nearer to the start of the concept life cycle does not waste money; rather, it generates money by increasing the potential for profit.

For example, Cadillac (1991) found that by creating interdepartmental teams in its simultaneous engineering process, it could reduce the time taken to make automobile styling changes. A process that took 175 weeks can now be done in 90 to 150 weeks, allowing new models to be on the market much faster.

Core Teams Increase Quality. Being first to market is not beneficial unless the product is top quality and meets or exceeds customer expectations. It is not just quickness to market that counts; being first to gain customer mindshare is becoming more evident and important. Mindshare results when the majority of the target market thinks of your products first and believes that your company offers the solutions that other companies must measure up to. Creating mindshare requires a dedication to quality, and creation of interdisciplinary teams with a customer focus is one of the cornerstones of quality management. Core teams serve that purpose on projects.

In addition, core teams that cut cycle time seem to add to quality in other ways. The arguments for faster product development cycle times through faster learning have recognized that productivity gains can improve not only cycle times but also product capabilities and quality. According to Schmidt and Finnigan (1992, p. 311), experts at Motorola claim that "one of the fastest ways to improve quality is to focus on reducing cycle time. They found that when they focused on cycle time, defects were reduced at a much faster rate than when they focused on defect reduction alone." This is because core teams reduce hand-offs from one department to another, reducing the information loss and quality decreases such hand-offs might otherwise cause.

Core teams also help implement a marketing-customer orientation. Because the team is involved from "concept to customer," there should usually be a representative from the marketing area on the team. Exposing team members to marketing concepts heightens focus on the customer for the whole team. Perhaps a customer or customer representative might even be involved with the core team, either as a member or through a focus group. In any case, the final project goal developed by the core team should have massive customer input, perhaps through quality function deployment (QFD) techniques. Also, teams should follow Total Quality Management (TQM) or Six Sigma guidelines to help ensure quality.

Core Teams Develop Better Project Plans. The core team refines project objectives, develops strategies for meeting those objectives, identifies critical resources, and develops the plan for the project. The plan becomes the daily guide to action for members of the project team. The core team should always be involved with the project manager in the planning process, so upper managers ought not to try cutting planning time by instructing the project manager to do it quickly and alone. Core team participation may take longer, but there are benefits.

By participating in plan creation, core team members better understand the goal of the project. A customer-driven requirements document helps set the project goal. A common, well-understood goal is a part of the team-building process that leads to a successful project; such a goal also helps reduce cycle time. In addition, core team participation in the planning process allows members to work with each other before the project begins, building trust among them that can develop further as the process proceeds.

Such participation also helps ensure that all necessary project components are considered, reducing the chance that something important is overlooked until near the end of the project. All core team members should know when to schedule help, from inside or outside the organization, to aid in deciding issues that fall in their area of expertise.

Upper management needs to encourage the project manager, the core team, and the project sponsor to hold a start-up meeting, sometimes called a project launch. It is important for developing a shared vision and for communicating, team building, and building relationships with stakeholder groups. Also, it can and should be used to develop trust between individuals and organizations and to define clear roles and responsibilities so that work can proceed. Experience shows that upper managers need to demonstrate support for the project during the start-up meeting but also allow the team to define how it will accomplish its goals.

Core Teams Can Overcome Organizational Design Problems. Without a core team, the final product may reflect the biases of organizational design, a problem inherent in organizations composed of highly autonomous divisions. As Bowen, Clark, Halloway, and Wheelwright (1994b) explain, when the HP 150 personal computer was first designed, four divisions were involved, each focused on a particular product line. No core team was developed, so overlapping projects arose. Senior management leadership was inconsistent. Because marketing was not involved early in the process, no one was sure if any customers really wanted the product, and critical components such as the keyboard and the disk drive were not high priorities for the divisions that made them. As a result, the final product reflected the independence of the divisions that manufactured the components and lacked a unity of purpose and design. The product was not a failure because it did get HP started in the personal computer business, but it did not live up to its potential.

Bowen and his fellow writers contrast that with the highly successful HP DeskJet printer project that skyrocketed the company into the inkjet market. This project used a core team almost from the beginning. The marketing department was involved early, and there was consistent top management ladder support. All team members were collocated, and the engineers worked closely with the marketing department and with end users: "The team produced a well integrated product because its members were located together for the duration, and they were an integrated bunch" (Bowen, Clark, Halloway, and Wheelwright, 1994b, p. 423). In this case, the use of a core team helped mitigate the organizational design of independent divisions and so produce an integrated product.

Core Teams Encourage Creativity.   Core teams are creative. Because they have members from different departments with different points of view, these teams embody requisite variety—the concept that creativity is encouraged when a variety of points of view combine to address a particular problem. It is not that teams of people from one department cannot be creative; rather, cross-departmental teams tend to have a larger variety of viewpoints, which encourages creative solutions. The principle of requisite variety states that having a number of different views fosters creative ideas. Requisite variety is a biological principle based on observations showing that species lacking enough variety and diversity tend to wither and eventually cease to exist.

Variety in team membership also makes teams more difficult to handle, so upper managers who support team training and provide the opportunity for extensive networking and robust interactions get greater creativity from core teams.

Core Teams Make It Possible to Develop Technical Expertise.   To be successful, a team must be able to use existing organizational expertise to produce the final product. The project manager may not have this technical expertise, so it must reside in the core team. Companies need people who can do two things effectively: serve as team members and lead the effort within their functions. Core team members do exactly that; they are themselves members of the project team, and they are responsible for directing the work of other team members. Core team membership is thus a pivotal position and should be highly regarded in the functional departments.

An important factor in making core team membership appealing is the existence of a dual career ladder in the organization. This means having two ways to advance in the organization: climb the traditional career ladder into management or climb a technical ladder and become a chief technical contributor. Consider adding a project management ladder. Core team membership is ideal for technical contributors: they can remain in their technical specialty and be part of the team without having to manage it, and they continue to develop technical expertise while contributing to team projects. (See Chapter Seven for more on dual career ladders.)

Core Teams Execute Project Plans. Once the plans have been established, the core team oversees the completion of the project, primarily by involvement in exception management and risk reduction.

Ellis (1994) described his experience with a core team at HP as follows: "The teamwork and alignment of the members of the core team is critical. This team will spend many hours together and will face many difficult challenges together. The project team and management group will look to this group to provide leadership. The extent to which we get 'out of our silos' [see Chapter Five] and act as a team will play a large factor in success or failure. We have had several off-site meetings with a variety of team building activities. We also have had a 'process quality consultant' available to help plan and address local teamwork issues."

Functions of Upper Management

Core teams are difficult to implement unless all upper managers agree on the concept of core teams (relatively easy) and pledge to do what is necessary to make it work (much more difficult). This is often a classic ends and means problem: everyone agrees on the ends, but no one can agree on the means.

One barrier is that implementation limits upper managers' freedom of action. If a person from a given department is put on a core team, that person is no longer available to the departmental manager until the end of the project. The departmental manager cannot pull the person off one project to work on some other "hot" one, as core team membership is defined as an obligation to work on the project from beginning to end. A person from R&D, for example, would stay with the project until the day the product was shipped to the customer, and maybe beyond, depending on the definition of the end of the project. Members of the upper management team must stand ready to limit their departmental prerogatives for the good of the organization as a whole. If they do not, the core team concept is doomed to failure.

Upper managers can again look to their own behavior for clues about creating an environment for successful multifunctional teams. Meyer (1993) describes good executive sponsors of teams as being like good driving instructors: they teach and guide without grabbing the wheel unless the situation is life threatening.

Sponsors help build capabilities and processes within the team to achieve the goal rather than solving problems directly. Meyer goes on to say that the critical roles of executive sponsors are teaching upper managers how to work with teams, transforming their own functions into centers of expertise, and learning how to lead a team-based organization: "It is very difficult to comprehend fully how these teams actually work until you've been on one. Making functional leaders sponsors enables them to see firsthand how the teams work and what they must change within their function to support them. Those who do not serve as sponsors miss this experience and rely on anecdotal reports picked up in hallway conversations" (p. 127).

To implement a core team process, upper managers are advised to consider each of the following.

Develop Project Priorities. Establishing project priorities is a first essential step, as discussed in Chapter Two. When upper managers work together to establish these priorities, they help core teams operate across organizational boundaries. This is important because core teams by definition cut across departmental lines. Any dissension in the ranks of upper management will be reflected in the behavior of the core team. If a given project has a different priority in each contributing department, the team members will reflect those priorities and have difficulty acting as a team. Thus, the project should have the same priority in each of the contributing departments, and that cannot happen unless the upper managers support the core team concept by defining project priorities.

Define the Core Team Concept as Important. Upper managers too often indicate the desire to cut cycle time and increase quality even as they deny project managers the means to attain those goals. The upper management team can support project managers by publicly declaring that the core team concept is important and will be implemented in the organization. When this is done, project managers can better implement the concept.

Agree on Assignment of Core Team Members. If upper management is serious about cutting cycle time and increasing quality, it will assign full-time core team members—usually. Some small projects may not warrant full-time assignments, but the team members even on these should still be occupied on them a majority of the time. The percentage of time may vary for each individual depending on where the project is in the process. However, the same people must remain on the team. For the core team to function effectively, its members need to be released from some departmental duties—that is, from "billable hours." Upper managers of contributing departments also need to realize the importance of the core team role and agree to the release so that members are not penalized for joining the team.

Normally, one project manager leads the team. It is possible to have rotating leadership within the core team; when this is so, the rotation should not come as a surprise, all project managers should come from the core team, and all should return to regular core team membership after leading it. At Allen-Bradley (Heckscher and Donnellon, 1994, p. 249), for example, "in general, leadership of project teams rotated according to where the project was in the milestone process. Marketing assumed the lead role for the business proposal and project definition segment, up through the first GM (upper management) milestone review. Engineering then guided the team through the design and development phases, followed by manufacturing's lead during pilot activity and full production. Marketing took over again for field performance reviews and the final GM evaluation, which occurred six months after the first shipment."

In general, project leader rotation from the core team can be done by assessing the key risk being encountered by the project at a given time. If marketing success is the key risk to project success, perhaps a marketing person should be the project leader. If technology is the key risk, consider a technology leader. Select a leader with talents and abilities strong in the skill sets required to overcome the important risks.

Resist Pulling Members Off the Core Team. Pulling people off the core team negates the entire concept. Cycle time is lost as new members must be trained and brought up to speed. Quality is lost as new members do not know the effects of decisions made before they joined or the effect that future decisions will have on previous decisions or on other departments. Thus, loss of continuity causes loss of both time and quality, the prevention of which is the very reason the core team was established in the first place.

Many upper managers attempt to mitigate the negative effects of pulling a core team member by replacing the person with someone of equal skill. But people are not interchangeable parts (see Figure 4.5); the assumption that they are may stem from managing departments where people do work that they have done many times before. In such an environment, there may indeed be only minor consequences to substituting one person for another, and the practice may even be considered good management, a way to maintain upper management flexibility at little cost in efficiency. A project environment, however, involves knowledge work, and such substitutions can cause major problems and setbacks; rotating core team membership is often cited as a major factor in project failure. Thus, upper managers best enable project success by developing the discipline to resist pulling members off the core team.

FIGURE 4.5. CORE TEAM MEMBERS ARE NOT INTERCHANGEABLE.

Motivate Core Team Membership. Core team members' attitude toward the project role is strongly influenced by the manager of their home department. If the department director is negative about it, the team member may carry that attitude into the team. Negative attitudes have a way of becoming self-fulfilling prophesies. According to Katzenbach and Smith (1995, p. 45), "Unbridled enthusiasm is the raw motivating power for teams." Upper managers and department directors need to show enthusiasm for project work to help motivate the core team.

Encourage Creativity. Upper managers need to be certain that people know that taking risks is okay. They must also drive out fear and create trust. This is often difficult to do in projects, given the triple constraints of schedule, outcome, and costs. However, upper managers can help in the following ways:

• *Schedule.* Project deadlines can be helpful in motivating completion of creative work. In fact, most creative work is done to a deadline. But it must be a believable deadline, and for core team members to really believe in it, they should be a part of the deadline-setting process, as discussed in Chapter Three. People are not motivated by artificial deadlines.

• *Outcome.* This is where the excitement of creativity lies in a project. Creativity is often needed to meet customer expectations and help solve customer problems. Upper managers encourage it by facilitating core team contact with customers and encouraging creative solutions to customer problems. Upper managers can help by finding the blocks to creativity in the organization and eliminating them for project teams. Look for triggers—key defining events that excite involvement and turn mild curiosity into commitment. These events are usually experiential; it is not usually possible to dictate them. Encourage team members to get firsthand unbuffered exposure to the source of urgency for the project, such as a customer's mission-critical problem. For example, many R&D managers at HP encourage their engineers to go with marketing representatives on customer visits. When they do, the engineers often discover creative ways that their products are being used and often learn of new customer needs.

• *Budget.* Research and experience indicate that one of the biggest barriers to creativity in organizations is overreliance on budget as a guide to action. Strict adherence to the budget may be sound practice in repeat process and product environments, but it is a creativity killer on projects. Stopping ideas because "they're not in the budget" sends a message that standard, safe thinking is wanted on projects. Certainly some projects that are very creative end up costing too much because of it. The key to avoiding this problem is to manage creativity; the actual cost of a creative solution is not as important as its effect on the final product. Continually direct thinking toward the final product, not toward the specific creative solution itself (see Box 4.2).

Stress Interdependence. Upper managers can help make the core team system work by constantly stressing team members' interdependence, a factor that leads to achievement of core team benefits. When a core team system is initiated, many of its members will be accustomed to working alone or in their own departments.

BOX 4.2. Creativity and Budgets.

Computer simulations have been used in project management training for many years. During a simulation, teams make choices among the most effective and often the most creative ways to solve typical project problems. Some organizations clearly make choices that rely on budget; they do not choose the most creative options, even though the team may want to, because these options are not in the budget. Questioned about this behavior, these teams invariably mention that their upper managers measure them on budget, not profit. Thus, if a more creative solution increases profit, the team does not benefit from it, and if the solution increases spending, the team feels the negative consequences. The net result is that many creative solutions are ignored.

They may feel more comfortable working alone than on a team. When reviewing team output, upper managers help by constantly asking how well the members have been working as a team. They also need to build a strong performance ethic and establish metrics for teams to measure performance. The project sponsor should meet with the core team often and review team output.

Provide an Environment to Support Teamwork. As previously mentioned, it is best for core team members to be collocated. The best environment for teamwork is where all team members are in the same area and interact daily. This enhances both team spirit and team communication. When collocation is impossible, a good environment can be approximated by providing a room that is available to team members at all times—a project room where they can meet, interact, and do project work. If having a "room of their own" is impossible, space should be designated where the team can meet at the same place, at the same time, on a regular basis. This is the minimum environment to support good teamwork.

In addition, much technology is available to help teams function. Linked computers with e-mail, shared files, project intranets, Lotus notes, and the like are just a start; core teams whose members are far apart should have access to facilities for conference calls and video conferencing.

Staff Teams for Success. Belbin (1996) reports from extensive research on why management teams succeed or fail that the classic mixed team is the most reliable variety of those studied. A team can more often find among its members the characteristics necessary for good management and leadership; few individuals possess all such characteristics. A winning team starts with a successful chair (project manager) who is patient but commanding, generates trust, and looks for and knows how to use ability in others. The team includes at least one very creative and clever member as well as at least one other possessor of a lively mind of similar caliber for the former to bounce ideas against. According to the research, teams where the remaining members have a wide range of mental ability pull together better than more intellectually homogeneous ones. Winning teams have a wide range of strengths to draw on and a good match between the attributes of members and their responsibilities. One team member or another should be suitable for any job that can come up, or the members should have the flexibility to adjust to and fulfill roles other than their primary ones. The research illustrates that a single addition to a management team can change the fortunes of a company, and a single subtraction from the team can have a momentous negative effect unless a balance is reestablished.

Change the Reward System. The goal should be to make team membership rewarding, as discussed in the next section.

Developing a Team Reward System

Probably the most difficult aspect of supporting core team development is changing the reward system to recognize the work of teams. Most organizational reward systems are deeply rooted in the bureaucratic assumptions of individual rewards for individual work. These assumptions require a narrow division of labor and a hierarchy of levels where an increase of level in the organization is rewarded with an increase in compensation. With experience, it is gradually being understood that the narrow division of labor and the vertical ordering of titles and authority do not tend to support teamwork. In addition, merit-based pay is theoretically tied to individual contribution to the value added by the firm. It is normally not based on team contribution. Because of this, most organizations end up extolling the virtues of teamwork but rewarding people for individual contribution. Heckscher and Donnellon (1994) say that because reward for individual contribution is seen as fair and desirable in the broader culture of the United States, the reward structure may be the most difficult aspect of an organization to change in pursuit of postbureaucratic organizing.

Determining Outcomes to Be Rewarded

There are several factors to consider when changing the reward system. The first is what behavior or outcomes will be assessed and rewarded. Upper managers need to define the criteria for success and make them very clear to all project team members. For projects, they should be based on the project goal statement. For example, is the team to be held responsible only for delivering the product or also for the ultimate profitability and support of the product? Is the team responsible for initial production of the product or for ongoing production? The reward system should be based on accomplishment of the project goal, and it should be public. Everybody on the team should know what the rewards are and how they are administered. For example, are all members of the team, or just the core team members, to be responsible for product success? Typically core team members are to be held more responsible for ultimate project success because they are the ones on the project from beginning to end. If they are more responsible, they should expect greater reward with success and greater disappointment with failure. The evaluations of everyone on the team should be based partly on total team performance. Most important, the system of rewards should be determined before teamwork begins and made clear to all team participants. A best practice is to ask teams and individuals what rewards they find important. Tremendous variability exists about how people view rewards, so asking them indicates care and respect for differing points of view. Also be sensitive to the cultural variations that exist around recognition in public.

Rewarding Teamwork in Reaching Outcomes

Individuals should also be rewarded for their contribution to teamwork. Most systems reward individual contribution, not teamwork. But if teamwork is desired, it should be rewarded; reward should be made for the behavior desired. The difficulty for managers in assessing individual contributions to teamwork is that they do not observe such behavior. The typical solution is to have team members assess each other on individuals' contribution to team performance. Of course, it is easier for core team members to assess each other if they are a continuous team. Members who come and go may do their part without full knowledge of other individuals' contributions. When this is the case, it may be possible for core team members to assess the work done by regular team members in their areas.

The important point is that upper management needs to create metrics that support and measure desired behavior; you get the behavior you measure. The metrics should be as objective as possible, and the criteria for a certain reward must be known in advance so people can strive to reach it. One example of a good metric for teamwork is given by Carlisle (1995). In the example, the upper manager wanted to develop teamwork among the refinery managers who reported to him. During weekly status meetings, team members reviewed operations and any problems that they had. They talked about the decisions they made to solve the problems and who on the team helped them solve the problem. When the manager is away, he picks as temporary manager "the man who is most often referred to as the one my subordinates turn to for help in dealing with their problems" (p. 76). When upper management positions become available, he also recommends this person for promotion.

In this example, teamwork is promoted by requiring team members to ask each other for help when they find problems. The upper manager literally refuses to help with problems until his subordinates consult with other subordinates. The metric is fairly simple: it measures how often people are referred to as helping others on the team. Of course, most upper managers do not have all team members doing the same or similar jobs as in a refinery; many different departments or functions are involved. However, from the perspective that all problems are team problems, such a metric could be effective in other settings as well.

Designing New Evaluation Processes

The project manager needs some control over the process of evaluation and reward, an important lever that can be used to motivate team members. One part of motivation is the intrinsic value of the project. Another is being included in the performance review at the end of the project.

If team members feel they will not be recognized in their departments for good project work, they will view joining a project as a risk. Thus, the project manager must be part of the performance review process. One way is for team leaders to provide feedback to functional or department managers who are responsible for writing performance evaluations for the people on the core teams. Base reviews on both individual contributions and teamwork, and the review form should have a section for evaluation of teamwork that grants it equal weighting as, if not greater weighting than, individual contributions.

This does not mean that the project manager must take over the performance review process. It remains the purview of the department director or, if there are no departments, of one person assigned the function for project team members. The person designated to do performance reviews should gather information from the project managers and other people with whom the individual works.

The project manager should have significant review input for the time people spend on the project, particularly that of core team members. This manager should fill out a detailed performance appraisal for each of the core team members that includes the appraisals of other team members regarding the teamwork of the individual. If possible, the project manager sits with the department director or other designated person during the project part of the performance appraisal. The core team members fill out performance sheets on other project team members in their areas, reducing the risk that team members might be penalized for their project work.

When upper managers appraise the performance of their project managers, stress not only the success of the project but also the project managers' teamwork with other project managers and how they worked as a team to implement the organizational strategy.

In addition, stress that individuals retain responsibility for their self-development and career management. HP made this clear with a CEO's objective for people development. Each person needs to take the lead in determining what he or she needs in a development plan: courses, conferences, reading, mentoring from others, or coaching from management, for example. Management has a co-responsibility to respond so that both parties, manager and subordinate, work together on people development. Career self-reliance is an important ingredient in building accountability in an organic organization.

Designing New Rewards

Finally, upper managers need to consider the rewards for good performance. In the past, it was usually assumed that performance was rewarded with pay or promotion, or both. However, not all rewards take these forms; furthermore, promotion should be based on the ability to do the new job, not on performance on the last one.

Even mediocre teams may have one or more outstanding performers. Such individuals can be rewarded with "most valuable player" recognition despite the team performance. If superior individual performance should be rewarded, consider bonuses and stock options. Promotion should be reserved for those who clearly can handle the job at the next level, not just for superior performance at the current level.

Many rewards are intrinsic in project work itself, such as recognition by senior management, learning a new skill, working at something new, working with different people, working in a new location, or having the ability to travel. One of the best rewards for project managers and team members is to get another good project or a larger project and continue doing what they enjoy doing. Different people like different rewards, and different people are motivated by different things at different times of their lives. The important thing is to have a variety of rewards, apply them according to needs, and allow the project manager to use some rewards to enhance team motivation. Some organizations enable individuals to award $50 to $100, no questions asked, to other individuals in recognition of contributions to the project.

Steele (1989, p. 151) commented on this important factor when discussing dimensions of reward systems in project management: "[One] dimension is allowing the project manager to have control over the process of reward. If the project manager cannot determine or at least strongly influence recognition and compensation, he faces an almost impossible task. Inability to promise and deliver rewards commensurate with contribution is a major barrier, even to recruiting capable people to work on projects, much less to motivating them to intense, dedicated effort. Being farmed out to a project, even a high-priority one, can make one an orphan when it comes time to reward performance—and it is a painful experience."

International and Cross-Organizational Teams

Employees at overseas branches of U.S. companies often complain about the home office, saying things like this: "We tell them everything. They never answer our letters, so we don't know what's going on in the States." The headquarters response is, "They don't listen, they don't answer our letters, so we don't know what's going on over there." Each believes it is sending lots of information to the other and getting little in return. Clearly, neither has defined what information the other side really needs.

The "distance doctor," Jaclyn Kostner (1994), focuses her work on describing how global or international teams can be effective despite the difficulties of bridging the distance between team members. In communicating, she advocates asking who is remote: you or the other team members? It depends, of course, on who is asking the question. Management may believe that empowerment means giving power to remote teams, but there is no guarantee that cooperation will take place. Instead, be prepared to gain access to the power possessed by others who are leaders of their own teams (see Box 4.3). You cannot, says Kostner, give away power you do not have. Success as a project leader comes from capturing power, not giving it away. Realize what contributions are needed from others, such as technical expertise, previous experience, or access to markets, and capture their power by establishing clear agreements on vision, roles, and responsibilities. The upper manager becomes a leader of leaders.

Kostner goes on to describe the glue that ties remote teams together: developing a powerful shared vision that vividly describes the end result expected. Look for evidence that people use this vision as "intellectual cohesion" that permeates all communications. People need to put out the extra effort it requires to check and recheck for understanding about where they are going. Be clear about what is expected from remote team members. Upper managers need to demonstrate a commitment to developing trusting relationships early in the process and maintaining them throughout the project. This means putting equal or possibly more attention on relationships than on tasks. Upper managers need to be clear about and reinforce through their own behavior the need to meet the "prime directive" that the team sets out to accomplish.

BOX 4.3. Why Empowerment Is Not Enough.

When James Kirk, captain of the starship *Enterprise* on the science-fiction television program *Star Trek,* went on a mission from the orbiting starship down to a planet, was he remote from the starship or was the *Enterprise* remote from him? In essence, the question is irrelevant because clarity of roles and the ease of communication kept the relationship continuous. Captain Kirk did not give power to the second in command while he was on the mission; rather, he put them in charge of the resources. When Kirk commanded, "Beam me up, Scotty," in order to be teleported back to the ship, he drew not on the empowered team but on the ability of the crew to engage the resources or power of the starship. (Of course, one could question if "upper manager" Kirk was foolish for leaving the ship instead of delegating the hero role to his project managers.)

How do you build trust with people who work off-site? Because other people look to leaders to organize the work, Kostner (1996) says leaders break the trust when they are not clear about the work. To correct this situation, start by giving a visual anchor—a way for people to visualize the end result. Then provide a hands-on anchor: a small model or prototype. Continue with a word anchor that provides description, definitions, and comparisons. The final step in creating crystal clarity is to create a clarity partnership, where both parties commit to work together to create understanding.

Addressing the topic of project and program management for large projects across organizational boundaries, HP Executive vice president Rick Belluzzo (1996a) advised being "very focused; pick those opportunities that you think have the greatest return, organize around it, but recognize it's going to take a lot of leadership, it's going to take a lot of getting around, talking to people and really working to develop an overall strategy that people can act on. That's what works best at HP. When you get a strong message out there that's very clear, people implement in incredible ways. That's a real strength of ours!"

Collocated teams are best, but if they are not possible, the teams should meet at a regular place at a regular time. For international teams, this is not always possible, so they can use conference calls or video. However, team members have to meet face-to-face to see eye-to-eye. Therefore, support occasional face-to-face meetings of international teams. They should meet at the beginning of the project, then perhaps every six months, and again at the end to wrap up and celebrate. Remember that the intent is to approximate the ideal, not to save money on airfare. Although it is important to plan face-to-face meetings carefully, the time apart should not (but often does) get short shrift; we are not as good at communicating at a distance. Recognize that remote team members thrive on information about the project and the company by supporting efforts that sustain and enhance the project management information system.

In the case of self-managed teams, know that core teams for projects do not run well without a recognized project manager. Self-managed teams run well when the process they are working on is well known, the objective is clear, and little cooperation is needed from outside the team. But this is usually not the case in projects, so a leader is needed. The enthusiasm generated by members of a self-managed team can result in the silo effect experienced by departments, such that team members become loath to work with outsiders. The project manager provides the liaison and ownership for the "whole product" result that facilitates collaboration among teams.

Telecommuting is an increasingly interesting option for enhancing employee productivity while adjusting the demands between work and life. Lew Platt of HP advised managers (1996) to sit down with employees and determine whether telecommuting really makes sense. As part of being a modern employer, delivering flexibility means to favor making equipment available so people can stay home a day or two a week. Do not get caught up in the issue of cost; it may be possible to balance the price of equipment, home loans, and other creative approaches against savings at the work site. These approaches give people an incentive to stay, helping the organization avoid the costs of finding and recruiting replacements and bringing them up to speed. The program manager for HP's work options program added, "We're moving from an approach where telecommuting was seen as a reward for top performers to more of an integrated business approach that balances an individual's need for flexibility with HP's business need" (Platt, 1996, quoted in *MEASURE, Hewlett-Packard*).

Moskowitz (1996) comments:

> Telecommuting and "hoteling" of offices [may produce] hidden advantages. For example, employees who are less tied to fixed workstations tend to lose their focus on intra-office concerns, such as procedures, politics, protocol, and rivalries. They stop jockeying for corner offices and turn much more of their attention outward, toward the customers they're serving and the work-related goals they're trying to achieve. . . . Among the many things telecommuters have successfully proven is that much of today's work can be "deconstructed" into individual elements, accomplished by various individuals working at separate times and locations, then reassembled again into a finished deliver-able with great savings in time, effort, and expense [p. 64].

The international presence enjoyed by multinational companies means that the sun never sets on some projects. It is increasingly possible for project work to happen by day in one country and to continue by night in another. Such non-stop work is one way to shorten cycle times. The environment to make this happen requires good project plans, clearly defined roles and responsibilities of people and their counterparts in the other country, and advanced communication capabilities.

Electronic meeting rooms are also becoming more readily available; they can allow core teams to conduct brainstorming sessions from remote sites. Team members may be at home or across the country and still connect into a central system. A question is posed on the computer screen, and people start typing in ideas that are visible in a common space on the screen to provide inspiration for further ideas. After a while, they may be asked to vote their preference for certain options. Technological tools such as these can help dispersed teams reap the benefits previously available only to in-person teams. Electronic meetings, however, are still weak communication vehicles.

To make cross-organizational and international teams work requires understanding cultural differences. People's actions, reactions, and perceptions are more often driven by their cultural values or shared beliefs as a group than by almost any other factor (Mead, 1990). Cultures may vary across disciplines, companies, and geography (Leonard-Barton, 1995). The differences may be frustrating at times, and they often slow progress, which may make some people view them as project liabilities. However, the benefits derived from the project outcome being applied globally may be massive. Upper managers can take the lead by viewing cultural differences as assets—ways of embracing a broad customer base—and seeking a shared understanding of those values that can lead to a result desired by all. Working with other cultures is not intuitive; people are genuinely different, and one's own experiences may not be preparation for understanding the thinking and actions of others. Upper managers support cultural diversity on projects by preparing and encouraging others to understand different cultures through asking questions, taking courses, reading, learning from others who work or have worked in other cultures, and immersing themselves in other cultures for sustained periods.

Belbin (1996, p. 136) summarizes the process: "Establishing the right climate in which well-designed teams can form and flourish is the foundation stone on which more effective teamwork in the future can be built." Even with the principles, concepts, methods, and techniques he uncovered for designing successful management teams, Belbin adds: "What turns team-building into an art is that the bricks, like legendary men, are made of different types of clay and not wholly predictable after firing."

Using Net Present Value as a Team-Building and Decision-Making Tool

An accepted best practice in project management is establishing core teams of people representing different departments who will stay with the project from beginning to the end. Although there seems to be growing acceptance of the core team as a concept, many organizations have found it difficult to develop and motivate these teams in the concrete. One way to help develop this team of people with varied backgrounds is to have them work together to make decisions regarding the project. This is a good idea in theory; in practice, however, project managers often express frustration in getting core team members to agree on a decision. Although each team member acts in a rational manner, the team itself does not act in a rational manner. What's the project manager to do?

Many organizations use net present value as a criterion for selecting projects. However, once the project is selected and funded, the expected net present value is soon forgotten as project managers focus on outcome, cost, and schedule. Project managers develop core teams to execute projects and concentrate on the outcome or project goal as a method for developing the team, developing a shared understanding, and resolving disputes. The basic idea is to have core team members concentrate on a common goal in order to develop a common view on how best to execute the project. While this is an excellent team-building technique, net present value can be used as an aid in making project decisions as well as an additional team-building tool for developing a shared understanding and resolving disputes. Not only does it build the core team, the practice also links a project selection criterion to project decision making.

Understanding the Problem

A first step in solving this problem is understanding the cause. Many people often assume that because the team is composed of rational people that the result will be rational behavior. This is not always the case, as shown in Box 2.1.

To illustrate the problem, assume a core team of three people: X, Y, and Z. Each of these rational people has to make a decision between choices A, B, or C. They rank the choices in the following way:

X: A > B > C; therefore A > C.

Y: B > C > A; therefore B > A.

Z: C > A > B; therefore C > B.

Now let the three rational people vote on the choice. When we compare A to B, we find that A > B by two out of three team members, X and Z. When we compare B to C, we find that B > C by two of the three team members X and Y. From our definition of rational behavior. we would feel that if A > B > C, then A will be preferred to C. However, when we compare A to C, we find that C is preferred to A by two of three team members, Y and Z. That is, the situation we see is A > B > C with C > A. Obviously, this team will have difficulty coming to a decision, for no matter which choice is proposed, there will always be two team members who prefer something else. The sum of rational behavior is not necessarily itself rational behavior.

Building a Team Even with Such Irrational Behavior

One expedient answer to this problem is for the project manager to express an opinion and give himself a vote. For example, if the project manager were to state a preference as A > B > C, then A > B by 3/4, B > C by 3/4, so it looks as if A is the choice. However, C > A by 2/4. This is not much better, so it might require the project manager to pull rank to break the tie between A and C, which would result in A as the winner. In this case, the team members may wince because A is the *project manager's* first choice, not *their* first choice. This situation will probably sour any developing team spirit. This is an expedient solution but not a good team-building decision. Having the project manager jump in and take over could demoralize the team and irritate team members, and it will not help them develop problem-solving skills.

A second answer might be the political approach, which is usually distasteful to project managers. For the political approach, the project manager tries to get one person to change one of his or her preferences. This might be done by making some sort of deal. Perhaps the project manager can tell person Z that he will give him extra budget to switch preferences between A and C, such that Z now states A > C > B. With this case, the vote is A > B by 2/3, B > C by 2/3, and A > C by 2/3, a seeming return to rationality. But at what cost? The project manager now owes something to one of the core team members, not a good position to be in. In addition, other team members will soon find out about the deal, not a good team-building technique.

A third approach is to appeal to a higher power, a shared understanding of what the project is meant to achieve. This approach begins with the project manager's working to understand why these people hold their preferences in the first place. In many cases, the reason for the irrational team behavior is that the individual points of view are being considered in isolation and based on individual departmental preferences rather than a project goal. To develop a shared understanding, consider these points of view in relation to each other while indicating how the different choices will affect the net present value of the project and its outcome.

An Example

Assume a core team of three people on a $3 million project to produce a new product in twelve months. Using the team, the product will cost $240 to produce and sell for $300 with an eventual market maturity of 20,000 units per month. Competitors will introduce similar products in twelve months. If this product matches the competition and is ready in twelve months, it should capture a 30 percent market share. The team is attempting to make a decision about adding a new feature that was not in the project scope to the product they are developing:

• Choice A is to have an outside firm develop the feature for a cost of $500,000 with no delay to the project. Because there will be no delay and the product will have the new feature, it is expected to capture a 30 percent market share. Using an outside firm adds $5 to the cost of producing the product.

• Choice B is to delay project completion by one month in order for the team to add the feature. This choice means a project cost increase of $250,000 but no increase in product production costs. Since the product will be delayed one month after competitor introductions, it expects to gain only a 26 percent market share.

• Choice C is to forgo the new feature so the project proceeds according to plan with no increase in project or product costs. Without the new feature, the new product expects to capture a 27 percent market share.

Now consider individual preferences for members of the core team:

X: A > B > C. The marketing manager feels that the new feature is important so that the product contains the latest technology. It is also important that the project should not be delayed in order to capture the most market share. Therefore, this manager prefers A over B and then C. A problem with choice A is that it adds to product production costs, but the marketing manager says, "That's production's problem."

Y: B > C > A. The production manager feels that the new feature is important because competitors will most likely have this feature. However, because competitors will have the feature, there can be no increase in price to cover extra production costs. Therefore, it is important that the product be completed at minimum cost.

Z: C > A > B. The financial manager wants cash flow to start as soon as possible and believes that early cash flow will make up for any cost increases.

You might be tempted to break the decision into two parts. That is, both choice A and choice B involve adding a new feature, and these choices are the first choice of the marketing and production managers, respectively. You might be tempted to say there is a preference for adding the new feature, so that the only real decision is to delay or not to delay; that is the choice between A and B. Here there is a clear choice because both the marketing and financial managers prefer A to B. Therefore, it looks as if the winner is to have the outside firm develop the feature.

However, the production manager is still concerned because he believes that the increase in product cost will decrease profitability. The team agrees to use the Business Systems Calculator (available at www.projectmanagersmba.com), explained in Cohen and Graham (2001), to estimate the net present value of each decision choice. Using a capital charge of 15 percent and a tax rate of 33 percent produces the net present value results in Table 4.1. Using this analysis, not adding the feature is now a clear winner.

The power of a net present value analysis is that it is able to take the three variables of project cost, product cost, and market share into consideration at one

TABLE 4.1. NET PRESENT VALUE OF THREE CHOICES.

	Choice A: Use an Outside Firm and Be on Time	Choice B: Use Team and Be One Month Late	Choice C: No New Feature and Be on Time
Project costs	$3,500,000	$3,250,000	$3,000,000
Duration	12 months	13 months	12 months
Product costs	$245	$240	$240
Market share	30%	26%	27%
Net cash flow with capital charge	$2,343,157	$2,079,146	$2,617,094
Net present value	$1,383,715	$1,226,186	$1,563,574

time and yield one numerical valuation. In this way, the results of the three different variables in each choice can be compared to one another, and the choice becomes clear.

Of course, there will always be arguments over the numerical values assigned to the variables, especially when one's favorite choice does not fare well in the evaluation. For example, the above analysis is particularly sensitive to market share estimates. Rerunning the analysis with market share for choice B at 28 and C at 25 results in net present values of $1,474,223 and $1,310,386, respectively.

In this case, it does not take much to change the rankings such that B is now preferred while previously preferred choice C now ranks last. This type of analysis can be manipulated by the types of maneuvers described in Chapter Two. Since the choices are so closely ranked and so easily affected by market share estimates, the team needs to obtain the best market share estimates possible.

When numbers are developed that everyone believes in, people will more likely abide by the results. Computed numbers raise suspicion and cause arguments unless the basis and means for the computation are clear. Use defensible, possibly conservative numbers, and take the time to explain them and get consensus on feasibility. A danger is that arguments ensue over calculations and detract from value-added decision making. Demonstrating a range of values that produce either different or consistent outcomes illustrates influence points. The aim is to accelerate dialogue about which decision best serves the team and organization. Encourage people to explore alternative points of view or ways of thinking.

A salient feature of a net present value approach is that silo thinking, such as "increase revenue" or "decrease costs," comes together in one formula. Both goals are important, and they interact. Some decisions affect the numerator and some the denominator; the interaction among all factors leads to optimizing the result. Use this approach not to drive people apart but to bring them together.

The Compleat Upper Manager

The successful complete upper manager:

- Defines a core team for each project.
- Specifies a project or program manager for each team.
- Supports the team by sponsoring a start-up meeting.
- Helps teams focus their work by prioritizing projects.
- Promotes trust among team members and across core teams.
- Recognizes that core team members are not interchangeable.
- Rewards teamwork.
- Supports the efforts of cross-organizational teams to communicate and work together.
- Uses a variety of techniques, including financial, to build core teamwork.

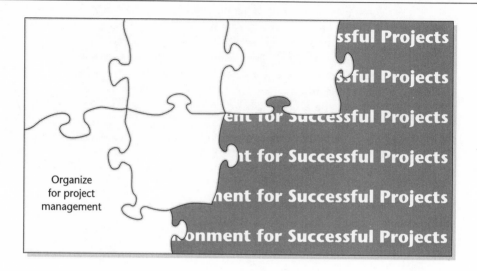

Organize
for project
management

ssful Projects
sful Projects
ent for Successful Projects
nt for Successful Projects
ment for Successful Projects
onment for Successful Projects

This chapter begins by looking at the role of organizational structure in project management. As projects tend to be fairly autonomous within organizations, an argument for decentralization is made. One option in organizing for project management is integrating projects into a functional organization. Another is moving to a fully projectized organization. A third option is creating a matrix organization, and a fourth is creation of a superfunctions unit. Another idea is a matrix diamond with a chief project officer. There are pros and cons to each of these types of organizations, so the discussions are followed by suggestions for organizing projects in your organization.

CHAPTER FIVE

ORGANIZING THE PROJECT MANAGEMENT EFFORT

There is nothing more difficult to take in hand, more perilous to conduct, or more uncertain in its success, than to take the lead in the introduction of a new order of things.

MACHIAVELLI, *THE PRINCE* (1516)

An important function of upper management is supporting project teams by designing the organization to support project management. This can be done by either redesigning the organization to emphasize projects or integrating projects into the current organization. Either way, the upper management team crucially defines the project manager's job, degree of authority and autonomy, and relationship to both the home department of the project and other departments in the organization. Upper management also plays key roles in specifying communication channels, methods of conflict resolution between the project and the rest of the organization, and how project management attention is to be directed— that is, the relative priorities of outcome, cost, and schedule.

The Role of Organizational Structure in Project Management

The term *organizational structure* is often associated with the organizational chart. Thinking about it in this way may be convenient, but organizational structure is more than lines and boxes. It has to do with groupings of people and reporting relationships, to be sure, but also with delegations of authority, empowerment, the criteria by which people are grouped together, the rules and procedures that determine what people in various groups do and pay attention to, and the patterns of interactions fostered by delegation, grouping, rules, and procedures.

CEO Lou Gerstner (2002), when asked how to revise the IBM organization chart, declared there would be no need for organization charts: "Anyone asking for one was focusing on the wrong thing" (p. Bu-11).

In toto, organizational structure induces certain behaviors on the part of individuals and inhibits others. For example, people grouped by function tend to pay close attention to narrowly defined roles and thus have difficulty with lateral cross-departmental communication. This is caused not only by reporting relationships but also by the total impact of the functional structure and the rules and procedures that accompany it. Lateral communications can be encouraged in functional structures such that people can be functionally grouped and not have cross-departmental difficulties. However, the functional structure by itself tends to produce such communications difficulty unless overt action is taken to alleviate it. This chapter examines how various structures can naturally help or hinder effective project management behavior.

The Argument for Decentralization

Robert Stoy (1996), formerly a vice president at Becton-Dickenson Company and then at Beckman Coulter, realized the extent to which much upper management control can hinder an organization's ability to reduce cycle time for new product projects. His question to upper managers is, "What are you willing to give up in order to reduce cycle time?" Stoy believes that if they are not willing to give up control over project decisions, they will not gain cycle time reduction even if they promote goal setting, project planning, core teams, and the like. One requirement of cycle time reduction is decentralization; another is implementation of good project management techniques. Stoy stresses that the goal of upper managers should be to have all project managers act like CEOs and treat projects as if they were a business. This cannot be done in a highly centralized environment.

Using this approach, Stoy brought project management to the quality and regulatory organization—something that had never been done before. The group is constantly involved in projects lasting anywhere from six months to two years. They had not approached the work as project management work. Stoy led an effort to institute consistent project and program management tools and techniques and use staff trained in these areas. The work now focuses on getting more staff in the quality and regulatory group to be fully trained and expert at project management. This is partly being done by bringing new people into the organization that have a project management background; it is also being accomplished partly by training.

At its most basic, the choice for upper managers is between control and results. If control is more important to an upper manager, the cost is lesser results. If results are more important, the cost is giving up some control. Getting more of one requires sacrificing a portion of the other.

An organization is considered centralized to the extent that authority is concentrated at relatively high levels of management. It is decentralized to the extent that authority is delegated to lower levels of management. Organizations centralize to the degree that the top managers want to maintain control over decision making. When economic times are tough, many firms move toward centralization to maintain better control over expenses. Decentralized organizations empower middle and lower levels of management to free top managers for strategic planning. A firm's degree of decentralization is greater to the extent that each of the following take place:

- More decisions are made at lower levels in the hierarchy.
- The number of important decisions made at lower levels increases.
- More functions are affected by decisions made at lower levels.
- Fewer decisions made at lower levels must be checked with higher management.

The advantages of decentralization are reflected in results, flexibility, initiative, and management development, exactly the areas important to project management. Project managers develop the broad perspective necessary for good decisions when they are empowered to make decisions themselves.

The disadvantages of decentralization are less upper management control and less efficient use of central resources. Control is probably the most important issue. When people are unsure of themselves, they tend to want to maintain tight control over situations for which they are responsible. Retaining most decision-making authority allows them to keep this control, or at least the illusion of it. Many upper managers are not fully versed in project management and feel unsure of themselves in project management situations; they may never have managed multidisciplinary projects before. Thus, they may prefer a more centralized organization, particularly if they are held responsible for the results of the project.

This exposes the dilemma of decentralization. Most of the advantages of decentralization accrue to the project managers, and ultimately to the organization as a whole. However, most of the disadvantages accrue to the upper managers, and these disadvantages can be individually severe if the projects they are responsible for are not successful. As the upper managers make the level-of-control decision, they may, to the detriment of projects and project managers, choose centralization. However more secure they may feel in the short run because of it, this decision will likely prove detrimental to the organization in the long run. Project managers need to be empowered if they are to manage projects well, develop the broad perspective needed for good decisions, and be able to develop into competent upper managers themselves. Therefore this chapter makes the argument in favor of decentralization.

Organizing for Project Management

Structurally, many functional organizations emulate military organizations. Returning after World War II, servicemen set up many of these organizations following a military model that itself essentially mimics the Prussian army's line and staff organization as developed by Bismarck for the 1870 Franco-Prussian War. In the line and staff organization, a few at the top (the General Staff) know the strategy. They advise the top echelon of officers, who then issue orders that must be obeyed by all others at lower levels. This is the ultimate centralized command-and-control organization.

In business, this most often translates into the typical line-and-staff structure where people are grouped according to the function they perform: the functional organization or bureaucracy (see Figure 5.1). Power, information, and money flow

FIGURE 5.1. A FUNCTIONAL ORGANIZATION.

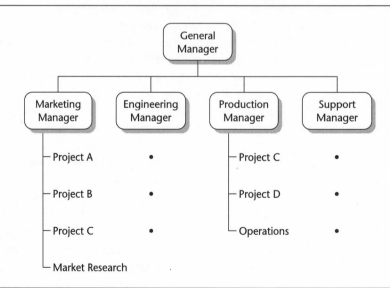

from the top of the organization into the various departments through the budget. The people in the departments minimize their costs while doing their assigned tasks as efficiently as possible. Coordination between departments is usually difficult, often handled by the staff and the upper echelons of the organizations. Information is mainly circulated vertically along the paths of the hierarchy. This type of organization works well when the major mission of the organization is to produce standard products and when problems are mainly technical. However, it tends to generate a professional culture where technical elegance is seen as more important than cost or schedule; conflicts often arise among specialist groups working on multifunctional teams, and the outside world of clients and other stakeholders tends to be neglected. In functional organizations, projects suffer in favor of standard products.

Integrating Projects into a Functional Organization

Functional organizations are designed to produce products, not to solve problems. Some saw this as an opportunity and began to develop project teams to address customer problems. However, projects do not naturally fit into functional organizations. Functions in organizations tend to isolate themselves by forming substantial bureaucratic barriers between themselves and other functions. This is sometimes called the "silo effect," as each department seems to operate in its own silo (see Figure 5.2). When this is the case, project work is seen as unimportant or even as an irritant. It will be done when it can be done, after all the important department work is finished, so progress is extremely slow or nonexistent. As a project proceeds through the bureaucracy, each department takes charge of its part, but often no one person is in charge of the entire process. As a result, new

FIGURE 5.2. AVOID FUNCTIONAL SILOS.

features may be added, and the project suffers "scope creep" and delay. With no real project management there is no real assignable penalty for delay, so the project wends its way to completion (if it makes it that far) in its own good time.

The principal strength of the functional design is its utilization of resources. The positive result is a gain in administrative economies of scale. This type of organization is particularly effective when a firm is a mass producer of items for sale from stock. Further advantages of this form include the following:

- It offers a simple communication and decision network.
- It facilitates measurement of functional output and results.
- It simplifies training of functional specialists.
- It gives status to major functional areas.
- It preserves strategic control at the top management levels.
- It makes it easy to understand how to progress in the hierarchy.

The principal problem with the functional design is that it complicates producing something new. The myopic perspective fostered by concentrating on functional activities can become a major shortcoming when attempting to complete projects, which require interdepartmental cooperation and communication to be successful. In a functional design, communication and cooperation often are problems, and departmental interests may take precedence over broader organizational goals. Typically, the functional form not only hampers cooperation because it provides no interoccupational contact; it also fosters a parochial emphasis on functional objectives with a minimal appreciation of or concern for overall organizational goals.

Projects can be accommodated in a functional structure if they can be executed almost entirely in one department or broken down into subprojects that need little integration. Hobbs and Ménard (1993) state that functional organizations tend to perform better on projects in which the development of technical content is the primary consideration. It would therefore be appropriate to integrate small development projects into a functional structure by assigning them to the appropriate department.

If projects are not mainly technical but still must be assigned in functional organizations, it often becomes necessary to assign someone to integrate the work of the departments. This person's job is to help overcome the communication and coordination problems inherent in functional organizations. For example, Rick Ellis (1994) at HP Medical identified many of the problems facing projects in departmental environments: conflicting priorities, poor communication, incompatible organizational processes, and loss of control. To meet those challenges, Ellis's organization devised a program manager role to coordinate the efforts of the functional areas for a particular project and to manage the product life cycle process and deliverables. Initially, the program manager authority was kept within the local business unit. Now the role has focused on managing the interactions between organizations, not the actions within each organization. Over time and with project success, the role was expanded to include increased authority and accountability for program success.

According to Ellis (1994), "Well-executed program management was a leading factor in several project successes. In particular, the identification and resolution of cross-functional issues by the program team, improved communication between the functional areas and increased decision making at the project level were identified as success factors" (p. 2). One key to this success was the gradual increase in scope of the job of program manager. Department managers may not see the need for such a role, or may see it as a threat to their power, influence, or status (or PIS, as it is often called). The legitimacy of the role is seen only after it becomes instrumental in project success. After initial success, the role can be expanded with increased authority to solve interdepartmental conflict.

Establishing a Fully Projectized Organization

Obviously, multidisciplinary projects that require integration of many different inputs, along with customer and other stakeholder interfaces, are not well accommodated by the functional organization. On the other end of the scale is the fully projectized organization (see Figure 5.3). This is a project manager's dream,

FIGURE 5.3. A FULLY PROJECTIZED ORGANIZATION.

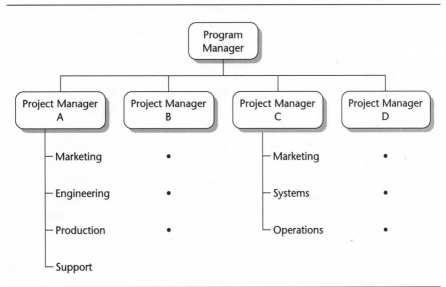

for in it the power, information, and money flow first to the projects and then to the departments. People in the organization see themselves as being on projects first and in departments second. The hallmark of this system is the project manager, who has more or less full authority over all project resources and is dedicated to project success and the attainment of project objectives. (The project manager's authority over resources does not usually extend to support functions such as accounting, however; these remain integrated into the larger organization's management system.)

The fully projectized organization is best when projects are the lifeblood of the firm. It helps ensure that projects are as high in quality as possible and done in the minimum time. This is because most resources are fully dedicated to projects only, not to departmental work. However, the fully projectized organization is expensive because of the duplication of resources among projects. As previously discussed, if the project is to be done well and done fast, it should not be expected that it can be done cheaply. But the new power structure, not expense, is what deters many firms from adopting fully projectized organization; most power in such organizations lies with project managers. For firms that have both projects and standard products, as most do, a further deterrent may be that standard products tend to suffer at the hands of projects. The fully projectized organization may be seen as a pendulum swinging too far in the opposite direction from the functional organization.

Integrating Projects by Developing Matrix Organizations

As noted, most organizations are a mix of standard products and new projects. The matrix structure addresses both by combining the project organization with the functional structure (see Figure 5.4). Generally defined, this is the sharing of power in the organization by project work and departmental work. One example is appointing both an operations vice president and a projects vice president. Matrix structures recognize the presence and importance of both projects and functional components by placing them on the same level and giving them equal access to organization resources.

This structure requires close cooperation of the two sides to meet organization objectives. In reality, however, conflicts often arise over the best use of resources, which too often must be resolved on the fly by the individual in the middle of the matrix who reports to two bosses in two organizations. This is often found to be unworkable. The problems with matrix structures are legend.

But the matrix design is good for organizations that have a variety of mid-sized projects that require cross-departmental cooperation. Most problems associated with the matrix design have to do with the inability of upper managers to

FIGURE 5.4. A MATRIX ORGANIZATION STRUCTURE.

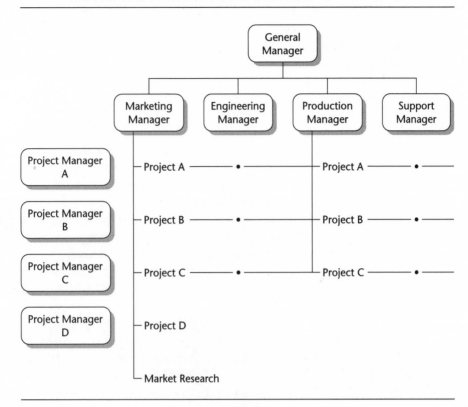

work out the required power sharing; imbalance of power between departments and projects inevitably causes conflicts to arise on the projects. The matrix structure contains no inherent methods for conflict resolution, so without proper power sharing among upper managers, project managers are left to fend for themselves. This brings on a classic abdication of the upper manager's responsibility: upper managers expect the project managers to resolve problems that the upper managers cannot resolve themselves. This puts the project manager into an impossible situation.

Resolving conflicts caused by upper managers takes time. Often the matrix structure is adopted with an expectation of a decrease in cycle time. Upper managers expect this result, and project managers are measured by it. However, if the upper managers do not act as a team and do not provide conflict resolution mechanisms, the project managers are not able to reach the cycle time reduction goals and are blamed for their inability to solve the problems the upper managers caused and could not solve themselves. This creates further animosity between project managers and upper managers, each side accusing the other of failure—which takes more time, causes more animosity, and so forth. Ah, such is the perversity of organizational life!

This is the main reason the matrix concept has been discredited. In moving to a matrix organization, the functional department managers often do not give up and share enough decision-making, resource-allocating, and conflict resolution power with the project managers. Project managers are not empowered and are thus impotent. Therefore, upper managers considering the move to matrix management first need to ask themselves if they are really ready to share their power with project managers. This is a difficult choice for those educated in the old school. The upper management team needs to follow a rational procedure for project selection, such as the one outlined in Chapter Two, and then elevate project managers to the same level of authority as departmental managers. If they are not willing to do this, adopting a matrix structure just invites disaster.

Using a Strong Matrix Structure

An example of granting sufficient authority to project managers is the strong matrix structure adopted by MacDonald Dettwiler and Associates (MDA) in Canada (see Figure 5.5). In this structure, all management aspects of the project are performed by the project manager, and all technical aspects are directed by the project engineer. The project manager has complete responsibility and authority for all aspects of project performance and deliverables. The project engineer re-

FIGURE 5.5. A STRONG MATRIX ORGANIZATION.

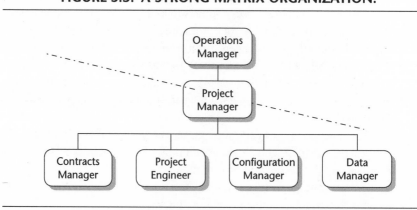

ports to the project manager for all technical aspects of the project. The project manager is the focal point of all communication between MDA and the customer and has full authority to resolve any issues. This puts the project manager in a strong position of both authority and responsibility. In addition, the core team is collocated as much as possible.

This is a strong matrix in that the project manager has responsibility and authority similar to that of departmental managers. Also, the engineering manager remains part of an engineering department but reports to the project manager for the duration of the project. With this and other strong reporting relationships within the project team, the matrix realizes some of the advantages of the fully projectized organization. An additional benefit is that the project manager is also a department member, as indicated by the slanted line in Figure 5.5. By developing a department of project managers, the strong matrix realizes some of the benefits of the functional organization.

This type of structure will not work unless project managers are thoroughly trained in the skills and practices of project management; furthermore, upper managers must design and support a project management system that they know and trust. Otherwise, project managers will be unsure about what to do, and the upper managers will understandably be reluctant to give them sufficient authority to be effective.

In designing a team to work in this environment, Belbin's research (1996) suggests making a priority of finding a first-rate technical person for a department where technical factors are critical and finding the project manager most likely to fit in and create a successful partnership.

Using a Matrix Diamond Structure with a Chief Project Officer

A strong matrix structure increases the authority and responsibility of project managers. However, as projects increase in number, size, and importance to the organization, the structure may appear insufficient because project managers eventually report to the chief operating officer rather than a chief project officer. The next step is to develop a matrix diamond approach balancing projects, with a chief project officer (CPO) on one side of the structure and the normal functional operations, with the chief operating officer (COO), on the other. A matrix diamond attempts to balance the needs of both the projects and continuing operations within the same structure, as shown in Figure 5.6.

In this structure, the chief project officer is at the same level as the chief operating officer and is responsible for the completion of all projects in the organization. All project and program managers report to the chief project officer, who is responsible for their training and development. Project team and core team

FIGURE 5.6. A MATRIX DIAMOND STRUCTURE.

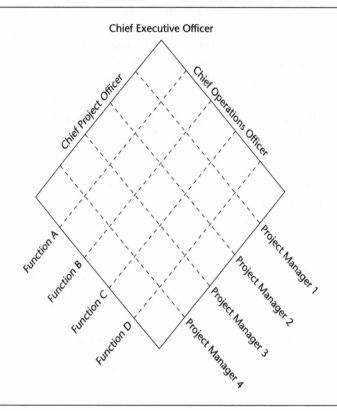

members continue to reside in departments that are responsible for maintaining their technical expertise. Projects continue being staffed using "borrowed resources," but the management of those projects has much higher status and authority. Since projects depend on borrowed resources, the matrix diamond structure may be untenable unless all upper managers are in agreement.

The creation of a chief project officer is a definite plus for the project side of the organization to ensure that each project is done well. However, creation of this position can be disruptive to the rest of the organization as a chief project officer represents a change in power balance, taking power away from the chief operating officer. It also means that program or project managers are elevated to the same level as departmental managers, which could take power away from the department manager position. Since the chief project officer and project managers now have their own budget and staff, this means that budget may be taken away from the operating side of the organization. In many organizations, budget size and controls indicate status and prestige. Reducing status can be very disruptive to the smooth functioning of an organization.

Although the matrix diamond looks good on paper, it puts team members into the "two boss" situation: one in the department and one on the projects. Unless these two bosses are in concert, the result is trouble for team members. In addition, time is lost when people shift focus between tasks. This means that if an individual does both project and departmental work simultaneously, there is lost efficiency on both tasks. This efficiency can be retained only if the individual does project work exclusively and departmental work exclusively, a sharing system that most departmental managers would find disruptive.

The process of making the shift to a matrix diamond is itself disruptive. The disruption can be minimized when upper managers work as a team to determine best ways to develop project management in the organization, as we suggest in Chapter Two. When upper managers get involved in selecting projects and assign responsibility for the success of those projects, they are ready to consider what organizational structure best supports those projects. With involvement of the entire management team to implement a matrix diamond structure, the amount of disruption is not eliminated, but it is vastly minimized. As we describe in *Creating the Project Office* (Englund, Graham, and Dinsmore, 2003), understand the sense of urgency, culture of the organization, formation of a guiding coalition, and the abilities and presence of enough supporters to implement the change. Be guided by people who realize the shift is necessary to achieve strategy and is not just something imposed from above. The matrix diamond requires a project management information system, project manager selection and development, a learning organization, and a project office—all topics we discuss in later chapters.

Due to the many problems we describe, the matrix diamond is often suggested but rarely implemented. Organizations find the change process difficult. Disruption is costly to production processes, and people generally feel the gain is not worth the pain. In addition, is it possible for one organization to be efficient at or facilitate both project management and process management simultaneously? Some organizations find it difficult to excel at both management types due to inherent differences between project and process, as shown in Table 5.1.

As shown in Figure 5.6, the matrix diamond approach could take emphasis away from production processes, which could bankrupt the organization. It is no wonder that people are reluctant to adopt a matrix diamond structure. Some organizations split the project function into a separate structure, like a wholly owned subsidiary or a separate company. Organizations that had two separate functions found it advantageous to split those functions rather than attempt to do two things in one structure. One example is when AT&T spun off Lucent Technologies so

TABLE 5.1. MAJOR DIFFERENCES BETWEEN PROJECT AND PROCESS.

Factor	Project	Process	Differences
Number of products	One	Many	Cost orientation much lower on projects
Certainty	Low	High	Attracts different personalities
Metrics	Few	Many	High ambiguity on projects
Reward	Project completion	Organizational	Project managers more independent of the organization
Procedures	Fewer	Many	More individual determination of action on projects
Team members	Multidiscipline	Unidiscipline	Higher communication need
Customer orientation	Make them what they want to buy	Sell them what we make	Customer as king
Individual expertise	Wider	Narrower	Project managers need not be technical experts
Creativity	Higher	Lower	The creative process looks chaotic to a process engineer
Attention to detail	Lower	Very high	Individual focus on completely different aspects of producing a product

that AT&T could concentrate on telephone transmission while Lucent Technologies concentrated on building switching equipment.

An example in Germany is Tenovis, formerly the private network division of Bosch Telecom. With the split, Tenovis could concentrate on projects regarding the merger of Internet and telecommunications technology so that Bosch could concentrate on the more traditional telecom business. Tenovis implemented a chief project office but does not have a chief operating office on its organizational chart. The chief project officer is responsible for shaping internal processes and managing strategic projects. Tenovis implemented an enterprise project management infrastructure as a trial project within its Program Management Office, which is responsible for conducting all large cross-company projects. The tangible business results they achieve allows them to deploy this infrastructure to other business divisions step by step.

Those of us in the project management profession find the chief project officer concept especially intriguing. However, its application is not yet widespread. Several commercial organizations show a project management career path leading up to a chief project officer, vice president of projects, or project executive, but the position remains empty. A Web search shows chief project officers occurring predominantly in government organizations, which apparently are taking the lead in a worthy concept.

Integrating Projects Through an Organic Organization

The organic organization is a combination of organizational types framed however necessary to support various projects. Most large organizations are of this type, as they require different structures to support different types of projects. Many have a variety of small projects, such as technical development projects, that can be wholly assigned to one functional department. Other projects that are larger or have high strategic importance can be assigned as independent units with full-time collocated staff; they may be run using the fully projectized structure. Medium-sized, medium-structure projects can be assigned as in a matrix structure, with permanent core teams but with other team members working part time on them; for these, it is better to fit the organization to the project rather than force the project into a nonsupportive type of organization.

Organizing for Project Management with Superfunction Units

In recent years, organizations have noticed that the rise in cross-departmental work has created problems in quality, customer service, and cycle time reduction. One attempted solution has been to group the departments that need to work together under a single senior manager in order to achieve better integration across a set of functions. Thus, a number of superfunctions—that is, combinations of functions—have appeared (see Figure 5.7). These usually include a performance measure that acts as a superordinate goal for the unit and assists in cross-functional trade-off decisions. The structural integration under one top manager makes coordination easier and more permanent.

The main object of the superfunctions unit is to foster interdepartmental cooperation by attention to a superordinate goal. It begins with the upper management team determining its biggest problem or best competitive advantage. The superordinate goal is derived from this consideration. The upper managers then determine what departments are most instrumental in solving that problem or creating that advantage. These departments are grouped together, and the superordinate goal is added to the goal of each department. This helps to foster interdepartmental cooperation, as each department is working toward at least one goal shared by all departments. In addition, people begin to think of themselves as members of the unit as well as of the department. Project teams within the unit can thus be much more easily formed, developed, and motivated, as most of the

FIGURE 5.7. EXAMPLE OF A SUPERFUNCTIONS UNIT.

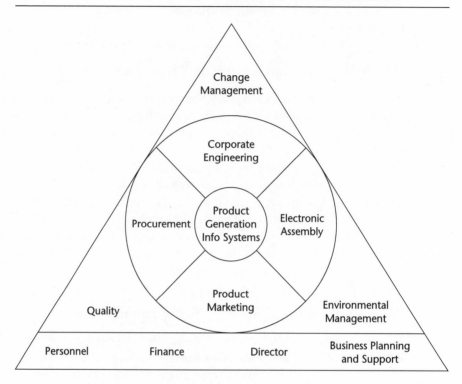

core teams are working for the same unit. In organizations that have many projects of a similar nature, such as new product development or software development, the superfunctions unit can develop into a considerable advantage.

HP has such a unit, the product processes organization (PPO). At the corporate staff level, HP combined engineering, manufacturing, product marketing, quality, and procurement under a single director. The goal of the PPO is to provide value to each functional area but across the company. For example, marketing develops training on building market-focused organizations that is available to all divisions. The engineering software initiative provides consulting services on identifying and deploying core competences. The change management department helps reengineer organizational structures. Procurement counsels manufacturing and engineering organizations on part portfolios and negotiates large purchase contracts with suppliers. Access to substantial discounts or short-supply parts provides competitive advantages for the company. Each of these would be difficult for one division to develop alone but is extremely valuable when available companywide.

An infrastructure team (IST) is the core team for PPO. Directors from each department meet regularly to address questions relating to programs, funding, and value-added issues. Most departments are shifting to the internal market plan for funding—that is, the departments are funded only if the people in the business units find value in the programs they offer and are willing to pay for them. The IST puts together program sheets to help business units understand the offerings. Directors have responsibility for liaison to specific businesses. Annual "road shows" are conducted to discuss needs of the businesses and the value offered by PPO programs. The IST has also established a goal to get more of the PPO departments working together on projects in order to increase the value of programs offered to the business units and to leverage greater value across more businesses.

Organizing Projects in Your Organization

Most organizations continue to revolve around departments, with project managers reporting to department managers. The problem most upper managers face is not which structure to choose but rather how best to integrate projects into the existing structure. The important consideration is how to set up the project in a way that mitigates the problems that the organizational design might cause. In highly centralized organizations, for example, specific lateral communication channels must be developed. Problems caused by the functional organization usually can be dealt with best by appointing someone in the proper department to overcome them.

In considering the design of projects, answer the following questions:

• How should projects be positioned in the existing organization, and how might the appropriate relationships between projects and departments be developed? If the organization does not have a history of doing projects, it is probably best to appoint someone on the core team to develop and cultivate good communication between departments and projects—similar to the program manager position described by Ellis earlier in this chapter.

• How should the status of project manager be defined? Should the project manager be recognized as a professional position? What level of authority and autonomy should the position have? The trend is definitely toward defining project management as a professional position with high levels of authority and autonomy. But if project management is new to an organization, the strong matrix organization can be the goal, beginning with a program of project manager selection and development as described in Chapter Seven. Upper managers should also begin to experiment with giving projects a more strategic emphasis, covered in Chapter Two. With experience and time, the organization can move toward the strong matrix.

• What management practices, procedures, systems, and measures should be used to manage the projects? One research study (Baker, Murphy, and Fisher, 1983) showed that a heavy emphasis on staying within budget has a negative effect on project success. In an organization that is very budget conscious, care must be taken to ensure that it does not overly constrict project practice. Project management practice usually stresses quality, schedule, and budget, in that order.

• What are the positions and responsibilities of various upper managers regarding the completion and success of projects? If upper managers are held absolutely accountable for the success of every project, it is unlikely they will grant the autonomy that project managers need. The responsibilities of upper managers may have to be changed to move toward the strong matrix design.

A Process for Determining Structure

People generally agree that the questions just raised must be answered in moving toward good project management, but the answers are not generally agreed on. Upper managers can begin by examining their existing system and contrasting the behaviors that structure generates against the behaviors they want. Any organizational structure directs, and therefore limits, individuals' attention, which affects their behavior. So part of the project organization design involves redirecting attention to influence the desired behaviors. For example, the departmental system may generate behavior that ignores the outside environment of customers and other stakeholders, whereas the behavior desired is for close and frequent interaction with that environment.

Some examples of behavioral differences include the following:

Current Behavior	*Desired Behavior*
Projects not real work	Projects as important work
Customers not important	Customers are reason for being
Project associated with department	Project associated with customers, strategy
Lateral communications difficult	Lateral communications easy
Project manager not desired position	Project manager desired position
Management systems thwart projects	Management systems facilitate projects
Ignore outside environment	Frequent interaction with outside environment

After listing the desired behaviors, organize to effect them. Following are some considerations for organization based on the list given above.

Place Projects on the Organization Chart. Project work must be seen as real, not as extra work. Thus, it should be assigned a budget and some space, and it should be listed as a part of what the organization does. Projects are the hidden element in many organizations. To help make them more real to project participants, they deserve space on the organization chart. This is a signal that upper managers take project work as seriously as departmental work.

View All Projects as Customer Projects. All projects are aimed at delivering value to some customer. The customer may be internal, such as another department, or external. It is first important to determine the project's customer or set of customers and then to associate it with that customer. The project may be called the "T-140 project," but all project team members should be well versed on the T-140's customer and what that customer will do with it. Upper managers need to support all core team members having contact with the customer, not just the project manager; the project becomes more of a customer project when the core team members see firsthand who the customers are and what problems they are trying to solve. Project core team members should meet with the customer early and often. Recognize that upper managers are typically not the customers for projects, and undue influence on their part may distract from successfully satisfying the real customers, such as prohibiting customer trials to save money.

Align Projects with Customers. Alignment is a problem with many systems development projects being developed for use in a functional area. Often the project manager in these cases is from the systems department; the projects then become known as systems projects, and the functional areas abandon much of their responsibility for them. Unfortunately, the systems people may also begin to see the projects as systems projects. When this is the case, they may concentrate on product features important to them but not to the customer. The disastrous results of this faulty direction of attention are well known. To affect this behavior, appoint the project manager from the user department. Another option is to set up the project independent from any department. This is an upper management decision.

Hobbs and Ménard (1993) suggest that the way a project is organized should be adapted to the specific characteristics of the project. They cite seven factors that influence the decision on project organization: the project's strategic importance, size of the project, novelty and need for innovation, need for integration (number of departments involved), environmental complexity (number of external interfaces), budget and time constraints, and stability of resource requirements.

The higher the level of these seven factors, the more the project requires an autonomous project organization. The lower the level of these seven factors, the higher the probability of project success is within existing departmental structure. Thus, the project that requires an autonomous structure is usually large, strategically important, new to the company (and thus requiring much innovation), and highly multidisciplinary (and thus requiring input from many departments); requires constant contact with customers to assess their expectations; must be completed under severe time constraints (usually because of competitor actions); and needs people working steadily on it from beginning to end.

A contributing department may become difficult when a project is associated with another department. It may withhold resources because its priorities are different from that of the project. This is definitely a problem that the upper management team must address. Helping to free resources from other departments is a good example of how upper management can support the project.

As Project Manager, Manage Across Organizations. The project manager needs considerable authority to implement the systems approach. In the past, it was sufficient to develop components to a solution, but now customers demand total solutions to problems. This requires a systems approach across organizations. Practices that are in place for high-volume, low-margin production are antithetical to low-volume, high-margin systems solutions. If the former practices are indeed in place, the project manager needs authority to change some of them for the good of the project. If resistance to this is strong and the departments are entrenched, set up the project manager as an independent unit with full control over the resources needed to complete the project.

Designate the Project Manager as a Professional. Taking projects out of departments means that project management needs to be designated as a professional position. With project management considered a profession, no longer will the best engineer be assigned to run the project. This eliminates the accidental project manager problem. (See Chapter Seven on selecting and developing project managers.)

Avoid Meddling in Project Processes. Too often upper managers want certain things done that are not in the best interest of the project. If the project manager is too closely aligned with (or reports to) that manager, the project goals may be subverted toward departmental goals. The power of the upper managers needs to be curtailed in that case.

If You Build It, They Will Come

In the movie *Field of Dreams*, Ray Kinsella searched for dreams all his life. Then one day, his dreams came looking for him. An Iowa corn farmer, he hears voices and interprets them as a command to build a baseball diamond in his fields. He does, and legendary Chicago Black Sox players come. The movie is about dreams and having the courage to go through with them.

Many writers point out that organizations are products of human imagination rather than some blind expression of an underlying natural order. The Greek god Helios symbolized the sunlight toward which all plants tend to grow, and an analogous process goes on in human organizational systems. Positive images are the seeds that can redirect people's minds. If you build an organizational structure based on internal voices and a projectized organizational "dream," chances are high that people will come.

David Cooperrider (2000), in developing his field of appreciative inquiry, provides a very positive and interesting organizational development approach to include when creating an environment for successful projects. He postulates strong arguments about the flexibility of organizational structures:

- Organizations as made and imagined are artifacts of the affirmative mind; we live in an anticipatory world of images.
- There is no such thing as an inevitable form of organization.
- The guiding image of the future exists in very observable and tangible ways in the living dialogue that flows through every organization.
- Organizations create their own realities; positive images whose prophetic, poetic, and normative aspects are congruent show the greatest self-fulfilling potential.
- Organizationwide affirmation of a positive future is the single most important act that a system can engage in if its real aim is to bring to fruition a new and better future.
- The greatest obstacle, and source of constant failures, miseries, and wickedness, is the inadequacy of the highest ideals.
- Organizations need not to be fixed but to have constant reaffirmation; organizations as heliotropic systems "grow toward the light."
- Creating the conditions for appreciative inquiry is the most important measure that can be taken to ensure the conscious evolution of a valued and positive future.

In a similar vein, executive vice president Rick Belluzzo (1996a) shared his frustrations about the elusive search for an organizational model:

I've spent a lot of time thinking about organizations and how to define the perfect organization, and I can't do it; I can't figure it out. I can't draw and develop a field model that solves one hundred percent of our problems.

What I've learned is you have to optimize your organization based on the problems you want to solve today, and determine what things you want to manage, what areas you're going to have to invest your time in and make work, because the organizational model doesn't do it naturally.

And that's where project management comes in. We need project managers to manage those areas you don't have direct authority over and that need to be integrated, and you make the decision to move things along. We're going to have a lot of that and that has to be a skill for us because that's what's going to make us better than other organizations if we can do it.

This advice from an experienced executive implies that the search is endless, so do not obsess over and make organizational structure the top priority. Do the best you can, but remember that it is the people who make things happen, sometimes in spite of the organization. Upper managers need to prioritize their time and craft the best organization they can. Ultimately, however, they depend on skilled, empowered project managers to manage fuzzy white spaces between the boxes and exercise creative judgment in operating across the organization. The best tools they have to make this happen are to set high ideals, appreciate strengths that exist in the organization, and share the vision.

The Compleat Upper Manager

The successful complete upper manager:

- Determines the appropriate organizational structure to support project work.
- Realizes that giving up control may be necessary to accomplish results.
- Provides the necessary scoping and authority to project managers.
- Designs a project management system that is known and trusted.
- Redirects attention to influence desired behaviors.
- Organizes to affect behavior.
- Supports the project management professional.
- Appreciates the vast possibilities that exist to reshape the organization.

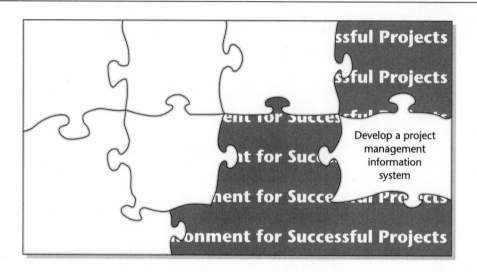

This chapter begins with a discussion of the importance of information and some of the behavioral issues of information. Following that is a consideration of system design and the contents of a project management information system (PMIS). The overall contents of a PMIS are examined by determining the questions to be answered—questions about outcome, schedule, and resource requirements. Other PMIS contents include facilities for communication and information for organizational learning. Final sections discuss PMIS software and hints for developing a PMIS.

CHAPTER SIX

DEVELOPING THE PROJECT MANAGEMENT INFORMATION SYSTEMS

Information is no longer simply a strategic asset; it is a critical enabler of success.

JOEL BIRNBAUM, HEWLETT-PACKARD SENIOR VICE PRESIDENT OF R&D

The goal of this chapter is not to make managers into information specialists but to make them concerned enough to make certain that an information system is put into place before projects begin. Thus, the approach is to stress the importance of information: how it is that good and flowing information helps alleviate mistakes and allows projects to run better, faster, and with higher quality. The chapter then suggests that upper managers ask themselves and their colleagues what questions they have about projects, when they have these questions, and how they like to see the answers. The emphasis is on answering questions, not supplying data.

The Importance of Information

In the old days, control of information was power. A few people had the total picture, kept it to themselves, and told others what to do. Individuals were not to make decisions; they did not know the possible effect on the total system. Instead they followed orders, and the integrating mechanism ensured that the totality of actions resulted in a final product. In this situation, the only information an individual needs is about the individual job. But this can work only in repeat product and process environments.

In projects, sharing of information is power. When a team is doing something new, individuals must be empowered to make decisions, and they must be informed decisions. People making decisions need to know the decisions others have made, and know the effect of their decisions on others on the project and on other projects in the organization.

People tend to make mistakes in times of anxiety, but with sufficient time and information, they can usually make good decisions. Typically, projects are tight on time; if information is in short supply as well, good decision making is unlikely. Even without much time, having sufficient and timely information can hold down the anxiety.

Empowering project team members often causes anxiety. That is, whenever something new is tried in an organization, people normally have some anxiety about the results. This is particularly true of project sponsors, who will be rewarded based on the success or failure of the projects. The usual way to relieve anxiety is to seize control: take over the project, micromanage it, and make sure it is done "right." But this is actually detrimental to the project. A better way to relieve anxiety is to have a sufficient flow of information so the upper managers can see what is happening and how things are going; this allows them to be more comfortable with empowering the project team. Information is thus critical to the proper functioning of a strong matrix type of organization. Upper managers need project information to help keep them from making the mistake of overmanaging projects.

An additional source of anxiety, and thus of need for information, is projects themselves. No one is certain what the final product of the project will be until the project is finished. Projects often employ new technology, which may or may not work. Or the project may require inventing new technology, always a questionable endeavor. The technology may also advance while the project proceeds, necessitating massive changes in product specifications. Customer trends or needs might also change as the project progresses. All these factors add to anxiety about the project outcome.

Another source of anxiety in complex organizations is the presence of multiple projects and how (or if) they are prioritized. Team members often wonder if the projects are launched opportunistically, on a whim, or if they indeed fit into a strategic plan. Does the whole organization agree on the relative priorities of projects, or are different agendas at play? Without good information, duplicate projects may be under way, often without the project team's knowing that others are working on the same or a similar problem. This makes team members wonder if their project will be canceled, which makes it difficult to motivate them. Project managers need to see the whole system of projects so they can answer questions from team members about them.

Another cause of anxiety is schedule uncertainty. Invention of new technology is notoriously difficult to schedule. A change in technology, competitor offerings, or customer expectations can obviate the best of schedules. Predicting product releases has proved difficult even in the most sophisticated firms. All project stakeholders need to know project schedules, schedule updates, and problems that may affect product release.

Additional schedule anxiety centers on members of the project team. These people are often needed elsewhere, on other projects or for work in their home departments. Contributing department directors want to know when their people will be done with the project so they can be scheduled for other work. For the organization to get the best use of their employees, this information is essential. In addition to department managers, the upper management team that is choosing which projects to perform needs the resource information to allocate the scarce resources properly.

Finally, there is always anxiety about the cost of the project. While a project is in progress, it represents expense, which sounds a lot like "expendable" to project team members. Wherever there is expense, there is interest. People continually want to know if the potential return on the project is worth the expense; return depends greatly on when the product will be ready (schedule) and what it will do (outcome). Thus, all three factors show a different side of the same anxiety: fear associated with uncertainty.

Such fear can be used constructively, to motivate performance that will help finish the project and alleviate uncertainty, or destructively, as a political tool for others to sow doubt as to the wisdom of continuing with this project (and, of course, of switching to another project they favor). Upper managers need to decrease the destructive use of fear. This is best done through sharing of information.

Most management mistakes are made in times of anxiety, usually over outcome, cost, or schedule. People often make mistakes because they feel they do not have the time or money to do the correct thing. These are individual mistakes. There are also systemic mistakes, where people think they are doing what is best, but the sum of their efforts is not best for the system. These mistakes are usually made because people lack information about the effect of individual decisions on the system as a whole. This is the problem of suboptimization, discussed in Chapter Two. Information can help resolve both the anxiety and the suboptimization problem. Box 6.1 addresses a common problem that is relieved by information.

Anxiety that leads to paralysis can be brought on by well-intended fear tactics. Project managers in a state government agency report that many upper managers come back from a "management charm school" or other training in a worse state

---

BOX 6.1. Information Relieves Anxiety.

The value of information and people's anxious reaction to the lack of it are easily seen when waiting for elevators in tall buildings. People push the down button, and if the elevator does not come fast enough, they push the up button. If an up elevator stops first, some people, amazingly, actually get on. They seem to feel better moving, even if in the wrong direction. Of course, they slow down the whole elevator system by doing so; the elevator has to stop to pick them up and take them the wrong way, and it has to stop again on the way down at the floor where they first pushed the button. These people make decisions that they think will speed their ride, but in fact they slow things down.

This behavior is rare where each floor has an indicator that shows where the elevators are and when they are coming. In this case, people push the button once and wait for the next elevator to arrive. With information, they do not have anxiety about when or if the elevator is coming, so they wait patiently.

These two examples show the value of information. Without indicators to describe status, people individually make decisions they hope will speed things up, but the sum of all these decisions actually slows things down. Providing information about the status of the system to everyone prevents them from slowing down the very system they are attempting to speed up.

---

than before. The managers get so inundated with concerns about legal, safety, individual responsibility, harassment, and procedural issues that they become ineffectual in making decisions or providing leadership. These issues are certainly important, but they need to be conveyed such that the information makes them aware of risks while helping them integrate the issues into a coaching environment.

Behavioral Issues of Information

Experience with information systems indicates that the way data are collected and used has an effect on the behavior of the people creating the data. Decisions are made based on the information in the system, and people shade the data or make their behavior look as if it conforms when it does not. People respond to what is measured and make their behavior conform to what they think are the best measurements.

The issue for upper management is thus to ensure that people know and understand the uses for the information in the system. But if one of the uses is resource allocation, which ultimately reflects on project success, there will likely be much fudging of the input data to make each project look as if it needs many more resources. Upper management needs to set up a system such that it is in everyone's best interest to supply accurate information.

One of the best ways to ensure honesty in communications is community. If people want to remain part of a given group, and everyone knows the information in the system and where it comes from, they tend to give accurate information. If they do not, they know they will be looked down on by other members of the community. Peer pressure from other members of the community is probably the best motivator to keep information honest. So the first step is to make all information public and identify the sources.

The next step is to gain information as part of the project process. Information is often filtered and distorted when recalled after the fact, so it is important to collect it as the work progresses.

The final step is to eliminate the benefits of poor communication (see Box 6.2). This means the end of the last-minute hero (see Chapter Three) and development of a culture where planning and sharing information is recognized and rewarded. Upper managers need to stop recognizing and rewarding the old heroes and begin rewarding those who demonstrate the behavior that they say they want.

The behavioral issues having to do with communication are mainly ones of motivation. People communicate when they see that it is in their best interest, and they do not communicate if they feel it would be detrimental. Poor communication is often considered a technology problem to which the solution is more telephones or computers. These can help, but only if the people using them really want to

---

BOX 6.2. Benefits of Poor Communication.

Asked what benefits accrue from poor communication and why people might withhold information, some upper managers are surprisingly candid. According to their responses, poor communication accomplishes the following:

- Minimizes impact of poor planning
- Cuts down on questions
- Easier to deny what you said later on
- Often a technique for gaining or maintaining power
- Good technique for masking true intent
- Helps you preserve mystique and hide insecurities
- Helps minimize opposition and criticism

communicate. Once people think about it, they have no trouble constructing lists of why people do not communicate, like the one in Box 6.2. Additional technology does not relieve any of the factors listed there. So before investing more money in computers and telephones, investigate the benefits of poor communication, and find ways to make good communication bring greater benefits.

Contents of a Project Management Information System

When determining the proper components of a project management information system (PMIS), first evaluate whom it will serve. Upper managers need the information on all projects regarding progress, problems, resource usage, costs, and project goals. This information helps them judge the portfolio of projects. They need to review projects at each milestone and produce a go/no-go decision. Project managers and department managers need to see each project's schedule, priority, and use of resources to determine the most efficient use across the organization. Project team members need to see schedules, task lists, specifications, and the like so they know what needs to be done next.

The PMIS should do the following:

1. Answer questions of the major stakeholders.
2. Facilitate communication between team members, between team members and other stakeholders, between all project managers, and between project managers and upper managers.
3. Help in "what if?" analyses to answer questions about project staffing, proposed staffing changes, and total allocation of resources.
4. Help organizational learning by helping the members of the organization learn about project management.

Standard information systems are not designed for projects. Normal information systems tell managers if they are on budget after the fact; they are unsuitable for "what if?" analyses to show the effects of staffing changes, proposed priority changes, or changes on other projects. A PMIS needs to give information on the following:

- Project activity progress
- Project costs as they occur
- Current and projected use of people
- Projected release dates
- Specifications and changes

An effective PMIS both cuts across organizational lines and develops information to be used as a basis for decision making. This information supports decision making by showing the following:

- Effects of changes in priorities
- Effects of changes in staffing
- Effects of project delays
- Effects of adding new projects to the portfolio
- Effects of changing resource allocations
- Effects of the loss of a key contributor

Developing a useful information system across projects is critical to the success of a project-based organization because people need to be able to do each of the following:

- Respond quickly to opportunities or threats.
- Get needed information efficiently.
- Avoid duplication of effort.
- Get help on a current project by considering information on similar past or present projects.
- Provide individual schedules, along with information on who is waiting for output, to support on-time delivery.

Questions to Ask About PMIS Content

Leaders will be known by the quality of their questions, not their answers. Leaders of project managers can best serve by asking challenging questions that support the goals of the project, not by attempting to solve all problems that come up; problem solving is the responsibility of the project team. The team feels empowered when it senses leadership and support from upper management; this support is engendered in part by being able to answer upper managers' questions. Thus, the team needs an information system that can help them answer such questions. If this system is not designed before the project begins, the project manager is forever in a reactive mode, chasing after information to answer upper management questions. A standard information system simply presents available information, leaving it to the users to glean answers to their questions from it. To support projects better, upper managers need to support the design of an information system that answers their questions rather than just presents them with data.

Information that relieves anxiety answers questions whenever necessary in a form that is easy to understand. Thus, an important step in developing a PMIS is to determine what information stakeholders need to answer their questions and relieve their anxiety. Some texts advise the project leader to begin with a list of stakeholders and ask each what information they need to know about the project. However, experience shows that the responses to such a question do not reveal all that is needed. Many people find it difficult to answer the question; they give an answer, but when the data are presented, they say the information is not what they really wanted, often leaving the project leader puzzled and frustrated.

For example, one newly formed organization commissioned a large number of task forces to make recommendations about how to work together. When they presented their work in progress to the manager, he said it was not what he was looking for. Asked what he was really after, he said, in essence, that he would know it when he saw it. Not surprisingly, this did not help. Most of the hard work expended by the task forces over the past six weeks was of little use; the participants were demoralized and glad to get off the teams. Rather than concentrating on a desired solution, they could have asked the manager what problem he was trying to solve. Understanding the problem helps in understanding the solution; in this case, people thought in terms of data and solutions instead of questions and problems.

Most people do not think in terms of data but rather in terms of questions. Therefore, instead of asking managers what data they need, ask what questions they have about the project. Also, ask how they will use the data to be provided. The provider then can help create a solution rather than being just a data reporter. Project customers or end users should also be asked what problem they are trying to solve.

People at different levels of an organization have different concerns. Department directors might be concerned about allocation of the resource pool. Senior management may be concerned about selecting projects that will respond to opportunities. Marketing managers want to know when products will be available. Project managers care about the effects of delay or changes or reallocation of resources. A perfect PMIS is designed to respond to all these concerns.

Upper managers need to think about what questions they have about the project and what questions other people will ask them about it. They then can work with the project leader and other stakeholders to develop an information set that answers those questions. Box 6.3 presents an example of the problems of presenting the information that is available rather than that which answers the question.

Good information answers stakeholders' questions, is easy for them to understand, and is there when they need it. Providing it requires that the project leader understand the questions and associated information from the stakeholders' points of view. The PMIS should then be developed to satisfy the information needs of all stakeholders, much as the entire project is developed to satisfy the needs of the customer and end users.

BOX 6.3. "I Need a Report."

I (Robert Graham) was working as a systems analyst when a manager said, "I need a report that tells me the current inventory levels." We designed a system that tracked the level of every part in the inventory and produced a massive report every two weeks. Eventually, someone asked the manager if he was using the report. No, he said, and added: "Last week someone asked me if I could deliver five hundred thermostats the next day. Your system didn't tell me that. I had to call Joe in production."

Obviously, we did not understand the problem he was trying to solve. Our problem was that we accepted his initial statement that he needed a report. But he did not: he was trying to solve a problem and thought a report would help. He stated the problem in terms of a solution, a common situation in many organizations. I should have asked him what problem he was trying to solve instead of just providing the information he requested.

Questions on Outcome

Questions about outcome are normally of three types. The first is about what the final product will do when it is completed. This is a concern of the project leader as well as the project stakeholders, as product specifications will likely change as the project proceeds. The project leader must guard against suggesting that a certain function will be available until it is certain that it will be. So answer questions about outcome in two parts: features that have definitely been decided on and those that are being considered. Regularly update the lists of each, and distribute them automatically to all stakeholders.

The second question about outcome is whether the eventual product will be successful. Stakeholders want to know how the product compares to that of the competition and how likely it is to gain market acceptance. The best way to address this is to summarize the expectations gleaned from customer and end user representatives, show how the product is being designed to address those expectations, and pass the information on to stakeholders. If this cannot be done for competitive reasons (because the information must be kept secret), the stakeholders need to be assured that expectations will indeed be met.

A third outcome question is about market segments. Stakeholders often want to know what market the product is aimed at satisfying. Thus, the project leader needs to be continually aware of and searching for potential applications and markets for the product and pass this information on to stakeholders. Therefore, the information system contains all information that the project team has discovered regarding customer requirements and potential markets.

Questions About the Schedule

A classic schedule question is about when the new product will be ready. Associated questions concern milestone reviews and the availability of prototypes. Make an updated schedule always available to stakeholders in order to answer these questions.

The chief source for information on the schedule is the project plan. Indeed, it is the central element of any good PMIS. The project plan is usually shown in two forms. One is the work breakdown structure (WBS), which shows activities and their durations (see Figure 6.1). This is a logical form of presentation of the activities that will be completed during the project. The WBS is the basis for the Gantt chart.

The Gantt chart in Figure 6.2 shows a project with ten activities. The column on the left side describes the activity, the length of the lines on the right show the duration of the activity, and the position of the activity on the graph relative to the bottom line shows the scheduled dates for that activity.

Another popular way to show schedule information is the network diagram. It shows both the activity duration and the activity dependencies—that is, which activities must be completed before subsequent activities can begin. The staffing levels and the person in charge of each activity can also be indicated. This diagram shows the project as a system of interrelated activities and indicates those relationships well. Because it is a visual map of the project, it is best for showing the big picture to team members and other stakeholders. Upper managers should become familiar with this type of schedule representation.

An important concept represented on this diagram is the critical path: the longest path by which the project can be completed in the shortest time. Activities on the critical path are said to be critical because any delay of them will certainly delay the finish date for the project. These activities require the greatest project management attention.

Also necessary is a diagram of the master schedule. This is a Gantt chart representation where each entry represents a project and shows the interrelationships among all projects in the organization. Enterprise project management software is becoming increasingly available to show the status of all projects in the portfolio.

Upper managers usually express many differing expectations of project schedule information. Some want to see aggressive schedules. Others want a variety of scenarios. A few know exactly what they want and tell the team when and how to do it. Most want to know what they can realistically expect so other projects can be planned accordingly.

FIGURE 6.1. SAMPLE OF A WORK BREAKDOWN STRUCTURE.

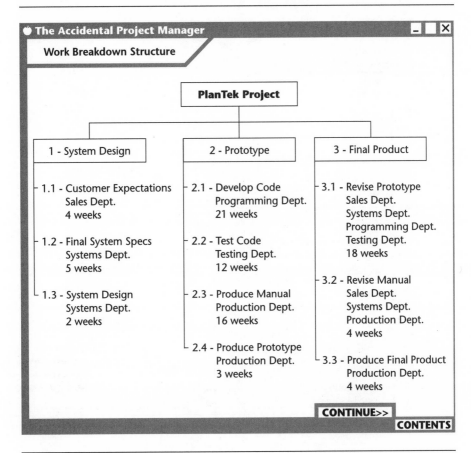

Source: Reprinted by permission of SMG Strategic Management Group, Inc.®

A computer program manager provided advice for project managers that is still worth following. Present a schedule you know you can meet; use everything possible—data from previous projects, statistical analysis, reconciled numbers from bottom-up and top-down forecasts, contingency considerations—to put together a credible schedule; get data and do your homework; use due diligence and negotiating skills to the hilt; and put your reputation on the line. Then work passionately to make it all happen.

This approach takes stamina, but it alleviates most problems in organizations. Completing a project when due makes it possible to move on to other projects that depend on its outcome or resources. Provide information that people can rely on to make this happen, and you become a hero.

FIGURE 6.2. SAMPLE OF A GANTT CHART.

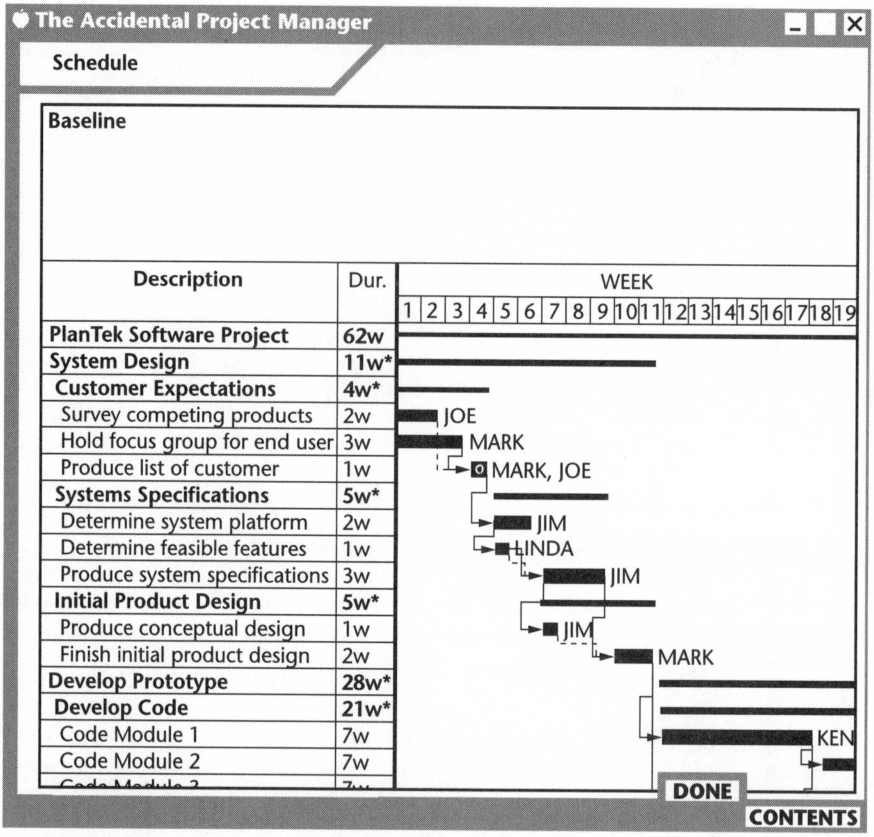

Description	Dur.	WEEK
		1 2 3 4 5 6 7 8 9 10 11 12 13 14 15 16 17 18 19
PlanTek Software Project	62w	
System Design	11w*	
Customer Expectations	4w*	
Survey competing products	2w	JOE
Hold focus group for end user	3w	MARK
Produce list of customer	1w	MARK, JOE
Systems Specifications	5w*	
Determine system platform	2w	JIM
Determine feasible features	1w	LINDA
Produce system specifications	3w	JIM
Initial Product Design	5w*	
Produce conceptual design	1w	JIM
Finish initial product design	2w	MARK
Develop Prototype	28w*	
Develop Code	21w*	
Code Module 1	7w	KEN
Code Module 2	7w	
Code Module 3	7w	

Source: Reprinted by permission of SMG Strategic Management Group, Inc.®

Questions About Resource Requirements

Projects have a way of using up countless resource hours, many of them unexpectedly. This often frustrates department directors who supply the resources. Their questions normally have to do with what resources a project needs and for how long—meaning they want to know when the resources will be available to the department again. Project leaders are understandably hesitant to address such questions; the answers are uncertain when a project intends to accomplish something new. Besides, initial estimates tend to be cast in stone by those who hear them, such that changes cause friction with the department directors. Thus, resource requirements should be presented as authoritative only according to today's view of the project. Project leaders should not just produce estimates and send them to the department directors; they should personally explain to each director the assumptions behind the estimates and indicate all factors that could cause them to change. Department directors, like everyone else, are much more amenable to change if they understand the reason for it.

It is important to be able to show individual schedules as well as resource loading for each project and across projects. "What if?" questions about resources can also be answerable using the system: What would be the effect on the project schedules of decreasing Joe's time by half? Are there enough resources to add another project to the portfolio? This information greatly enhances the ability of the upper management team to make decisions regarding optimum allocation of resources.

Information That Is There When Needed

Information sufficient to answer questions does little good unless it is available when it is most needed. Upper managers need to work with the project leader to determine when the information will most likely be needed. Asking stakeholders when they usually discuss a project or what meetings they attend where project questions arise should suffice to make this determination. If regular meetings of senior managers take place where the project is discussed and decisions are made, provide the information the day before the meeting so that stakeholders arrive with up-to-date data. Timely information is current information that arrives just before the person needs it. Intranets now make it much easier to provide and get updated information. Use e-mail messages to inform stakeholders when updated information is available on the intranet, and set up expectations that everyone regularly updates their information before coming to meetings.

Information That Is Easy to Understand

Even if information is accurate and timely, it is useless unless the person using it understands it. Many people are not familiar or comfortable with Gantt charts and network diagrams. Thus, the first few times information is supplied in these formats, the project leader may need to review them personally with others to ensure that they fully understand what is being presented. If they prefer not to work with network diagrams and the like, develop a different format that they are comfortable with. Always remember that information is being produced in order to relieve anxiety and uncertainty. If people cannot understand the information, it increases the very anxiety it was designed to reduce. The information should conform to the person rather than expecting the person to conform to the information.

PMIS and Communication

An important function of any PMIS is facilitation of communication within the project team and between the project team and other project teams and outside stakeholders. Examples of technology available to aid communication are e-mail, teleconferencing, Lotus Notes, the Web, and a variety of database sharing programs. Much of this is readily available in larger organizations.

Technology can help project managers communicate with each other in a variety of ways. Upper managers should support the creation of a project manager's communications network, through which project managers have access to each other to share best practices and other project information. The idea is to have an electronic meeting place for project managers throughout the organization.

3M (Storeygard, 1995) developed an electronic post office (EPO) for such communication and performance support. The EPO is available to all project managers in the organization and contains the following information:

- General reference material, including a project management glossary, book reviews, article summaries, and other more static or unchanging information
- Project initiation material that provides best practices for quick start-ups on projects
- Working reference material that provides practical matter to download, such as plan examples, methodology procedures, and tool guidelines
- Management material for ongoing projects, such as metrics information, team-building advice and ideas, and multiple project considerations
- Specific information on techniques such as project partitioning, user analysis, and prototyping
- A "meeting place" for project managers to share information and ask for help

PMIS and Organizational Learning

The PMIS should be designed not only to provide information but also to gather data as feedback about organizational learning. To generate more accurate deadlines and schedules in the future, for example, track experience versus projection on today's projects, and then analyze and seek the cause of the differences. Were the differences due to wildly optimistic or pessimistic projections? Wrong staffing level? People not having enough time? Analyze differences to get better at estimating durations and project completion dates.

A PMIS should also have the ability to make visible the accuracy and stability of schedule and budget estimates. It should be able to track how far off the original estimates and reestimates were. It should track how often schedules and budget estimates change and why they slip. Record and archive causative factors for use in project reviews, as input to planning process improvement efforts, and for input on future project planning efforts. These features are necessary to support quality improvement in schedule and budget estimation techniques.

Birchall and Lyons (1995) also see technology assisting team learning in many ways. In particular, they cite the following:

- Communications technology can substitute for face-to-face contact in the case of dispersed teams.
- When given access to communications technology, people will pay attention to different things and communicate in different ways. This could help enhance team performance.
- Communications technology can complement other team-building activities by helping to maintain relationships and show progress on group tasks.
- The technology can provide teams with a wealth of information from both inside and outside the organization.
- Communications technology will change interaction patterns in ways that are difficult to predict. People will begin to think in new ways and work together differently, as well as do completely new things.
- Teams can have much better access to a shared memory. With much enhanced team memory, team learning can focus on the areas of nonroutine activity that are of greatest intellectual challenge and offer the highest added value for the organization.

It is important to remember, however, that systems and technology never truly substitute for the personal touch. People need to interact directly with others to be most effective with them. Support efforts for people to meet in person initially and periodically, and then use the technologies to supplement communications throughout the project.

Software and PMIS

Exhibit areas at project management conferences are overflowing with a variety of software packages claiming to solve project management problems. The feature sets of these packages have become quite robust. Unfortunately, it often takes a guru to understand and use all the features. The software may do "favors"—change data on a task, for example, and the end date moves out of sight; after an hour of fiddling, it turns out that an inconsequential linkage created the movement. People can record immense amounts of trivia about every conceivable task on the project. It becomes easy to spend more time managing the software than managing the project.

Project management software is like religion: most people have their own, many believe in it fervently, and some become evangelists. A constructive approach to the software challenge is to ask, "If you were given project management scheduling and tracking software, how would you use it?" Possibilities include the following:

- Improving the estimating process
- Determining realistic end dates
- Capturing all tasks, owners, and start and finish dates
- Showing interdependencies
- Managing deliverables and dependencies
- Identifying critical paths
- Reviewing progress

By focusing on how the software output will be used, project managers can be more selective in what they use and how they structure the information.

The solution to this challenge is more behavioral than technical. Sharing information makes for successful projects. Reports and graphs become meaningful when the creator keeps asking, "How can I make this information clearer to the recipient?" Upper managers help by describing how they will use information about a project. Focus on action-oriented information that helps guide action or make decisions, not on control-oriented information that is burdensome to collect and of dubious value.

Many managers have favorite software that produces reports that are clear to them, so any PMIS should be able to support a variety of software applications.

The software side of PMIS is basically a database problem; all programs and reports should draw from the same projects database. Project schedules are one way of looking at the data, and resource schedules are another way of looking at the same data. If all are drawn from one database, customized reports or custom software can draw from the data in real time. People can use their own software to have their own view and might share these views with others who may not have thought of them but may find them helpful.

Upper managers are advised to be involved in and direct the process of database design. A PMIS database must cover the entire organization in order to be useful, so upper managers' participation from all affected areas is needed. Otherwise, individual groups will continue to suboptimize—that is, design databases only for themselves and not for the entire organization. Individually designed databases are difficult to use when information must be summarized across different entities. To ensure most efficient use, the PMIS database requires coordinated design.

Developing a PMIS

Upper managers need to agree up front on the specifications of the PMIS and the use of the data. This means that the upper managers determine what they want from the PMIS, and then they work together to get the required input and determine the required output. Box 6.4 describes a simple low-tech approach to the display of information.

BOX 6.4. The Value of Information.

I (Randall Englund) sat in on a number of hardware team weekly meetings. The project manager reported the good news that the computer processor board was due back from the vendor that week. Much technical discussion ensued, and most people left the meeting satisfied. Only later did I wonder if the board was early, late, or on schedule; no information about overall progress had been presented, and no schedule was evident or referred to. The manager and team felt good about the current events, but their approach did not provide enough information to management about the probability of a credible completion according to a project schedule.

Later, chairing a program team responsible for resolving issues about the computer architecture, I used a wonderful low-tech idea suggested by an experienced manager. I plotted the schedule on transparency film and inserted it in a transparent document cover. For the weekly status meeting, I drew a black vertical line representing the current date on the document cover. I highlighted in green all tasks that were on or ahead of schedule and in red all those that were behind schedule. Using an overhead projector to display the chart, I presented a visual picture of the status of the complete project. Team members instantly sensed whether red or green dominated the landscape. We then discussed problem areas. For the next meeting, I took the master schedule out of the document cover, put it in a new cover, drew a new time line, and again highlighted status in appropriate colors. Previous covers formed a historical record for the project. At one point, I used blue markings to present a bridge on how we would work on behind-schedule tasks in order to meet the completion date.

Meetings of this project team were tremendously effective as a result of the use of this simple technique. The project was completed on schedule to the exact day.

One way to think about required output is to visualize a dashboard of information, like the dashboard of a car. Meyer (1993, p. 150) says this is a "model for helping teams develop a guidance tool. A car dashboard only tells you the minimal information required to drive the vehicle safely to any destination you choose. By design, it limits the information to the absolute minimum. The best dashboards have highly visible, graphic analog gauges that display the necessary information so clearly that one hardly has to take one's eyes off the road to read them." The information is immediate, with no lags of weeks or months: "The goal is to have as many real-time response gauges as possible." What should be on the project information dashboard? Possibilities include measurements of critical path status, stress, motivation of project managers, staffing plan versus actual staffing, projects on target to meet objectives, progress in resolving design issues, progress in resolving defect issues, yellow flag and red flag issues, and program cost to date.

To compare data on different projects requires design of a common database system. Project managers have to use discipline and a central list to define such things as names of people who are working on their projects. Without a common numbering system, it is difficult to compare and summarize information about people and other resources. It is the job of upper managers to persuade project managers to use a common system. Use the Web to display real-time information.

Project managers may resist all this, viewing it as extra work, until they see the benefits. To influence them, find a champion who agrees that the problem needs to be solved, contacts the project managers directly to get their inputs, and helps them understand the benefits and that they can participate in the design. Iterate this process until all people develop consensus. People will participate in the database system if they understand why they need to work with it, see it as a common problem, and are able to influence the design and get the benefit.

Extra effort to discuss the proposed PMIS is the investment required to achieve participation and commitment from project managers. The person contacting the project managers needs to listen to the pain expressed and be empathetic. Demonstrate in vivid terms important to the listener the benefits that will accrue to the project manager from using the PMIS. Convince the person that the system is an investment with beneficial returns, not simply an additional cost. The design needs to accommodate as many of the concerns expressed as possible. Take the time to explain why some concerns may not or should not be incorporated into the design.

In addition, consider explaining these benefits to a common system:

- It allows seeing the big picture and knowing how each project affects others.
- Data collected by the system help in developing more credible schedules.
- It helps speed decisions about changes from weeks to days.
- It holds down the need to remake decisions.

- It improves the quality of decisions because upper managers are better informed.
- It saves time: fewer arguments over projects with other managers occur.

The development of an information center can be a project management process involving a series of unique projects. Marjorie Smink, manager of the Knowledge and Wisdom Center for the Project Management Institute (PMI) in Newtown Square, Pennsylvania, used the five process groups (initiating, planning, executing, controlling, and closing) and management skills described in the PMI standard publication, *A Guide to the Project Management Body of Knowledge* (2000), popularly known as the *PMBOK Guide*, as she developed the center.

Smink is convinced of the importance of applying project management to information center development. "I implemented an increasingly more disciplined approach in applying the *PMBOK Guide*'s process groups, especially the planning process, to projects such as the grand opening of the center, the implementation of an integrated on-line library system, promotional projects, and the creation of an archives program." Furthermore, Smink believes, "I can apply the techniques to any project I tackle. The project management discipline fits in well with the work of an information center, for it is a natural adjunct to what we already do. It gives us added focus to organize materials, develop a working schedule, document the projects and our progress, and achieve our goals. The project team has clear objectives and a self-enforcing mechanism to stay on track; therefore, we become more efficient. Learning project management has helped me accomplish projects more effectively and confidently."

Representing one form of an information system, the Knowledge and Wisdom Center is a resource for relevant, reliable, and timely information for the global practice and profession of project management. As described at www.pmi.org/info, the center's services include:

- Reference services for answers to project management–related questions
- Document delivery services of articles from PMI-published journals and conference proceedings
- A quarterly electronic newsletter of practical tips and tools
- Hot topics—pathfinders to information on topics of interest including benchmarking, project templates, and the value of project management
- A knowledge base of books, journals, Web sites, and reports held in the center, as well as abstracts of articles from PMI literature, capturing the intellectual capital contained in the institute's literature and in the minds of project management experts
- A collection of reference tools for developing education and training programs for PMI certifications
- Proceedings from seminars and symposiums

Named in honor of James Snyder, founder, fellow, and chair of the PMI Educational Foundation, the PMI James R. Snyder Center for Project Management Knowledge and Wisdom officially launched operations on December 6, 2001, with a grand opening ceremony. The center ultimately will become a totally electronic information center. It currently houses a strong collection of books and journals related to project management and minutes of PMI board of directors meetings.

The center serves as a source of project management information for all stakeholders in the profession and the institute: PMI members, project management practitioners, consultants, students, academic-business-government entities, the media, and the public.

Measuring Progress

Sharing of information is greatly facilitated by models that people understand and use as short-cut communications vehicles. One helpful concept borrowed from engineering is to measure project progress by a vector approach. A vector has magnitude (α) and direction (θ). (See Figure 6.3.) Of course, the ideal for project progress is large magnitude in the direction of the project outcome statement. However, there are times when the direction gets altered, such as priority interrupts or executive requests that send people moving in different directions or on other tasks. Sometimes the magnitude or amount of progress gets altered, as with morale and motivation setbacks brought on by "integrity crimes" or by reorganization announcements that paralyze work in process.

All managers need to be conscious about the impact of information on the ebb and flow of project work. Timing is everything. There are times when magnitude may be down—progress is slower than expected—but the vector is still going in the right direction—the team is still together and working toward the project goal. That is okay and may be the natural energy of the group for that

FIGURE 6.3. A VECTORED APPROACH TO PROGRESS.

moment, because the right work is happening, albeit slowly. A manager could mess things up if he or she pushed too hard at that time, so the advice is to "go with the flow."

If the manager or the information system senses the vector turning in an undesirable direction—missed milestones, retracing old decisions, unconstructive conflict—that is the time to step in and turn things around. The magnitude of the vector determines what type of action to take. If the misdirection is small or slightly off target, gentle coaching and reminders are sufficient. When major shifts occur that appear to take the project way off track, directive action and commands may be necessary.

Facilitating team progress can be guided by getting quantitative and qualitative inputs from the information system as inputs to the vector concept, gauging what is happening, and taking appropriate action. Progress can be measured and communicated by reporting the direction and magnitude of the vector. Good news is when the vector points in the right direction with a magnitude appropriate for the stage of the project.

Creating an Environment for Project Success

All professionals help create an environment for project success by modeling desired behaviors. If on a project team, prod and support the project manager to initiate and plan the project well and design a communications plan. Develop reports that are simple and clear. Follow through on action items and deliverables. Act with authenticity and integrity. Support team processes that get issues on the table for discussion and resolution. Demonstrate how projects link to organizational strategy. Where these actions are not evident, ask why and what you can do to help. Demonstrate success through small actions; then use the information system to share the results and the process that created them.

Take the time to reflect on project work and information flows within the organization. Learn the process and techniques codified in the project management body of knowledge. Take the initiative, experiment, and act on proven theories of project management. Celebrate successes, and learn from projects that are less successful. Create opportunities for this knowledge to be shared. Be sensitive to the importance of people—the attitudes and support of top administrators, the commitment of team members, and the inclusion of input from customers, users, and stakeholders. An environment for successful projects depends on people collaborating instead of competing, sharing instead of hiding. Start with a personal commitment to excel in this worthy endeavor; ask and expect others to do the same.

The Compleat Upper Manager

The successful complete upper manager knows that:

- Projects create anxiety in organizations; the PMIS should relieve anxiety.
- Management mistakes are made at times of anxiety, so the PMIS should minimize mistakes.
- An effective PMIS cuts across organization lines and provides information for decision making.
- The information system should be based on the questions of upper managers and project managers.
- A good information system is one that answers stakeholders' questions, is there when they need it, and is easy to understand.
- Most stakeholder questions have to do with outcomes, schedules, and resource requirements.
- The PMIS should support organizational learning and provide feedback to managers concerning their performance.
- Software can help collect and display information, but a PMIS for decision making requires more than just software.
- Developing and running a PMIS require extra effort on the part of project managers. Upper managers need to convince project managers of the benefits of putting in the extra effort to get the extra information.
- Because the PMIS is systemwide across organizations, it will not be implemented unless upper managers push to make it happen.
- The value of information is to guide appropriate action.

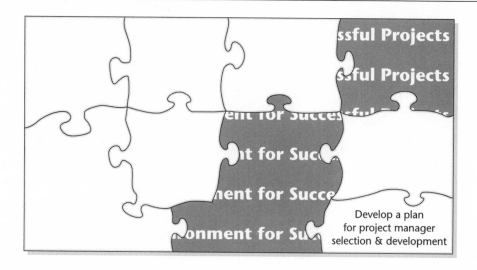

ssful Projects

ssful Projects

ent for Succe**s**ful

t for Suc**c**

ent for Succe

onment for Su

Develop a plan
for project manager
selection & development

This chapter begins with a review of the problems that develop when an organization uses the accidental project manager approach to project manager selection. Many people take the job because they see no other career development options. A first step in project manager selection is to provide an attractive alternative: thus, the need for a dual career ladder.

Several studies are reviewed and summarized to yield five important criteria for project manager selection. Given these, a project manager selection process is proposed, an important part of which is helping potential candidates determine if they really want the job. Finally, the chapter reviews a project manager development process, including the role of upper management in it.

CHAPTER SEVEN

SELECTING AND DEVELOPING THE PROJECT MANAGER

*The best leader is the one who has sense enough to pick good
[people] to do what he wants done, and the self-restraint to keep
from meddling with them while they do it.*

THEODORE ROOSEVELT, *AMERICAN IDEALS*

M ost people become project managers by accident. The usual path to the
job is through expertise in a technical specialty. In the past, those with technical skill were told to run projects that used it. The best systems analysts or pro-
grammers were put in charge of software development projects, and the best
engineers were put in charge of product development projects. However, the technical part of a project is often the smallest and easiest part. Technical success does
not necessarily lead to project success; it is necessary but not sufficient. Upper
management needs to take the lead to put into place a system that selects and develops those people with the greatest potential to manage projects. This chapter
covers the processes necessary to select and develop exceptional project managers.

The Accidental Project Manager

Accidental project managers are alive and well—or at least alive; many do not feel
so good about themselves or the job they are doing. Asked informally during workshops to rate their job satisfaction on a scale of 1 to 100 (where 100 means they
are totally enthusiastic, love their job, would still do it if they were independently

wealthy, and are doing exactly what they want to be doing), very few project managers give themselves 90 or higher. A small percentage are in the 70 to 90 range, many say 50 to 70, and some say less than 50. People below 50 are in trouble; it is very difficult for them to achieve outstanding results when their enthusiasm is so low. The star performers usually rate their satisfaction at 85 or higher. People with high enthusiasm and motivation find the energy, ideas, and resources to overcome the obstacles that block their path. Research (Baker, Murphy, and Fisher, 1983) indicates that the personal ambition and motivation of the project manager is the most important success driver during the formation phase of the project.

Most organizations want project managers who come from the ranks of star performers. Technology companies typically promote people to project manager based on their outstanding performance as engineers. But do these people make outstanding project managers? Will they be enthusiastic about their new responsibilities? Do they have an aptitude for the requirements imposed on them to lead and manage projects? It is imperative to recognize that the skill set of project managers is different from the skills exercised in other professional disciplines. Managers who select and develop project managers are well advised to understand the competences required from these people and adjust selection criteria accordingly.

Box 7.1 tells the story of learning a lesson about how engineers do not naturally make good project managers. A big difference occurs when training, selection, and implementation process steps are added.

It would seem that the first requirement of a potential project manager is the desire to be one, including the desire to be a manager in general. It makes sense that the people who are selected and developed to do a particular job should really want that job. A colleague once described newly hired HP employees as "brilliant adolescents." The company hires the best people it can, usually from the top ranks of technical graduates. And indeed, they have all the energy and enthusiasm of adolescents, applying themselves to many new opportunities, putting in long hours, going from one task to another with minimal guidance and even less formal training, moving from project to project. Most learning is on the job. They enjoy the excitement of exploring new technologies. They know from the "next bench" that other engineers also love the esoteric products they develop. All that talent in a seemingly disjointed environment is the reason that some amazing products finally get released to the market.

But management talent is not always obvious. The glamour of 25 percent yearly growth by high-tech companies in the 1970s and 1980s was evident in the youthful cadre of managers. Promotions came early for them, often before they developed much in the way of people skills. Project managers counted on their

BOX 7.1. Trained Project Managers Make a Difference.

In the early stages of developing a new computer system architecture that was to lead HP to market prominence in the 1990s, problems were detected in the development of new products such as interface boards that were ahead of the architecture definition. A massive effort was mounted to design a process to resolve these issues, drawing on a large group of technical experts from several divisions and multiple projects. Engineers were formed into study groups to investigate and propose solutions. Because architecture decisions are far reaching, the process had to include thorough reviews from all projects developing products. Resolution of issues also had to take differing organization priorities into account.

The first phase reached resolution seven weeks beyond a nine-week schedule. Too much time spent by too many people on a process that had many inefficiencies made management nervous. A retrospective analysis at that point highlighted the role of study group chair people, who were lead engineers, as an important area for improvement. A typical report at the weekly control group meeting was, "We're still working on the problem and need more time." They maintained a low profile and did not ask for help. It turns out that these people had no training on project management; they were trying to approach problems with strictly technical solutions. The real problems, however, were not technical: there were two or three possible technical solutions, and each organization favored a different one. The problems were organizational: no clear decision-making processes or ways to assess impact when operating across organizations were evident.

For subsequent issue resolution phases, trained project managers were assigned as study group leaders. They did not need a great depth of knowledge in computer architecture. Their role was not to argue for a position but to concentrate on an effective and efficient process for bringing technical experts into consensus. When tough issues could not be decided, they were passed up to the control group and eventually assigned to functional managers, who would make a business decision. Better estimation, scheduling, and communication techniques were also applied. Selecting leaders from people committed to exercising project management practices resulted in a shorter schedule met to the very day using fewer technical experts.

technical knowledge to make decisions, not on their ability to influence or motivate people.

Unfortunately, retaining an adolescent mentality in a growing organization is like carrying around a time bomb; it eventually explodes. The problem is exacerbated in difficult times, when stress levels run high. After a while, long working hours take their toll. Call it burnout. Disappointment sets in when customers do not purchase products according to optimistic forecasts. Projects are canceled after project teams expend dedicated effort on them for six months or a year or longer. The fast track up the management chain is very narrow or nonexistent. People are redeployed, as happened during the late 1980s, and must search around their company for other departments that need them. This was not supposed to happen to technical professionals, but it did. It happened again in starting the twenty-first century, with dot.bomb collapses and terrorist attacks. Violation of basic business fundamentals and loss of confidence in the economy put many people out of jobs.

And so the adolescents grew up. The realities of highly competitive markets require maturity, and maturity means that people do not fight the same fire over and over; they learn from past mistakes. Market "misses" cannot be covered by charging a premium for top-of-the-line products, so mature people learn to fix the process, not the product. An opportunistic approach to launching projects still appears chaotic, but it features an overarching strategy as well as criteria for making decisions. Project managers prove their efficacy when ambitious projects produce delightful products, meet schedules imposed by tight market windows, and use a lean staff of dedicated professionals. At the helm are leaders who have an aptitude for producing results by working with people because they are trained in the practices of project management. It also means that organizations need skilled managers who get the right work done with fewer people.

In the light of all this, appointing accidental project managers is no longer appropriate, if it ever was. Upper management needs to insist on and assist in the development of a process that selects and develops individuals with the best aptitude to become successful project managers.

The Need for Dual Career Ladders

Managing is not engineering. According to one project manager, "Someone once told me that management was a lot like engineering, except that you solve problems with people. Sure. And bow hunting for grizzly bear is just like target practice, except it involves real animals. The analogy entirely misses the raw adventure of the real thing." He added: "A manager's accomplishments are measured differently than an engineer's. . . . I was creating an environment that allowed the engineers to succeed. When the engineers were successful, I was successful" (see Platt, 1996, quoted in *MEASURE, Hewlett-Packard*). Another project manager once remarked, "Project management is too important to be left to amateurs."

The first important criterion for project manager success is the desire to be a manager in general and a project manager in particular. Many organizations, however, force people into the position even if they are not adept at it and do not desire to become one. True, the project management position may be the only way to promotion beyond the job of technical specialist; the step from technical specialist to project manager may be the assumed progression when there is no way to move up a technical ladder. It is far better, however, if alternative upward paths exist: one through technical managership and one through project managership.

With dual promotional ladders, technical managers can stay in their departments and become core team members responsible for the technical portions of projects. They must have many skills and interests, as they will work on project teams that include a variety of departments. They have to be able to see the whole picture, not just have a view of their own specialty. Dual ladders also allow progression through project management. Project managers must be able to manage technical specialists while handling the behavioral and administrative tasks that motivate the specialists to do their best work.

Project Manager Selection Criteria

Changing the project manager selection and development criteria is critical to the maturation process. Fortunately, studies and research are starting to identify the competences needed by project managers. An effective project manager is more than a brilliant engineer; research indicates that technical knowledge is not paramount to being a successful project manager even in a technical organization.

Research points to the enthusiasm of the project manager as a key criterion for project success: the project manager not only must want to be a project manager but must want to manage the project in question. Thus, part of the selection process, beyond finding people with the aptitude to be project managers, is matching them with particular projects that they will be interested in managing.

David Packard, a cofounder of HP, stated as part of the corporate objectives in 1961: "A high degree of enthusiasm must be encouraged at all levels; especially the people in important management positions must not only be enthusiastic themselves, they must be selected so they will engender this enthusiasm among their associates. There can be no place, especially among the people charged with management responsibility, for half-hearted interest or half-hearted effort" (p. 126).

One definition (Wheelwright and Hayes, 1994) says that an effective project manager is a "technological entrepreneur" who can do each of the following:

- Invoke the inner confidence to ask dumb questions and keep asking them, plowing through the jargon, implicit assumptions, and unstated relationships that often surround technology.
- Thrive in the ambiguity that surrounds working in an unstructured environment without clear lines of authority or specific resources.
- Operate through interpersonal ad hoc agreements and understandings, on the basis of personal credibility, good will, and mutual advantage rather than relying on organizational loyalty or rank in that organization.
- React instinctively to opportunities and crises, and thus maintain the credibility of the project and keep it progressing inch by inch, rather than waiting for . . . (fill in any excuse).
- Identify the people whose support is crucial to the success of the project and win their allegiance.

A keynote paper presented at the World Congress of Project Management (Gadeken, 1994) identified from research six competences that distinguish outstanding project managers from their contemporaries:

- *Sense of ownership and mission.* Sees self as responsible for the project; articulates problems or issues from broader organizational or missions perspective.
- *Political awareness.* Knows who influential players are, what they want, and how best to work with them.
- *Relationship development.* Spends time and energy getting to know project sponsors, users, and contractors.
- *Strategic influence.* Builds coalitions and orchestrates situations to overcome obstacles and obtain support.
- *Interpersonal assessment.* Identifies specific interests, motivations, strengths, and weaknesses of others.
- *Action orientation.* Reacts to problems energetically and with a sense of urgency.

These competences fall almost exclusively within the category of managing the external environment, which means managing relationships outside the project office.

To support the emphasis on managing the external environment, the same study compared importance rankings of the project manager competences with those of other professional specialties. Other professionals considered technical expertise (ranked 1 by them, 21 by the project managers), attention to detail (7 versus 22), and creativity (3 versus 15) as far more important than did the successful project managers. Key areas that project managers ranked higher than other professionals were sense of ownership and mission (ranked 1 by the project managers, 17 by the other professionals), political awareness (4 versus 21), and strategic influence (14 versus 23).

These data support the idea that technical expertise is not the most important requirement for successful project management. The project managers ranked this aspect twenty-first out of twenty-seven (it does show why technical expertise was so long considered the most important: other professionals rank it number 1). Clearly, the practice of promoting the best engineers to manage engineering projects was ill founded. This study indicates that far more important is a sense of mission, the sense of really wanting the project to succeed, and a political awareness of how to get things done. Technical expertise is necessary on the core team, but not necessarily by the project manager.

Gadeken goes on to say that "the transition from functional specialist to project manager may be conceptually quite difficult, mainly because project managers need external interface skills to a much greater extent than their counterparts in operational commands."

One of Gadeken's recommendations is especially striking: "The preferred alternative for project manager selection is to assess which candidates have or can more readily develop the critical leadership and management competencies. Training can then be provided or tailored in project management functional disciplines (knowledge areas) to augment the candidates' prior knowledge and experience base." We usually do it just the other way around.

Another firm did a competency analysis to define a project manager (PM) model (Sarna, 1994). Results from surveys and focus groups were validated by firsthand observations and ratified by managers of project managers. Even before entering individual development planning and training strategies, project management candidates must fit this firm's PM Competency Model by showing proficiency in the following areas:

- Business development
- Client relations management
- Communications skills
- Finance
- Monitoring and reporting
- Personal self-development
- Planning
- Problem detection and resolution
- Staff development
- Staff management
- Quality management
- Organizational utilization and support

Candidates with this profile are then eligible for training and development in curricula covering methodology, planning and control, client relations, project administration, staff management, and integrating workshops.

Keane Consultants employed a behavioral research firm to identify the key project management qualities that make the difference between average and superior performance (Edgemon, 1995). From this it developed the Project Manager Competency Model, which has four clusters:

- The problem-solving cluster, which includes competence in diagnostic thinking, systemic thinking, conceptual thinking, and information gathering
- The managerial identity cluster, which includes competence in strong project manager identity, self-confidence, and flexibility
- The achievement cluster, which consists of concern for achievement, results orientation, initiative, and business orientation
- The influence cluster, which stresses the importance of organizational and interpersonal astuteness, skill in the use of influence strategies and team building, along with a client orientation and self-control

Continual studies on PM competency sponsored by the Project Management Institute (www.pmi.org) largely support the diversity of skills needed for this profession. One focus on membership study (*PMI Today*, June 2001) points out that the greatest challenge to the future of project management is public perception and acceptance of the profession and acceptance by top management. The top capabilities needed from project leaders are leadership skills such as vision and motivating others, people skills and getting along with others, and management skills for directing and managing others.

David Frame (1999) used the guidelines he helped develop for the Project Management Institute to define the most important competencies for individuals, teams, and organizations. He concludes, "Higher levels of management should do everything possible to create an environment that enables their employees to shine. The key word here is support. . . . Moral support means that management creates a culture that encourages employees to excel in their tasks. High performance is encouraged, and slacking off is seen as unattractive. One way to create a healthy environment is to empower employees to make a wide array of decisions. By being part of the decision-making process, employees incur an obligation to perform their tasks effectively. This is the essence of ownership" (p. 214).

Reward based on performance and promote based on ability, advise Hammer and Champy (1993, p. 74): "Advancement to another job within the organization is a function of ability, not performance. It is a change, not a reward." Managing is a particular skill. Too often people are promoted to project management as a reward for past performance; these are accidental project managers. Changing to a project management organization means assessing the potential of a candidate to perform the project management role based on competence in the skills that job requires. Often these candidates will not have distinguished themselves as individual contributors or in technical roles, because these are not their greatest skills. But put them into project management, and they shine!

Belbin's research (1996) on successful management teams singled out effective leaders as those who are trusting, accept people as they are, have a strong and morally based commitment to external goals and objectives, are calm and unflappable in the face of controversy, are geared toward practical realism, possess basic self-discipline, are naturally enthusiastic, and have a capacity to motivate others while being prone to detachment and distance in social relations. The successful team leader is someone tolerant enough always to listen to others but strong enough to reject their advice. Such individuals show approval of people who accomplish their goals, like people who are lively and dynamic, know how to use resources, never lose their grip on a situation, and reach their own judgments. They are adept at drawing out the potential of the group and get high marks on skill in consultation, delegation of work, and firmness of decisions. Belbin reports that leaders of project teams appointed on the basis of this profile rather than on the basis of experience and seniority achieve more favorable outcomes and the most reliable results. Belbin, who observed these leaders play an important part in teams that encountered the usual difficulties but overcame them to finish strongly, also cautions: "It is quite difficult to identify individuals with this gift for it belongs to some deceptively ordinary people."

Technical ability is not an overriding indicator of the effective project manager. It certainly provides increased credibility on the job in a high-technology environment, but has been elevated in importance beyond what it deserves.

Project managers need to have leadership potential. Some do have this potential; others are followers. A manager who is a follower simply takes the assignment from upper management and passes it along to the team. A leader develops a personal vision about the assignment that includes a vivid description of the significance or the value-added contribution to be made by the team. These leaders are able to inspire team members to share the vision and get excited by it.

An upper manager who successfully brought complex programs to completion shared that effective project managers need three things: vision, focus, and resources. If they have those, they possess immense power to get things done, and unfortunately may therefore be perceived as threatening by other managers. Organizations may respond by not giving such people control of the resources they need and requiring that they manage multiple projects. What they cannot take away, however, is personal vision. Project managers need to cultivate a personal vision of a desired future state associated with project success. The ability to create motivating visions is perhaps their most powerful project management tool.

The Five Top Criteria for Competent Project Managers

The results of research and experience so far seem to point to five characteristics possessed by people who make successful project managers.

They Have Enthusiasm. The most important criterion is the desire of the person to do the job. This means that the person knows what the job entails or is willing to learn, and wants not only to be a manager in general but to be a manager in a project environment and on specific projects. Make determining the level of enthusiasm part of the interview and selection process. Potential project managers can take a transitions course to ensure that this job is what they want to do. If the enthusiasm and aptitude are there, they can be trained in the skills of the job.

They Have High Tolerance for Ambiguity. Project managers must be ready to work with very ambiguous authority. People who need clear-cut authority do not do well as project managers. They must be ready to work in situations where absolute authority is nonexistent, roles and responsibilities are uncertain, and measures of success depend on customers who constantly reevaluate their expectations. They also need to be comfortable with the ambiguity that exists at the beginning of a project and possess the ability to turn that ambiguity into concrete deliverables.

They Possess High Coalition and Team-Building Skills. The project manager needs considerable skill in building coalitions of external stakeholders and teams of internal members and in translating the vision of the project to all. The power to get a job done is granted by external stakeholders, and the ability to get the job done lies only in the project team. Project success depends heavily on the project manager's ability to build the coalitions and the team.

They Have Client-Customer Orientation. Although coalitions and teams make it possible for projects to get done, the final measure of success is the satisfaction of customers. Customer expectations and problems continually change, so the better the project manager understands the customer situation, the better the chance is that the final product will solve customer problems. The project manager must be able to take customer needs and craft them into a vision that can be used to motivate and direct members of the project team.

They Have a Business Orientation. According to Collins and Porras (1994), an inclination toward business is a highly important factor in building a sustainable and visionary business. Project managers need to understand the business of the organization; they will make many decisions that will affect many parts of the organization, so they need to know the effects of those decisions. In addition, they will make decisions affecting the final profitability of the final product, so they need to understand how the organization makes and maintains a profit. Business orientation will determine the final success of the project. The project must meet the strategic objective of the organization, help the final customers and end users solve their problems, and make a profit.

A Project Manager Selection Process

How do you find good potential project managers? The first step is to know what you are looking for by using the criteria just outlined. The next step is to use a critical behavior interview process where candidates are asked what they would do in given situations. Situation-based tests might also be used to get similar results. For both, the responses are best evaluated by successful project managers. Of course, people do not always do what they say they would do, so an extra validation would be to watch the results of experiential exercises and behavioral simulations. That way, it is possible to watch what candidates actually do.

Few candidates will be proficient in all five of the top criteria for competent project managers. But remember that the key is to discover the candidate's potential. Successful candidates may then be assisted in putting together a development plan. However, potential is very difficult to ascertain and to judge. It might help to ask the candidates what obstacles they overcame to get where they are and how they did so. Their responses would give some indication of enthusiasm and tolerance for ambiguity.

Having a process for project manager selection is very important. In one highly effective interviewing process at HP, an open requisition is posted on the electronic notice board. The hiring manager interviews respondents by phone and (based on a set of questions prepared in advance or simply on visceral reactions) selects a few for in-person interviews. Peers and team members who will work with the winning candidate conduct the interviews; the candidate who receives the job offer must not only be competent for the position but also fit in with the group or provide talents that do not currently exist within it.

Each interview avoids duplication of effort by covering different ground. Each interviewer is assigned specific job areas to cover, such as teamwork, goal setting, conflict resolution, work style, and technical proficiency. This process is inherently more interesting to candidates, as they do not answer the same questions repeatedly. Because the team members who do the interviewing are involved in the process, they take more accountability for the decision. The group also appears much better organized to the interviewee.

Each interviewer fills out an evaluation form after the interview, and all meet to discuss their perceptions. These discussions provide a forum to bring to the surface subtle feelings that one person may be hesitant to write down or bring up alone. When such a concern is shared, someone else may recall the same or another area of concern. The group decides if the concern is relevant and important. Further research may be needed; the candidate may be interviewed further, or associates of the candidate may be interviewed. There must be a consensus decision for an offer to be made. Sometimes the final set of candidates is so compelling that a process similar to prioritizing a project portfolio is followed (see Chapter Two).

This process consumes a lot of time and may involve people in discussions that make them uncomfortable, but it greatly reduces the risk of bringing in someone who will not be a good fit. No person alone could detect all the positive or negative qualities of the candidates, but group discussion makes it clear if one candidate stands out. If no candidate does stand out, a gap in the credentials of an otherwise excellent candidate may be bridged by training or by reassigning responsibility for a function to somebody else. The group may choose to pick the best from the group of candidates or to keep looking.

The Transition to Project Manager

The project management initiative at HP assisted the selection process by offering a course to potential project managers called "Transitions to Project Management." The course explains to candidates what project management requires of the individual, how being a project manager differs from being a project contributor, and how the ability to lead projects can be developed.

In this one-day course, participants learn the many elements of managing and leading projects. The intention is to develop awareness of the differences between individual contributors and project managers. The course explores the transition from individual contributor to the roles and responsibilities of project management in today's environment of flattened work groups.

It also identifies key attributes of successful project managers and provides a forum for participants to discuss best practices with successful project managers from their site. It does not explain how to define, plan, or manage projects; these are covered in another course on project management fundamentals. It is, however, designed for people from all functional areas and may benefit current individual contributors who are taking on more responsibilities as well as new or aspiring project managers or leaders.

The objective of such a course is for participants to learn to do the following:

- Identify key issues new managers face when making the transition from individual contributor to project manager.
- Identify and discuss new personal perspectives and realizations about project management.
- Refer to a participant guide to identify available on-site management workshops, courses, and consulting that can strengthen management skills and project team functioning.

Course delivery is classroom based and features guest project manager presentations and stories, facilitated interaction, case studies, questions and answers, and discussion. Announcements of course dates are sent out periodically by internal e-mail.

The comments of course participants are generally positive (for another experience, see Box 7.2):

> "This course has caused me to think about which career path I really want to pursue: project management or technical contributor."
>
> "I highly value the opportunity we have in the course to hear from successful project managers."
>
> "I never really appreciated the scope of project leading and how difficult it can be."
>
> "I really resonate with the job of the project manager. It's definitely what I want to do."

After taking the course, some people decide they do not want to be project managers. This is a positive response; the alternative may be promotion to project manager, a year or two of hell for everyone involved, and an eventual return to the role of individual contributor. Much more productive is preventing that scenario. This also indicates again the importance of the dual career path; the technical career path offers an alternative to the management path, which is preferable for those who do not want to be project managers. It also helps organizations not lose the technical contributions these people make. If a dual path is unavailable, these people may elect to leave the organization or to stay and become ineffective project managers.

BOX 7.2. A Trip to St. Louis.

I (Robert Graham) remember well my own version of the HP transition course. I had received my degree in systems analysis and was running a small computer center at the time. The next step would have been to run larger computer centers in larger and larger organizations. To check out the possibilities, I went to a conference of computer center directors in St. Louis. There I learned just how much management was involved, how extensive were the politics involved, and how much emphasis was put on installing and maintaining ever-larger computer systems. The knowledge made me physically ill, which I interpreted as a sure sign that I did not want such a job. It gave me the impetus to complete my doctorate, go to the University of Pennsylvania, and get a job that I absolutely wanted. My "transitions course" saved me and many others a lot of grief.

Another testimonial came from one site where interviews were conducted for a project manager position. Interviewers commented that the quality of persons applying for the position and the interview discussions were much more impressive because the interviewees had attended the transitions course.

During occasional presentations at the course, I (Randall Englund) shared my belief that project managers should have an aptitude for managing projects. My career included doing service calls as a field service engineer on medical equipment. Later, as a sales development engineer, I responded to calls from the field about sales opportunities for computer systems. Each day brought new problems to solve, but I was in a reactive mode. My performance was adequate but not outstanding; I needed something different. As far back as I can remember, I am most alive when doing projects.

I try to explain aptitude by describing what I am doing when I feel I am making a significant contribution. Although I was trained as an engineer, I am not happy digging deep into technical complexities or doing maintenance tasks. People make things happen. To me, a good day at work includes helping a team of experts solve organizational problems. Behavioral issues affect organizational effectiveness far more than technical problems. My contribution may be to refocus efforts on the real problem, remove obstacles, or design a process. I need to identify important challenges, prepare a plan, adapt and execute that plan, and produce concrete results. Then I look around for a larger project to tackle.

Managers of project managers need to search for people with this aptitude wherever they exist in the organization, for these are the ones who should be in charge of projects. Availability alone is not a skill set.

The Project Manager Development Process

Project manager development follows the basic model outlined in Figure 7.1. At stage 1, a person is unconsciously unskilled, not even knowing there is such a thing as project management. One day, however, this individual is appointed (perhaps accidentally) as a project manager and is abruptly at stage 2: the person now knows that project management exists but does not have the ability to do the job and knows that too. This consciously unskilled person, with any luck, is able to begin a development plan by taking some courses and applying the lessons learned to the job. Now the individual is at stage 3, consciously skilled, applying the learning but with deliberate effort.

Developing truly seasoned project managers takes more development effort, but unfortunately, many development efforts stop at this point. People at stage 3 need to move beyond deliberate effort into habit, perhaps by taking on larger projects and talking over problems and experiences with a mentor. They work at becoming stage 4 project managers, who are unconsciously skilled and carry out

FIGURE 7.1. THE PROGRESSION PATH OF DEVELOPMENT AS A PROJECT MANAGER.

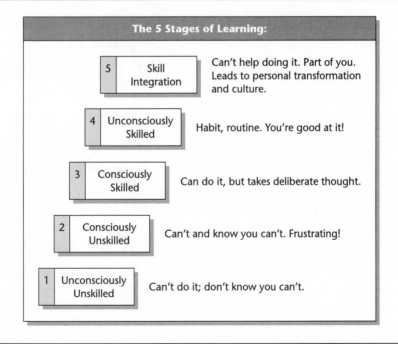

best practices through habit. The final step is skill integration, where best practices are integrated into their complete work life. Stage 5 is best reached by discussing experiences with peers and by teaching others, becoming part of a network of project managers; attending and giving papers at company and external conferences; attending best practice forums; seeking outside certification; and becoming a project mentor.

All of the following may be components of a good development plan for project managers:

- Taking courses for skill development
- Entering a mentor program
- Becoming part of a network through e-mail connections, company conferences, outside conferences, and the Web
- Attending forums on specific practices and gaining the ability to share best practices
- Obtaining certification from the Project Management Institute, which helps the individual and is becoming a standard for experienced project managers

Courses for Skill Development

Most project management development curricula cover the following five topics for skill development:

- *Project techniques.* Normally a project management fundamentals course teaches basic project planning, estimating, and risk analysis techniques. When participants finish this course, they know how to put together a project plan.
- *Behavioral aspects of project management.* This course covers such areas as team building, motivating team members, developing effective project teams, and dealing with upper managers, contributing department managers, and other stakeholders.
- *Organizational issues.* This course covers techniques for managing across organizations when the project manager has all the responsibility and little of the authority. It teaches participants how to get projects done in spite of the rest of the organization.
- *Business fundamentals.* Many project managers have a technical background but lack basic business knowledge. This course teaches the business of the organization, how decisions affect the bottom line, and how to run a project as if it were a business. David Packard (1995, p. 44) says he learned much about running a business from courses outside his engineering major: "I gained a lot from two classes I took at Stanford: business law and management accounting. I had

signed up because I thought they might be of some use in our new business. Looking back, they were among the most important courses I ever took." To have project managers think about projects as a business, business fundamentals courses are important.

- *Marketing and customer issues.* In the end, there must be a market and a set of customers for the final product of the project. This is true even of internal projects. This course focuses on the techniques of defining and developing a market, as well as understanding the needs and desires of the project's customers and end users.

The Project Manager Mentor Program

When Odysseus, king of Ithaca, went off to fight the Trojan Wars, he left behind his trusted friend Mentor to look after his son, Telemachus. The word *mentor*—meaning a wise and trusted friend—has been part of the vocabulary of relationships ever since. A mentoring relationship involves seeking or giving advice to help the "mentee"—the person being mentored—grow, develop specific competences, and tap the experiences of others. New project managers often find themselves in highly stressful situations as they try to make the transition from technical contributor to team leader. Many successful project managers say that this was the most difficult time in their careers. A newly appointed project manager may encounter informal mentoring spontaneously or through luck; historically, this was a primary means for learning from those who had gone before. A more formal program strengthens the mentoring process by guiding and supporting volunteers who want to improve their mentoring relationships and increase the benefits they give and receive.

Facilitated mentoring can be defined as a structure and series of processes designed to create effective mentoring relationships, guide the desired behavior change of those involved, and evaluate results for the mentees, the mentors, and the organization. The reason to begin a mentoring program for project managers is to reap the advantages of a sustained one-on-one support activity. A mentoring program improves the performance of persons responsible for managing projects and increases the opportunities for cross-organizational networking.

A mentor's role is to provide guidance or advice, or both, but does not substitute for or replace the management role. There is a distinct difference between mentoring and managing: a mentor does not sit in judgment on a mentee and is not involved in performance appraisals of the mentee. Ideally, the mentor is in another organization and has no direct impact on the mentee's job position. Mentors can give advice from their perspective, but the mentees must ultimately judge the value of this counsel for their particular environment and have the option to take or leave it. A good mentoring program has advantages for both parties:

Benefits for the Mentor

- The chance to help someone acquire skills
- An opportunity to help someone achieve results
- Self-esteem enhancement
- Job enrichment

Benefits for the Mentee

- Higher performance and productivity ratings
- More pleasure in work and greater career satisfaction
- More knowledge of the technical and organizational aspects of the business
- Unbiased advice to solve specific problems
- Access to impartial perspective on issues

A successful mentoring program has these ingredients:

- People who volunteer to be mentors and to describe their areas of expertise
- Potential mentees who ask to be mentored and are willing to identify their coaching requirements
- Mentees calling mentors to establish a relationship
- Conversations that are positive experiences for both parties
- A central organization that facilitates connections and monitors results
- Complete confidentiality between both parties

Not all mentor programs need be as formal as described here. Upper managers can encourage informal contact and exchange between new and veteran project managers, and individual project managers should seek out mentors.

Elements of a Project Manager Network

In addition to learning basic skills in class and from a mentor, project managers continue to develop by networking with each other. This network can take on several forms:

E-mail connections, where every project manager is connected to every other project manager through an e-mail folder. A project manager who has a question or wants to know if others have experienced a similar problem can ask others in the network.

Company conferences, where all project managers in the organization can get together in person to discuss mutual problems of project management. (See Chapter Nine for a full discussion of how this was done at HP.)

Outside conferences, such as those of the Project Management Institute (PMI) and the Product Development and Management Association, give project managers a chance to meet and listen to others in the same profession. Society membership is also an important source of information.

The Internet and the Web, which provide additional opportunities for interaction.

Project Management Forums

These companywide forums for practicing project managers are normally half-day sessions devoted to a specific project management topic. Specific issue forums allow for more advanced discussion of topics and the opportunity to share experiences among practicing project managers. Virtual seminars may also be conducted over the Web and telephone lines so people conveniently get exposure to more good ideas.

PMP Al Gardiner participated in a Creating an Environment workshop and shared efforts he was part of at his company to help PMs develop each other: "As you know, [my company] is in the middle of a major cultural shift. We have not been able to hold the Friday Learning and Sharing (L&S) sessions for the past eight months or more. However, I can elaborate on the benefits we gained when we were doing them."

Here are his responses to our questions:

• *Can you describe a specific benefit they have brought, either to individuals or the organization?* "The L&S sessions were specifically designed to gain knowledge of industry practice in various areas of Project Management. The benefits were many including understanding new methodologies and tools, enhancing soft skills, and gaining a deeper understanding of our own capabilities. The L&S session also included a period of PMP prep study. The attendees would step through a learning tool (in this case, PMIQ's CD) and do practice questions. Wrong answers were researched and an explanation of the correct answer was distributed to the team."

• *Who organizes them?* "My group [IT Service Delivery] was responsible for the logistics. This is essentially having a conference room and teleconferencing capability, preparing material, researching answers, and distributing communications."

• *How do you communicate about them across the organization?* "Via e-mail. First, my team was required to attend (and present articles) as part of their performance measurement. Through our contacts with other PM organizations in [our company], we invited others to attend. . . . While I am no longer in a position to arrange these sessions, the Director of the IT Project Management organization may be interested in doing something. Our CIO's [chief information officer's] strategy seems to be geared towards a projectized organization so he may be interested in your work."

Project Management Certification

Some organizations now use the project manager certification process of PMI as a way to ensure that their project managers have exposure to a broad array of topics and subject areas. In the process of obtaining this certification, the candidate encounters a wide variety of project managers from a spectrum of organizations. Obtaining certification does not guarantee that people can manage projects, but it does mean that they have studied and passed a test on fundamental and advanced project management practices. Although it is rarely required by organizations in order to become a project manager, it is often recommended for those who wish to pursue a career in the field and usually required to manage projects for clients.

The Upper Management Role

The project manager selection and development process described in this chapter probably cannot happen without direction and support from upper managers. A project management council could run it, but with little chance of success. A group similar to the HP Project Management Initiative (Chapter Nine) could be formed to develop and oversee the process. Perhaps it could be assigned to an existing department such as human resources, but this is not recommended unless someone very knowledgeable about project management is in that department. The recommended approach is for a project management initiative or project office to see that the program is properly developed, implemented, and staffed to develop a cadre of trained project managers.

The Compleat Upper Manager

The successful complete upper manager:

- Stops the appointment of accidental project managers.
- Develops a dual career ladder to allow people to stay in technical positions.
- Determines proper project management selection criteria for the organization.
- Develops and installs a project manager selection process.
- Supports the creation of a course on transition to project management.
- Supports and oversees a project manager development process.

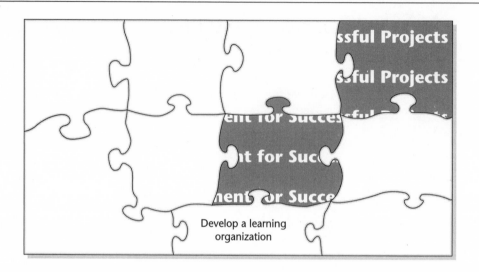

Develop a learning
organization

This chapter begins by describing examples of learning experiences. It explains the principles of adaptive and generative learning in organizations and discusses the role of leadership in learning organizations, along with the new leadership skills required. Project audits and project reviews are techniques for retrospective analysis, so the chapter includes both the rationale and a process for project reviews. The chapter concludes with a questionnaire that serves as a project review form.

CHAPTER EIGHT

DEVELOPING A PROJECT MANAGEMENT LEARNING ORGANIZATION

To know that you do not know is the best.
To pretend to know when you do not know is a disease.

THE WAY OF LAO TZU, SIXTH CENTURY B.C.

Managers can view the project team process as a learning opportunity. A part of the environment for successful projects is developing a practice of learning the best project management practices. Upper managers need to initiate and guide this practice, or it will not happen.

The first level of learning is adaptive learning: helping project teams adapt to new environments and learn how to do project management better. Most adaptive learning comes from examining successful and unsuccessful practices on projects within the organization. The second level is generative learning, which results in developing new practices that had not previously been considered. Upper managers can look on project teams as a front guard with information about how the "battle" is going. The project team is "out there" doing the project and is close to information about latent customer desires. Team members often do not see the situation this way, so they may experience latent customer desires as wishful thinking. Organizations that support the process of transformative learning can mine this experience and use it to transform their thinking about customers. This may lead to new practices that had not previously been considered. Upper management needs to take the lead here to develop the learning organization. Projects are a natural place to start, and project audits and reviews are a good first step. Upper managers are advised to design a process of reviews and help present and future project managers learn from past experiences.

Examples of Learning Experiences

A Hewlett-Packard (HP) division hired a productivity manager to help improve the product development process. He identified a model that describes a progression of skills and competences to achieve significant improvement in project planning. The model was implemented in an evolutionary fashion on pilot projects. By measuring the amount of variation in project completion predictions over the life of the product development effort, he learned how the predicted completion time differed from the actual completion time. With this information, he could adjust predictions to match reality better, and planning on subsequent project phases improved by more than three times. Improvements greater than four times were noted when compared to projects not using the model.

In another example, complexities of the computer operating systems business led upper management at an HP lab to realize that they could not succeed by doing business the old way. With the help of an internal project management consultant, they decided to implement consistent planning processes throughout the lab and set clear expectations:

- Use of a common life cycle and training on project management practices
- Centralized schedule management and integration
- Rigorous schedule tracking, updating, and issue management
- Rigorous dependency identification

They surveyed the results and learned that significant changes in organizational and individual behaviors on the job led to more reliable schedules, less stress, better communications, and an estimated time savings of four weeks on a project expected to take six months.

Many organizations have a regular process of conducting employee surveys. Entities often use consulting assistance to respond to specific issues identified by low scores on surveys, such as project management for executives, operating across organizations, and empowerment. Surveys are an important learning device to understand current reality in an organization, but employee surveys are effective only if upper management responds to them. Therefore, it becomes imperative to take action to schedule training or focus efforts on how to create a different future. Offsite meetings provide the opportunity for managers and employees alike to "discover" the issues themselves and to propose action in areas such as getting to know the customers better and developing a shared vision (Graham and Englund, 1996).

The project management conferences that HP ran internally (described in Chapter Nine) used a minimal staff because they leveraged from the work breakdown structure, experiences and data that they had documented, and continuity from previous conferences. The process became streamlined, and the quality continuously improved.

Another example of a learning process is the case of a field installation solution at General Electric. The district office scored low on efficiency metrics and had a poor process for installing rooms of complex equipment. The supervisor began tracking data on how long it took to do the work, analyzing where problems were often encountered, reviewing sales proposals in advance, taking the time for planning, and putting a complete schedule together. The results allowed the district to rise to the top in statistical standing. Site preparation problems were avoided, and customers were delighted to get their equipment installed faster and with fewer frustrations. At first, sales representatives resisted the new process because it introduced another step before getting their proposals typed. But they came to appreciate the value created through shorter installation times and a service department committed up front to the customer project. These results were achieved by having a district service manager who was extremely supportive and empowered a dedicated project manager to try new approaches. He also kept the district sales manager at bay, unable to muck up the new process.

Then again, anyone could have the kind of manager often depicted by that eminent "professor of project management" Scott Adams, creator of the Dilbert cartoon strip, which chronicles the organizational perversities of life in high-technology companies. In one episode, the boss offers two hideous fates to Dilbert the engineer: he could receive high pay forever but all his work would be burned in front of him each day, or he could be in eternal poverty but all his work would be useful and appreciated. Dilbert responds that either option is better than his current job. In this case, the manager learns that all perceptions are relative and that the current situation may be even worse than imagined.

Lessons such as those in the preceding examples start to permeate an organization and positively affect its ability to produce successful projects when there is a focus on learning and people are empowered to operate in an organic organization. "We have no metrics" or "We don't know how long things take" are telltale signs that an effective process for creating a learning organization is not present. It also means the organization is not tapping the wellsprings of knowledge available from an effective project management information system. It is important to collect reliable data (see Box 8.1), but be wary of becoming too analytical or reliant on the power of the computer printout or too dependent on data collected from people whose attitude is "give the kid a number"—providing bogus or questionable data to make the data collector go away. Much priceless information can be learned from projects, and most of it is free. Upper

---

BOX 8.1. Getting Reliable Data.

Managers depend on data to help them make decisions, and they seem to assume that the data provided to them are somehow real—that they represent reality. However, I (Robert Graham) have long argued that data represent what most people wish was reality or want you to believe is reality (Graham, 1982). Then again, the data may represent nothing at all; they may be manufactured to satisfy someone's demand for information.

When I was director of a data center, people asked me for all sorts of statistics, many of which I had no way of providing. Once I was asked how many of a particular type of student were enrolled at the university. I told the person asking that it was illegal for me to collect that number, but he persisted. I explained that because no one classified students that way, the computer could not report what he desired. Still he persisted, sure that I had the number somewhere. Finally I asked what *he* thought the number was. He made a reply, I agreed with it, and he went away.

I had discovered a useful tool I called "giving the kid a number." Whenever people asked for the impossible, I gave them something, and they would go away. Usually I had no idea what the "information" would be used for or what the consequences of the fabrication might be; I just knew that when I gave the kids their numbers, they went away. This reminds me of a story attributed to Sir Josiah Stamp, Her Majesty's Collector of Inland Revenue in 1929:

> The Government are extremely fond of amassing great quantities of statistics. These are raised to the nth degree, the cube roots are extracted, and the results are arranged into elaborate and impressive displays. What must be kept in mind, however, is that in every case, the figures are first put down by a village watchman, and he puts down anything he damn well pleases!

---

management action is essential to develop a learning organization that can collect this information and use it to improve project management practices.

Principles of Learning in Organizations

People are learning organisms, and experience is a primary teacher. The innate desire to learn is a powerful force that is highly visible in each of us as children. People use their experience to learn basic rules for themselves, on the order of "if this happens, do that." In cultural groups, the rules are formulated into procedures, often called recipes. The recipes are handed down through the generations, and they become "the way things are done" in that cultural group. Recipes are based on the experience of a particular cultural group, so they are different for different cultures. For example, some cultural groups deal with snow, while others deal with sand. In their native situations, the recipes are valuable guides to behavior. However, when the climate changes and the sand culture has to deal with snow, its recipes become more of a hindrance than a help. To survive, the members of the sand culture must first learn about snow, then adapt their recipes to help them deal with the new set of problems. In organizations, managers first dealt with departments. Now they must deal with projects. Changing a group's long-held practices is the process of cultural transformation.

Adaptive Learning

Organizations are cultural units, so they face the same processes. People in organizations have always learned from their mistakes and have adopted basic rules that help them survive. If the rules seem to work well over time, they are usually codified into company procedures. In the past, employees attempted to "learn the rules" in order to be successful. Those who followed the rules were often the most successful in the organization. Those who questioned the rules or suggested changes were often forced to leave the organization. As long as the rules correctly matched the environment of the organization, the organization was successful. When the environment changed, the organization was forced to learn new rules and adapt, or it perished.

There are many examples of both succeeding and failing to adapt. British Airways was able to completely change many company procedures when it changed in 1984 from a government service with no responsibility for profit and loss to a freestanding, competitive organization. It dramatically changed its procedures to match the new environment (Desatnick, 1993). PanAm, in contrast, was not able to adapt to new competition and perished.

The major difference between those who survive and those who do not is the organizational ability to learn, a desire to survive, and the ability to adapt. Arie de Geus (1988) of Royal Dutch Shell says, "In the long run, the only sustainable competitive advantage is your organization's ability to learn faster than its competition" (p. 70). Most people have the ability and desire to learn, and all organizations are composed of people. Therefore, most organizations have the raw material it takes to learn and to adapt. The difference is in leadership, which must set up systems that encourage people to learn and adapt.

Learning organizations foster a spirit of learning from failure, questioning practices to see if they are still valid, and valuing experiential learning. This means that practices such as shooting the messenger who brings bad news, punishing those who question traditional methods, and fostering a spirit of fear must be discarded. Upper managers intent on developing a learning organization can begin by welcoming those who bring bad news to their attention, encouraging those who question traditional methods and assumptions, and demonstrating that learning from experience is an important part of personal success. It is difficult to learn in a culture of fear. An enlightened person views every occasion to answer "I don't know" as an opportunity to begin a learning process.

Learning organizations also provide ample feedback to people, similar to the thousands of feedback units per hour kids receive playing video games. Compare that to a typical rate of one feedback unit per hour they are lucky to receive in traditional classrooms or in organizations, and you get a picture of how far we need to go to improve those learning environments. Upper managers can lead the way by structuring procedures and situations that give project team members sufficient feedback on how they are doing. Feedback is an essential part of the learning process. One trait practiced by influential people, including those who influence without authority when operating across organizations, is that they provide more feedback to people whose cooperation they seek than those people get elsewhere. Everybody has multiple activities competing for their attention, and they are more likely to direct that attention to people who help them learn through constructive feedback.

Learning organizations are built on the assumption that people are designed to learn. Not only can they learn, but productive behavior depends on it: people do not follow orders well unless they see a reason for it. For example, people tend to follow medicine dosage advice more closely when they understand that minor deviations from the plan may cause major illness or death. Upper managers need to ensure that team members know why they are asked to follow procedures for organizational learning.

In school, the game is to get the answer right and avoid making mistakes. This is also true in business organizations. "Getting it right" often means behaving according to the norm or the accepted organizational myth. For example, many automakers used to believe that safety would not help to sell cars and that people would not pay extra for seat belts and other safety features. This has now been shown to be a myth, but those who initially acted outside it were scorned or even fired. Behaving within the myth draws kudos but results in no learning; behaving outside the myth develops learning opportunities but normally draws no kudos and may eventually result in exiting the organization. Upper managers foster a learning organization when they allow questioning of assumed organizational myths. Otherwise, the behavior of people will be forever directed by old assumptions.

Generative Learning

Adaptive learning is about coping—learning from changes in the environment. Generative learning is about expanding one's capabilities. This level shift represents the impulse to learn. Peter Senge (1990) points out that adaptive learning is important for the short run, but generative learning leads to long-term survival. Generative learning, unlike adaptive learning, requires new ways of looking at the world, but this could be hazardous to one's career in many business organizations. It also requires seeing the production process as an integrated system. For example, while the United States concentrated on inventory and production forecasting, Japan built up networks of relationships with trusted suppliers and became able to make changes quickly. Generative learning requires seeing the systems that control events, not just the events themselves. When people fail to grasp the systemic cause of problems, they are left to work on symptoms rather than eliminating underlying causes, and the best that can be hoped for is adaptive learning.

The evolution of project management is like the evolution of the quality movement in Japan. First there was fitness to standard, when project managers built to the specification of architectural drawings to ensure success. Then came fitness to need: understanding what the customer wanted and providing products that reliably met those needs. Now project managers need to understand latent need: what the customer might truly value but has never experienced or would never think to ask for. HP refers to this process as probing for the imaginative understanding of user needs. The development of "The Complete Project Manager" (Box 8.2) is a good example of discovering this latent need and meeting it with a product. Generative learning expands capabilities beyond what is currently known or assumed.

BOX 8.2. Leading the Way.

The creation of "The Complete Project Manager," a project management training simulation, is an example of generative learning. Customers used to lament that training fades fast and that people do not implement what they learn in project management classes. There are several reasons; this book is an attempt to remedy one of the problems, but there are others. For example, if people do not experience problems in the classroom, they do not relate the suggestions given there to problems on the job. What was needed was a way to experience the problems in the class. The solution was a simulation. However, at the time, few thought to ask for a simulation because they had not yet experienced one and thus did not realize its potential. In fact, when asked if they wanted a project management simulation, customers said no, as they had not experienced learning in a simulated environment. However, I (Robert Graham) saw the problem as one of latent need and imagined and then developed a product that had not previously existed. That product is now successful in helping to meet the training needs of project managers.

The upper manager's new work is to change the hero story prevalent in many organizations in order to reward leaders who demonstrate a commitment to learning and generating new knowledge. Our traditional view of leaders is deeply rooted in an individualistic and nonsystemic worldview. Leaders are heroes—great men and women who rise to the fore in times of crisis. This is why we need crises: to create heroes. This myth focuses on short-term events and keeps the crises coming. Software development often rewards the heroes who can fix software defects and neglects the people who prevent them. Generative learning means an all-out attack on such organizational perversities that keep people behaving in ways that are not effective, are not in line with organizational goals, and ultimately are self-destructive.

Peter Senge (2003) says the way to get a critical mass of people doing things differently is "through the sharing of generative ideas, ideas that can change how people think and act." He adds, "One of the most effective means of spreading such ideas, is through stories. . . . Even more powerful is a reinforcing pattern of stories that gradually starts to build an idea in people's heads." The more opportunity that project people have to get together, whether formally or informally, the more stories are shared. Take the lead through "management by storying around." Look for, tell, and constantly repeat stories about how project managers and teams effectively and efficiently practice their profession. We can listen to these stories all day long and not be bored.

See project teams as possessing a wealth of information about changes in the environment. They are "out there" when they are doing projects. They are the ones in the organization who are experiencing something new as they proceed through the project. They are in contact with the customer, so they are in a great position to pick up trends in customer needs. The problems that happen to them are the ones that signal things to come. They are the ones who can discover not only the stated needs of the customer but also the latent needs—what the customer might truly value but has never experienced or has never thought to ask for. Discovering latent need is one of the true values of generative learning.

How might this happen? Many times the team reports to management that the customer "wants everything but doesn't want to pay for it." This is a standard lament and usually causes smiles all around. But to learn from it, managers should ask what customers are asking for. What is this "everything" that they want? This represents an attempt to think like the customer. Perhaps what is being asked for is not available now but represents a trend in customers' perceptions of their requirements. Because the core team is "out there," they can pick up these bits of information if upper management encourages them to.

Understanding what lead users are doing is an excellent source for innovation and generative learning. 3M shows that products following this process have much higher success rates than others. Familiarity with existing product attributes and uses interferes with an individual's ability to conceive of novel attributes or new uses or markets. Upper managers striving to create an innovative learning organization can get away from "business as usual" by tapping von Hippel's description (1988, p. 107) of lead users: people who "face needs that will be general in a marketplace, but they face them months or years before the bulk of that marketplace encounters them" and who "are positioned to benefit significantly by obtaining a solution to those needs." They serve as a need-forecasting laboratory for marketing research. Also, because they often attempt to fill the need they experience, they can provide new product concepts and design data. Market experience with diffusion of innovations, however, shows that the early adopters of a novel product or practice often differ significantly from the bulk of users who follow them in their needs and in solutions that appeal to them. Thus, the lead users are a valuable source of trends in knowledge and markets but may not be the arbiters of what will appeal to the whole market.

The lead user approach was used within HP as a way to decide on and disseminate knowledge about best practices for project management. A process was documented based on literature research by members of the corporate Project Management Initiative. Surveys and interviews were conducted with early adopters—people struggling to meet the needs of fast-moving entities within HP. Their practices were captured and used as a basis for learning by others in the company just coming upon the need to manage their projects. The design for each step in the process involved finding users doing that step and then gathering examples of their deliverables. These structured examples become powerful motivators for others to understand and immediately apply the process. Questions continue to come up about how to optimize the practices; these questions become the basis for new research or models that can create new learning. A learning organization has been created, reflecting steps in a maturity model for processes: document a process, share the knowledge with others, apply the process as a way of repeating success, improve the process, and identify opportunities or gaps where new knowledge can be generated.

Geoffrey Moore (1991), a master at creating analogies to explain high-technology market trends, talks about management's responsibility when "crossing the chasm." The traditional Technology Adoption Life Cycle, to use his formal term, portrays the purchases of a new product by visionaries and then by pragmatists as a smooth transition, following the gentle uprising slope of a bell curve. In fact, it is a dramatically discontinuous development. Between the time that visionaries finish making their early buying commitments and the time that the wait-and-see pragmatists are ready to buy typically extends several years or more. During this period of transition, the new product has no market. This period is the chasm.

Many projects get canceled during this period because management is disappointed that sales of the product do not follow the upward bell curve slope. They fail to recognize the existence of the chasm state. Upper managers who have patience and follow certain steps that Moore prescribes can achieve a sustainable leadership position in an expanding mainstream market.

Moore (1995) describes another kind of problem as being "inside the tornado." It might take a "bowling alley" strategy to pick niche markets that get products across the chasm. If the product gets chosen by the market as the leader, or "gorilla," it hits a furious acceleration period that feels like being in a tornado. The problem becomes how to ship products fast enough. Later in the life cycle, the product hits its stride in a mature market that feels more like being on "Main Street." This is the time to enhance the product and enjoy the fruits of your labor.

The message for all managers is to recognize the market forces at work in the different stages of the life cycle and adopt leadership styles consonant with success in the market. For example, to get market acceptance and cross the chasm, build the infrastructure that supports a "whole product." When product sales exhibit tornado-like characteristics, it is not the time to introduce new technology or pay attention to specific customer requests. Just ship the product. It is not common for a gorilla company to commit suicide during the tornado, but it has been known to happen when upper managers force their organizations to focus on projects that do not support the market needs. These learned strategies help organizations avoid problems of the past and generate new approaches to competition.

Leadership in Learning Organizations

In learning organizations, leaders are not heroes but rather designers, teachers, and stewards. These roles require the skills of building shared vision, bringing out and challenging prevailing mental models, and fostering more systemic patterns of thinking. That is, leaders are responsible for learning. Project leaders do this when they work cooperatively on a goal statement, foster thinking about what is best for the project rather than what is best for the department, and focus on the entire project process from concept to customer.

Creative Tension

An integrating principle is creative tension, a way of viewing the gap between the vision and the current reality. It occurs in every project. The goal is the vision, the plan is the path, and the start of the project is the current reality. The principle of creative tension holds that "an accurate picture of current reality is just as important as a compelling picture of a desired future" (Senge, 1990, p. 9). Use the energy that comes from that tension and the conflict it generates to propel the project toward the vision; tap the diversity of project team members as an asset to make this happen.

Many people in organizations are motivated to change only when problems are bad enough (see the revitalization model in Chapter One). With this approach, the change process often runs out of steam as soon as the problems driving the change become less pressing. In this case, the motivators for change are extrinsic. With creative tension, the motivators are intrinsic. This mirrors the difference between adaptive and generative learning: adaptive is extrinsic, and generative is intrinsic. The more powerful motivators to perform are the intrinsic factors.

Leader as Designer

People who aspire to lead out of a desire to control, to gain fame, or simply to be the center of action will find little to attract them to the quiet design work of leadership. However, organizational design is much more than just moving boxes around on a piece of paper.

The first task of organization design is to design the governing ideas of purpose, vision, and core values by which people will live. This is like the goal statement of project management. It gives a clear sense of purpose and values that can affect key decisions. Consider the credo of Johnson & Johnson:

> Service to customers comes first;
> service to employees and management comes second;
> service to the community comes third; and
> service to stockholders, last.

If leaders state the vision and do not follow it, cynicism takes root in the organization. Thus, the second design task is to develop policies, strategies, and structures that translate guiding ideas into business decisions. Guiding ideas are visions of a future state consonant with the purpose and values of an organization, a description of the end in sight when success is achieved. The key is not getting the right strategy but fostering strategic thinking. Leonard-Barton (1995) espouses strategic improvisation, citing upper management in companies like HP as concentrating on strategic recognition rather than strategic foresight, that is, "on the ability to identify and support high-potential ideas rather than on the ability to plan out future moves in detail" (p. 116). Where this thinking prevails, there are stories of individual product development projects that altered the course of the corporation. It is the same in project management: the strategy and structure that translate guiding ideas into business decisions are the planning process and resulting network plan. We all know that things often do not go according to plan and that the value is in the planning rather than in the plan itself, so the key is fostering the thinking that goes into planning. This is strategic thinking about the project.

Upper managers encourage the leader as designer when they guide project managers to design the project infrastructure: the core team, meetings, decision making, change management, communication processes, and rewards that govern projects.

Leader as Teacher

Project leadership does not mean the leader is an authoritarian expert whose job is to teach people the "correct" view of reality. Instead, it is helping everyone in the organization to gain insightful views of current reality. The role begins by bringing to the surface people's mental models on important issues, that is, the assumptions underlying how they think. "Our mental models control our ability to generate possibilities and our ability to understand one another" (Marshall and Freedman, 1995, p. 17). These models must be brought forward and challenged. Then the leader helps people restructure their views of reality so that they can see beyond superficial conditions to the underlying causes of problems and to a different future. A director of corporate engineering described his mental model of the organization as an orchestra: each position needs a master musician, and all positions must play together on the same piece of music. This model conveyed his vision that each person needs to have a defined expertise that he or she brings to the organization, but it is not enough to apply that expertise solo; people need to work together across the organization synergistically. Working together is often a challenge when most projects are conceived and executed on a stand-alone basis.

To be a leader and teacher, the key question becomes, "Where do leaders predominantly focus their own and their organization's attention?" If upper management asks only about cost and budget, that will be the mental model that people have. Research (Baker, Murphy, and Fisher, 1983) shows that this model has a negative effect on project success. If time is the main focus, then time becomes the model and quality may suffer due to pressures to show progress. Team motivation has been shown to be the most important focus for projects, yet top management rarely asks about that. Upper managers can change the mental model to focus on the most important aspects by asking questions in the following order:

1. How well is the project team understanding and meeting customers' expectations, both stated and latent?
2. How motivated is the team?
3. How well served are the other stakeholders: top management, department directors, legal, marketing, and others?
4. How well are quality standards being met?
5. How is the project proceeding according to the schedule?
6. How are you doing according to the budget?

Leader as Steward and Motivator

Lawrence Miller (1984) wrote, "Achieving return on equity does not, as a goal, mobilize the most noble forces of our soul" (p. 15). The first part of stewardship arises from keen appreciation of the impact one's leadership can have on others. A manager can never fail to influence; even doing nothing places priority on the status quo. The other part arises from the leader's personal sense of commitment to the organization's larger mission. People's natural impulse to learn is unleashed when they are engaged in an endeavor they consider worthy of their fullest commitment. A leader's role is to take care of the people who follow or who place their stewardship in the leader's hand; the leader should not just use them to look good upward. The leader as steward helps others see the big picture and how they relate to it.

Many managers believe that their power and authority come from above. In today's and tomorrow's project-based organizations, however, more power will come from below or the sides—from the support of project team members. These are the people doing the work; their motivation to perform is tantamount to project success. As David Packard verbally responded to an employee's thanks for his leadership at HP, "No, it is you the people of this company who Bill Hewlett and I have to thank for making it great."

Leader as Maverick

Leaders of learning organizations often go against accepted customs, so they are often seen as mavericks. In addition, they often support other mavericks who may be able to teach the organization something. David Packard writes:

> Management's turndown of a new idea doesn't always effectively kill it. Some years ago, at an HP laboratory in Colorado Springs devoted to oscilloscope technology, one of our bright, energetic engineers, Chuck House, was advised to abandon a display monitor he was developing. Instead, he embarked on a vacation to California—stopping along the way to show potential customers

a prototype model of the monitor. He wanted to find out what they thought, specifically what they wanted the product to do and what its limitations were. Their positive reaction spurred him to continue with the project even though, on his return to Colorado, he found that I, among others, had requested it be discontinued. He persuaded his R&D manager to rush the monitor into production, and as it turned out, HP sold more than seventeen thousand display monitors representing sales revenue of $35 million for the company.

Several years later, at a gathering of HP engineers, I presented Chuck with a medal for "extraordinary contempt and defiance beyond the normal call of engineering duty."

So how does a company distinguish between insubordination and entrepreneurship? To this young engineer's mind the difference lay in the intent.

"I wasn't trying to be defiant or obstreperous. I really just wanted a success for HP," Chuck said. "It never occurred to me that it might cost me my job." As a postscript to the story, this same engineer later became director of a department . . . with his reputation as a maverick intact [1995, pp. 107–108].

New Skills for Project Leadership

Here is a summary of the new skills that are needed for project leadership:

- Building shared visions. This is working cooperatively on goal statements. Each person shares responsibility for the whole, not just a piece. Ask, "What is best for the project?"
- Encouraging personal visions and tapping each person's passion and enthusiasm. When people write a part of the shared vision, they get something personal—a personal values approach.
- Communicating and asking for support from other departments and divisions.
- Visioning as an ongoing process, refining project plans, and using the vision as a daily guide to actions.
- Building extrinsic and intrinsic value to achieve customer satisfaction.
- Stressing positive visions, not threats.
- Thinking systematically—by seeing the process from start to finish. Be cautious that today's solutions do not become tomorrow's problems.
- Developing a learning organization, performing project reviews, summarizing results.

Creating an open learning organization requires leaders who are skilled in reflective openness. This means a willingness for each manager to look inside and reflect on his or her own behavior. One sign of reflective openness is a match between actual and espoused actions and upper managers who act with integrity—walking the walk as well as talking the talk. Consider the true story of a general manager making a presentation where 60 percent of the words on his slides (we engineers are always counting!) refer to a strategy for the division to supply systems and customer solutions. But at that time, every project that attempted to address system problems or customer usability was canceled or failed to come into existence. The business was clearly focused on developing hardware boxes. That gives the upper manager low credibility and makes him a candidate for a fate similar to that of the man on the street in Figure 8.1.

Other managers who are effective leaders are able to avoid getting defensive. A manager who was faced with the frustration of departmental members at

FIGURE 8.1. THE IMPORTANCE OF WALKING THE WALK.

Source: Non Sequitur © 1995 Wiley Miller. Dist: By Universal Press Syndicate. Reprinted with permission. All rights reserved.

changes in the project status sat down with the team and listened to and empathized with their concerns. He also shared his own similar concerns and described his battle scars and his decision not to fight certain battles. He then described how the team could be successful and what other changes for the better could take place. He articulated a future that was not so threatening. His openness and lack of defensiveness turned around a potentially emotional encounter. Many upper managers are able to apply this concept in a truly gifted manner and be quite inspirational; many others seem totally unaware of its power.

The systems thinking loop in Figure 8.2 helps explain a process that leads to reflective openness. The model is an embellishment of the revitalization process described in Chapter One. The purpose of the model is to chart a path of actions and results reflecting both the current situation and changes that lead to a new steady state.

This double loop model starts in the center with recognizing a current reality: a need for people in the organization to be more open. For example, upper managers feel the impact of "high muckety-mucks mucking it up" because "senior managers don't tell us what's going on or where the organization is going." People feel left out of the communications loop; they suffer individual stress (moving up and to the right on the upper loop in the figure). "We don't manage projects well—they take too long and cost too much" is a battle cry that triggers an improvement effort.

The first step is often toward a new steady state when managers go through the motions to adopt a behavior of participative, or outward, openness. Meetings are scheduled to discuss the problems and get people involved. They give the impression of soliciting inputs from others but do not act on or respond to the thoughts that are shared. In the vernacular of Senge's systems thinking models, participative openness becomes a "symptomatic solution" that "shifts the burden" away from the "fundamental solution," which is developing the skills of inquiry, reflection, and dialogue (Senge, 1990, p. 278). Because this is often just an intellectual exercise and therefore lacks authenticity and integrity, people do not internalize or take action on the ideas. People in the organization then find themselves back around the loop to the same problem: "We need to be more open." Moving on to the lower loop in Figure 8.2, there is often a long delay before this behavior manifests itself in problems serious enough that actions become necessary, when people sense disaster lurking in the shadows. Discussion sessions now need to focus on looking at the mental models of how people perceive and sort things—laying all the dirty laundry out on the table. By acknowledging that "something is rotten in the state of Denmark" and making a commitment to create and act on new models, the organization begins to recreate itself. Team learning takes on new importance, and people gain the ability to generate new possibilities.

FIGURE 8.2. OPENNESS IN ORGANIZATIONS: AN EXAMPLE OF CLOSED LOOP ANALYSIS.

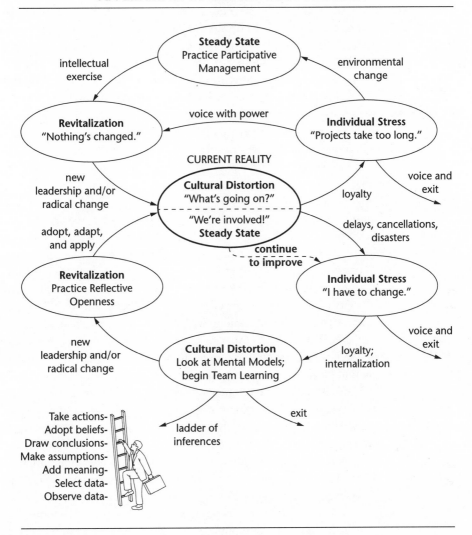

The skills of reflective openness, according to Senge, include modifying defensive behavior, walking the walk, and understanding when people are somewhere up the ladder of inferences—making assumptions and jumping to conclusions based on limited or filtered data. When any of these behaviors occurs, people need to reflect on their own thought processes, share those thought processes with others, and inquire of others what thought processes they are going through. Break the loop by stopping current behaviors and trying something different. Schedule training sessions or staff meetings to focus on behaviors that hinder or support teamwork. Draw loops that reflect current reality, and discuss alternative interventions. When all of these steps are working, the negative spiral effect in an organization turns positive, and the systemic process has a positive, reinforcing effect on the effectiveness and efficiency of an organization. Teams in a learning organization continue going around the lower loop, each time getting better and better.

Consider using discussion sessions based on each of Peter Senge's five disciplines for creating a learning organization: personal mastery, mental models, shared vision, team learning, and systems thinking. One group in the information systems community put together a series of creative sessions that included role playing and skits. Its training program used case studies to encourage team learning and the conscientious practice of basic project management skills by all members of a work group or department; its goal was to make project management a core competence of every member of the work group. The group learned that to manage the change to a new system in the service center, it had to facilitate the learning that takes place among project team members and work groups. It further learned that project management excellence comes only from the disciplined practice of good project management. The conscientious application of these two ideas enabled this group to raise the level of its project management expertise.

Daniel Goleman in *Primal Leadership* (2002) argues that the fundamental task of leaders "is to prime good feeling in those they lead. That occurs when a leader creates *resonance*—a reservoir of positivity that frees the best in people. At its root, then, the primal job of leadership is emotional." In contrast, "toxic leadership poisons the emotional climate of a workplace" (pp. ix-x). Goleman quotes results from a range of industries that link leadership to climate and to business performance. Results show that in 75 percent of companies studied, climate alone accurately sorted companies into high versus low profits and growth. "The climate—how people feel about working at a company—can account for 20 to 30 percent of business performance" and "50 to 70 percent of how employees perceive their organization's climate can be traced to the actions of one person: the leader. More than anyone else, the boss creates the conditions that directly determine people's ability to work well" (pp. 17–18). The recommendation: "Gifted leadership occurs where heart and head—feeling and thought—meet" (p. 26).

"Resonant leaders," writes Goleman (2002),

know when to be collaborative and when to be visionary, when to listen and when to command. Such leaders have a knack for attuning to their own sense of what matters and articulating a mission that resonates with the values of those they lead. These leaders naturally nurture relationships, surface simmering issues, and create the human synergies of a group in harmony. They build a fierce loyalty by caring about the careers of those who work for them, and inspire people to give their best for a mission that speaks to shared values [p. 248].

The emotional intelligence of a leader and of project teams can be improved through open and honest sharing during project reviews, systematically addressing issues that arise, and banishing previous "undiscussables" so that every topic is open to discussion.

Project Audits

Lucent Technologies found that one way to develop organizational learning is the use of a project audit. This audit is usually performed after the definition phase of the project, when the project team has developed a baseline business case, the project plan, the baseline architecture, and initial requirements. The idea is to have a team of experienced project managers from outside the project and the organization review the plans and proposals before the project team begins performing the project.

The audit is usually done at the location where the work is being performed, at the request of the project manager, and it provides feedback to management on the technical and managerial feasibility of the plans, including suggestions for change. Project management auditors are normally at or above the level of project manager, have technical and managerial experience associated with the project, and are not in a position to influence any team member's performance evaluation directly. In this way, the audit team is like a group of expert consultants, but with experience on projects in the Lucent organization.

The members of the team use their knowledge and experience to discern potential problems in the project plans that a less experienced project manager may overlook. In addition, the audit team members may be able to supplement the plan with ideas that the project manager had not thought of, perhaps in areas where the project manager lacks experience. Using this project audit device, Lucent Technologies is able to pass on learning from within the organization and foster both adaptive and generative learning.

Project Reviews: Retrospective Analysis

Project reviews are another important step in developing learning organizations. These take place at the end of the project and summarize important project learning. The reviews need to be summarized and put into a report or file that is available to new project leaders. A new project leader can read the reports before starting a new project and learn from previous projects.

A project review is an excellent vehicle for promoting adaptive learning in an organization. It allows project participants to learn from their mistakes and to suggest procedures (recipes) so that others who follow do not have to repeat the old mistakes. (They can then focus on making new mistakes!) Unless a project review process is in place, those who follow never get that advice. It is upper management's responsibility to develop such a process and to make sure it is followed. Upper managers need to require that reviews be done at the end of every project, they need to look at the reviews for lessons learned, they need to take action on findings, and they need to have these lessons made available to future project participants. They should also require that each project team consider the lessons of previous teams when they do their project planning. (A recommended format for project reviews is given later in this chapter in Exhibit 8.1.) But be aware that memos about who did what to whom are counterproductive; rather, encourage and participate only in processes that attempt to learn from the experiences and seek corrective actions leading to improved processes.

In addition to assessing what went well and what did not, reviews allow team members a cathartic experience to reflect on and vent their feelings. This is a healthy practice that supports an open, trusting organization. People feel better for the experience—they may find out they are not alone in their reactions or thinking, and serendipity may happen in a precious (unplanned) moment. Encourage these opportunities for reflection, because all real learning involves movement between reflection and action.

Workshop surveys reveal that project reviews happen more often than they used to. This is a good thing. Issues that come up become part of the planning process to improve predictability on future projects. Workshop discussions also surface recurring problems such as system crashes and interfering behavior from upper managers. We urge people to take what they know about past behaviors and plan for them to occur again. It may be difficult to know exactly what and when, but probability is high that they will happen again. Wise project managers find ways to include these soft "tasks" (that is, tasks that are not planned but are treated as though they are because they consume resources and time) in the work breakdown structure and schedule.

The big challenge from project reviews remains about how to get the learnings into a knowledge management system and disseminated across the organization.

A Project Review That Saved the Day

One experience that demonstrates the learning organization process in action is that of a retrospective analysis completed at the end of the first phase of a massive project at HP. The project involved hundreds of key engineers to resolve a large number of computer architectural issues, an effort where the first phase went seven weeks beyond a nine-week schedule. Members of the program team responsible for coordinating the efforts did a detailed analysis of the process. They looked at the growth in work scope during the period, the complexity of issues being resolved and corresponding time durations, the reporting and communication processes used, and management anxiety.

The engineering teams had focused on resolving the first tier of 150 issues. However, during the course of investigating, proposing, and assessing the impact of some issues, engineers uncovered related issues. The nature of these "new" issues required that they be solved at the same time instead of being deferred. In other projects, this phenomenon is known as "scope creep" or "creeping elegance." The retrospective analysis showed approximately 20 percent growth in work undertaken during that phase.

The reviewers also analyzed the complexity of each issue as high, medium, or low and determined on the average how long it took to resolve issues at each level of complexity.

Looking ahead to the next phase, the program team now had a statistical basis to improve its estimating process. Planners analyzed the new set of issues by estimating the complexity level, applied the formula for the time it took to resolve each type of issue, and increased the projected work load by 20 percent. The next phase targeted fifty issues for study and resolution, but the team scheduled for sixty; no one knew in advance what the extra ten would be, but the extras showed up as anticipated. As the engineering teams began work, they prepared bottom-up schedules that were compared with the statistical schedule. The program team reconciled these two to come up with a realistic schedule. This was the schedule used to manage the project.

The retrospective analysis uncovered a problem with e-mail: the sheer volume of proposals and replies sent bogged down the network. Reviewers did not have access to responses from other reviewers. For the next phase, the program team set up an electronic bulletin board where basenote proposals were posted. Engineers posted their comments or impact assessments as replies to the basenote; they were required to read the bulletin board every day, and every engineer could view the comments of every other engineer. This process led to dramatic improvements in dialogue flow, timeliness, and quality of the effort.

The program team also discovered that engineering team leaders were not separating technical issues from organizational ones. The leaders reported week after week that the engineers needed to keep working on the issues, but a review found not the lack of a technical solution but multiple solutions available. No clear process existed for making a decision on trade-offs, nor did the engineers always have the perspective or skills to solve these organizational issues. The program team thus trained the engineering team leaders on project management and set up a process to send organizational issues promptly up to the management team or to upper management if necessary.

By applying these lessons to the next and subsequent phases, each phase was completed exactly on schedule, used fewer resources, and calmed much management anxiety. Upper managers became supportive and were impressed with the use of a repeatable process. Having a documented process also meant all the teams could continuously improve the process, and they did.

Another important point is that the same team that did the retrospective analysis carried the findings into planning and implementing the next phase. To maximize the application of the learning process, upper managers need as much as possible to keep teams intact or at a critical mass for subsequent projects and also to get as many people as possible trained simultaneously on a new process. Otherwise, it is like taking some water out of a polluted pond, purifying it, and placing it back into the pond: the intent may be to purify the pond, but the effect is that the purified water becomes polluted again too.

Purpose of the Project Review

The project review performed at the end of a project is designed to learn from the project experience, find underlying causes of problems, and make suggestions to correct them and thus minimize problems on future projects. It is also an outlet for people to vent emotions stirred up from working on the project, a necessary and healthy step. A project review is not a "witch hunt" or "stupid who" exercise to find and chastise those who caused the problems, but rather a chance to look back on the project process, reflect on the experience, and answer the questions, "If we had it to do all over again, what would we do differently? What should we do the same?"

A project is an excellent learning opportunity. Projects have beginning goals and final products; analyzing the difference between them forms an excellent basis for discovering what was learned during the project. Projects are new and different and thus go against standard procedures. They normally require thinking and behavior that is outside the organizational norm. Behaving outside the norm develops learning opportunities because people see things in a different light. View each project as producing two deliverables: a result and an improved process. The goal of the project review is to facilitate and codify this new learning for use in future projects, for both current project participants and future project teams in the organization.

Midproject reviews are another good practice. They may be less formal but still allow sharing of ideas about what is happening, what needs to change or be accelerated, and how to make real time course corrections.

The Project Review Process

The process of a project review is often facilitated by an outsider—someone who is knowledgeable about project management and skilled in group dynamics but otherwise unrelated to and unaffected by the project. This is particularly necessary if the project has been deemed a failure or if a high level of animosity or bad blood exists among the project core team members.

The main participants in the review are the project manager and the project core team members. Having participated in the project from beginning to end, they have the best overall view of the project process. Input from regular team members who were present for only a portion of the project is usually solicited by the core team member who was responsible for the individual. However, a regular member might also participate in the review discussions, particularly if the member was involved in a critical incident that is important to the lessons learned. Remote partners also provide input.

The process begins with review participants' individually reviewing what they learned from the project by answering the questions on the survey in Exhibit 8.1. The questions are broken into four topic categories: project management practice, critical incidents, project results, and suggestions for the future. These questions cover the major categories of importance for most projects. However, if for a particular project an important category is missed, additional questions can be proposed by team members.

Consider giving the survey to participants at the beginning of the project so they are aware of the questions they will be asked and can fill in notes as situations occur. In any case, the survey should be filled out by the end of the project, while the situations are still fresh in their minds. The review should be one of the last steps in the project process.

Participants will discover that they benefit individually from the analysis, which helps to codify what they learned from project participation. The final questions help them think about what they might do differently on the next project.

EXHIBIT 8.1. THE PROJECT REVIEW QUESTIONNAIRE.

A. Project Management Practice

Begin by answering all the questions in this section, and then analyze those answered no.

Was the project goal clear?

Was a core team established?

   If yes, did it remain together for the entire project?

Was a detailed project plan developed?

   If yes, did the core team participate in developing it?

   Did the plan cover the entire process from concept to customer?

Was the project deadline truly negotiated with project sponsors?

Were core team members aware of the benefits of the project:

   For themselves?

   For the organization?

Were core team members continually aware of what was expected of them?

   And when it was expected?

Did top management support the project throughout its duration?

Was the customer or end user (or customer representative group) involved early in the project?

Was the customer fully informed of:

   Project progress?

   Project changes?

   Project setbacks or failures?

   Project delays?

Were customer expectations:

   Solicited?

   Included?

   Met?

   Exceeded?

EXHIBIT 8.1. THE PROJECT REVIEW QUESTIONNAIRE, Cont'd.

Was project communication sufficient?

Were regular meetings held?

Was timely project information readily available?

Did team members know whom to contact if there was a delay or other problem?

Did the core team meet regularly with:

　Upper management?

　Customer(s)?

　Contributing department managers?

　Other interested parties?

Did the project have a detailed budget?

　Was it a help during the project?

Now review those questions answered no:

What problems do you think may have been generated by the lack of that factor?

What could you, or did you, do to rectify those problems? What changes or procedures would you recommend for future projects?

What practices that worked well would you recommend continuing?

B. Critical Incidents

Were there things on the project that seemed to go wrong due to a variety of outside forces?

　Describe these critical incidents.

What could have been done (for example, what signal heeded, data tallied, or meetings held) to avoid or minimize these incidents?

What do you recommend for future projects?

C. Project Results

How well do project results relate to the original plan?

What were the major deviations from the original plan?

EXHIBIT 8.1. THE PROJECT REVIEW QUESTIONNAIRE, Cont'd.

Of the major deviations listed, which ones were caused by the following?

Lack of planning or planning technique skill

Lack of foresight—not seeing entire project process

Change in technology

Change in customer specification or expectation

"Random" events

D. Suggestions for the Future

What suggestions would you make to help minimize deviations from the plan?

What suggestions would you make to help discover necessary changes faster, especially in the beginning of the project when making changes is much cheaper?

What suggestions would you make for project management in this organization?

Follow individual analysis with a team discussion, which focuses first on the points from the review questions and then moves to general discussion. The purpose of team discussion is to learn further by sharing insights, clarifying points of view, summarizing key learning points, and developing suggestions for future project teams. If there has been trouble on the project team, an outside facilitator would be most helpful here.

The next step is to develop a list of recommendations for the continual improvement of project management in the organization. Distribute this list to other project managers in the organization. It is less important to have a comprehensive list of possible improvements than it is to focus on a few key areas for improvement and then take action on those findings. The team's job is not complete when it fills a room with ideas on flip charts. Find those areas where the organization can and will make changes. Consider using one of the processes described in Chapter Two to prioritize the improvement list.

A recommendation for getting these practices into widespread use is to require the project manager who is just starting a project to review previous projects. Translate this reflection into action by having the person present to an upper management team or at least to the core team what was learned and what will be adopted, adapted, or applied to the current project.

The Upper Manager's Role in Reviews

The project review process can form the basis for generative learning, which is why it is important for upper managers to be so involved in it. The questions in sections B, C, and D of the review begin to look at underlying causes of problems. Upper managers demonstrate commitment to learning when they take the time to review these findings in detail with project participants. Several projects relating the same type of problem or experience flag an underlying cause that needs to be addressed.

Upper managers need continuous demonstrations of their commitment to learning and to action. They should participate enough in retrospective reviews to set expectations, design a healthy process, and establish a supportive environment. They should also be alert to bow out when management presence may inhibit open discussion.

Reviews should be required as a part of a product or project life cycle. Set expectations for areas of learning from projects:

- Better estimating of schedules and resources
- Better knowledge of the impact of changes
- How to communicate more effectively and efficiently in project teams
- Guides for leadership in keeping on schedule
- Processes that need to be in place, such as escalation processes that involve upper managers sooner rather than later to get difficult issues resolved
- Types of data that foretold disaster but were ignored
- Significant events that were not expected
- Random events
- Evidence-based decision processes
- New best practices to adopt, adapt, and apply

An Organic Approach to Project Management

An organic approach to project management adapts effective concepts from nature to make organizations more project friendly, leading to greater value-added and economic results. This approach encompasses the behavioral, technical, business, system, and change management aspects that create an environment for project success.

For example, training that seamlessly blends metaphors, multimedia, examples, concepts, and tools better motivates people to action and attain desired results. It takes all the research into account about multiple intelligences, preferred sensory styles, and how people accelerate the learning process.

Accelerated learning is critical to creating learning organizations. Commenting on her example in *The Accelerated Learning Fieldbook* (1999), I (Randall Englund) said, "Lou Russell offers an energetic style and systems approach that is invaluable for accelerating the learning process. Her skillful blending of research findings with personal examples is immensely informative, and, best of all, immediately useful!" Russell offers the advice, "If individual learners can become more effective in their ability to learn (create new knowledge) and communicate with others (exchange new knowledge), the business will become more innovative and flexible. Knowledge cannot be created through technology. Once people have increased their knowledge, they may then appropriately use technology to enable more knowledge acquisition" (p. 9).

Russell warns in workshops against overdoing technology and creating "death by PowerPoint." Include graphics and animation in presentations to enliven bulleted text slides. It is also possible to create "death by metrics" if they impose unnatural forms or controls that go counter to people's instincts and preferred ways to operate in organizations. Because people vary in their learning styles and reactions, use a variety of techniques that motivate them to learn.

One metaphor Russell uses to describe information technology leadership is alchemy. Practiced primarily in the Middle Ages, alchemy brought together various essential elements toward the formation of something greater and more valued. Russell and Feldman (2003) say, "Alchemy is change. It is a process of transformation, taking what is and creating what can be. The alchemical process blends multiple inputs—material elements, heat, time, pressure—to induce transformation and a hoped-for output, something of value. Leadership alchemy is much the same. There are various inputs: self-insight, a solid skill base, technical competence, organizational culture, and constantly shifting external forces. Blended together, these create an environment for transformation that not only induces change, but demands it" (p. 209).

Complexity science is a new field that adopts chaos theory to organizations. It recognizes that small initial conditions create unpredictable results. However, patterns exist for how this happens. Behavioral patterns exist in organizations. For example, people respond to energy; otherwise, entropy sets in. This pattern guides project and upper management leaders to tap their passion for the contagious effect it has on the self and others. Another pattern is the role of experiential learning as a requirement for achieving and sustaining positive business results.

This chapter builds on a cycle of knowledge creation that sees theories as a plant's root system; nutrients flow from the roots up the plant or tree and into branches, leaves, and fruit as the methods and tools that are used to create results; the practical knowledge that is created recycles back to the roots and helps form new or revised theories. Success becomes repeatable because it builds on a known foundation while also adapting to changing conditions. Upper managers are like successful gardeners: best results occur when creating an environment for the system to perform the way it innately knows how to. This calls for a learning organization.

The Compleat Upper Manager

The successful complete upper manager:

- Makes individual and organizational learning a priority.
- Develops a critical mass of people trained on new processes.
- Mines the project management information system for data to fuel the learning process.
- Asks project managers for project reviews, both before and after the project.
- Takes action on findings.
- Immediately applies findings to new projects, preferably with the same team or team leadership.
- Avoids short-term fixes that may lose sight of objectives, not work, solve one problem but create others, or fail to solve the problem that needs to be resolved (the real solution may be elsewhere).
- Surveys and acts on employee feedback.
- Demonstrates a continuous commitment to learning.

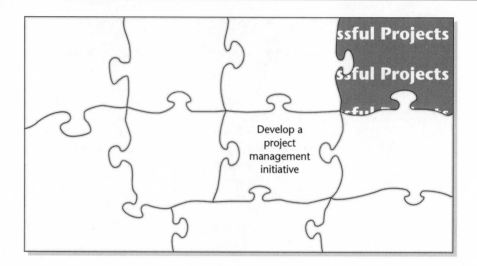

ssful Projects

ssful Projects

Develop a
project
management
initiative

This chapter begins by describing the purpose of a project management initiative and goes on to describe the components of and actual experiences with the Hewlett-Packard Project Management Initiative. We discuss the results achieved by an initiative within the organization and suggest ways from these learnings to make a concerted effort that improves project management across the organization.

CHAPTER NINE

DEVELOPING A PROJECT MANAGEMENT INITIATIVE

This they tell, and whether it happened so or not I do not know;
but if you think about it you can see that it is true.

BLACK ELK, *BLACK ELK SPEAKS*

To create an environment for successful projects, research the practices that correlate with project success, get that knowledge implemented across the company, and develop a project management curriculum. These steps constitute a project management initiative. This chapter describes an initiative that Hewlett-Packard (HP) used to develop and market products, realizing that project management is a key enabling factor for rapid cycle times. Other forms of a project office convey similar benefits.

The perspective comes from one who was there, Randall Englund. As the preface to *The Blue Cat of Castle Town*, Robert Graham's favorite book, says, "It is all true, but there is not a word of truth in it" (Coblentz, 1974). Peculiar as it sounds, this statement is often correct. From a cultural anthropologist's point of view, when people describe "what's going on," perhaps not every word they speak is true; but as Indian historian Black Elk indicates in the opening quotation of this chapter, if you think about what is being described, whatever chords of truth shine through are the important realities—the real truth.

A project management initiative represents corporate resources expended to help people anywhere and everywhere in the organization improve the environment and skills for effective project management. It is a group of people continually present and available to help project managers and upper managers alike. It helps organizations make ongoing improvements and survive changes. The people in the initiative are experienced project managers with the ability to motivate, develop, and coach others. They become a conduit to provide and accelerate the flow of information. The initiative may also seek out breakthroughs or competitive practices that can significantly change the organization. To achieve and sustain a project-based organization requires some form of initiative or project office.

A project management initiative provides the following:

• Conceptual models for project management
• Curriculum for project manager development
• Help in project manager selection and development
• Consulting services
• Continuing development opportunities
• The latest information for project managers
• Forums for developing best practices
• Forums to help upper managers
• A central information source for project managers entering new areas

The origin of HP's Project Management Initiative was a 1989 breakthrough objective set at the highest level of the company. HP's senior management, realizing that time to market was increasingly important as a competitive weapon and that the company needed to get the right products to market quickly and effectively, set out to establish the necessary systems and processes.

The executives asked corporate engineering what would help. Working with the R&D Productivity Council, corporate engineering created a prioritized list of factors that were hindering time to market. Insufficient project management skill was high on the list. The chief operating officer then created a project management objective to reflect corporate engineering's assessment. Marvin Patterson, as director of corporate engineering, became the upper manager sponsor. He delegated to one project manager the responsibility for meeting the objective.

The Purpose of an Initiative

If left to their own priorities or those imposed by short-term organizational pressures, upper managers often spend little time on project management. Even if they do, the efforts often atrophy when the individuals are promoted or transferred or the entity is reorganized. Establishing an initiative at the corporate level helps project management efforts survive these changes. Because the efforts at continual improvement, organizational learning, and cultural change usually take several years to have an impact, it takes structural change to make behaviors change. HP often uses initiatives supported by cross-organizational councils to implement these changes.

The Project Management Initiative focused at its beginning on project management in the research and development or engineering function, and later recognized the need to address managers of projects in all functional and staff areas.

Where the initiative resides in the corporate organization chart is very flexible. HP's Project Management Initiative was in corporate engineering, which merged with manufacturing to become the engineering and manufacturing processes, themselves part of the product processes organization, a group consisting of many corporate staff activities roughly paralleling most of the functional areas in a typical division (see Figure 9.1). The logic for this has to do with being an engineering-driven company where the typical project manager resides in the R&D function.

FIGURE 9.1. THE HP PRODUCT PROCESSES ORGANIZATION.

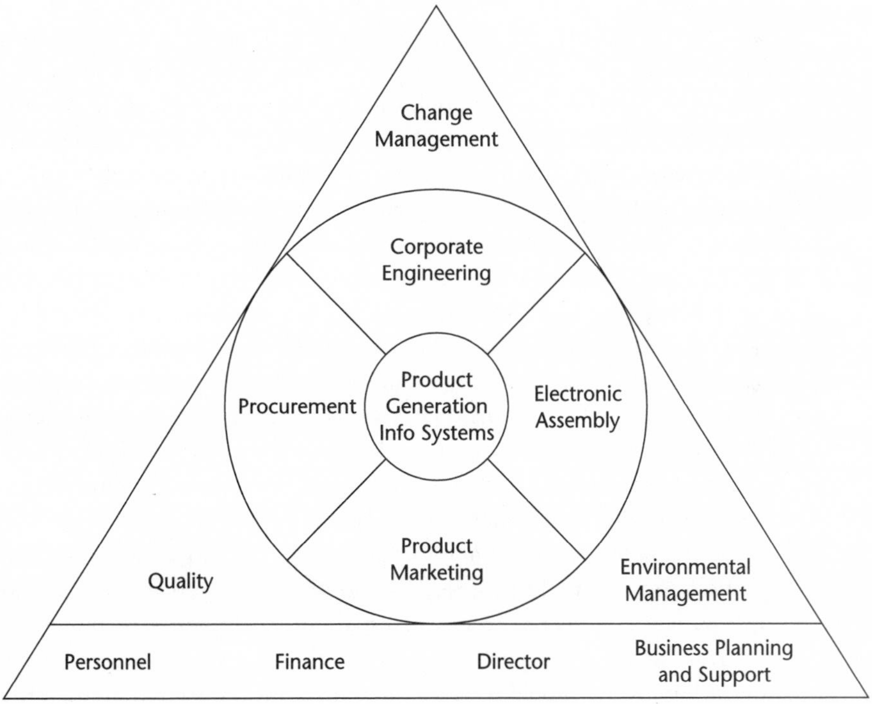

The placement made sense even with the broadened audience of all people managing projects because it gave the initiative a mainstream focus. The director cared about and strongly supported the initiative, believing that engineering managers greatly benefit from it. Managers in other functional areas are more than welcome to participate in the offerings of the initiative, as project management goes across disciplines and participation from people in all functions is thus important. Later, the parent group renamed itself as product generation systems.

The initiative manager enlisted the help of others by forming a council of people interested in project management—a Project Management Council. These representatives were drawn from each major business in the company. Although the intent was to have each business represented equally, actual levels of cooperation varied. Some groups where project management needs are clearly recognized may have several representatives, whereas multiple groups may be represented by one person. The overriding objective was to have individuals on the council who care about making a contribution rather than insisting that each business name a representative. About twenty persons attended each council meeting. Initially, the council met quarterly; as the initiative gathered steam over several years, the council met less frequently.

Discussion at an early meeting resulted in a purpose statement—an enduring reason for existence—that says: "Lead the continuous improvement of project management throughout the company." Several permanent staff members were added to develop courses and publications that would help inculcate the practices of project management into the heads and hearts of all practitioners.

Perhaps obvious but worth noting is that for an initiative to succeed on an ongoing basis, the support of senior management and achieving status as a core competence are vital. In times of reengineering and downsizing, anything lacking these ingredients is subject to being contracted out.

When a new chief executive, Lew Platt, took over in 1993, the initiative sought his continuing support. He was invited to address the council and answer a series of questions submitted to him in advance. He stated during that address: "One chronic problem is that HP typically promotes people to management who have many years of training in some other discipline. . . . I want to make sure training is encouraged and given more priority than it is today." Regarding the place of project management within HP, he said, "I think project management is a core competence and a real important one. I'd like to see it 'best-in-class.' To be the best and to stay the best requires continuous improvement." He went on to say that HP must keep current with what other companies are doing to stay competitive. The initiative staff strove to fulfill this imperative. Asked how much training each manager should receive, Platt answered, "Any job training [on] the order of a couple of weeks a year is a reasonable investment to make."

These statements are examples of valuable public evidence of senior management support, not only for the initiative's sake but to motivate managers in the company to pay attention to the training needs of their people. (Platt's mention of two weeks' training per year referred to maintaining and updating skills; a new project manager needs much more when beginning to manage projects.)

The vision statement developed over a long series of staff meetings describes a desired future state in which the practices for project success are identified, concisely documented, widely understood, appropriately adapted, and enthusiastically applied. Rigorously applied, the vision allows people to continually improve how they do their work and to lead others to achieve excellent results quickly.

Over time, the team found that it needed to articulate its basic values and beliefs, as it found it could contribute in more ways and places than its resources allowed. Besides, a corporate activity is subject to intense scrutiny: Is it necessary? Can anybody else do the same thing? Why is this group doing what it is doing? Articulating values and beliefs helps a team focus on the most important issues when making decisions—and, of course, helps justify its existence. For HP's Project Management Initiative, these beliefs included the following:

- HP's competitive business success needs timely, excellent results from projects.
- For HP to get timely, excellent results from projects, competence in project management is necessary.
- To get the necessary competence in project management, a concerted effort is required.
- A concerted effort is particularly needed in project management because most HP project managers were educated in other disciplines.

Components of the Initiative

The Project Management Initiative (see Figure 9.2) consisted of the following elements, each discussed further in the next sections:

- The initiative team, comprising permanent staff members dedicated to the initiative
- The Project Management Council, an advisory group
- Consulting services on general project matters, project start-ups, assessments, project plans, and tools
- Training resources such as courses and workshops
- Information resources: a survival kit, videos, proceedings, cassettes, and referrals
- Conferences for project managers and upper managers.
- WebShops to provide distance learning

FIGURE 9.2. THE PROJECT MANAGEMENT INITIATIVE
AT H-P AND ITS COMPONENTS.

The Initiative Team

A vision statement is supported by a mission statement that lists specific goals the team hopes to achieve. The mission varied each fiscal year but always included metrics on customer satisfaction, number of people affected by the initiative, strategies and tactics, revenue, results achieved, and ongoing contributions. The team was composed of full-time staff members who previously practiced project management in entities within the company. Team members need to bring experiences from a wide range of activities: R&D, marketing, factory and field, programming, program and system management, and productivity management. Thus, they are members of an interdisciplinary project team with a wide breadth of experience, such that if one person cannot solve a problem, another can. They are capable of developing and delivering courses, and they are communicators. Some of their time may be spent in classroom training, but they view themselves first as experienced, practicing, knowledgeable project managers. Consulting and facilitation skills are very important. The team is supported by several other people who provide logistics and instructional design knowledge.

Goals, responsibilities, and due dates for each individual were developed, maintained, and updated at one-on-one weekly meetings with the initiative manager and shared with the extended team. An extended team includes partners in other functional areas who provide marketing, logistics, and instructional design support. Team members develop and maintain competence by working with practicing project managers, attending courses and conferences, developing a network of professional contacts, and staying current with management literature.

A stated goal of all activities was that they follow espoused practices; the initiative team cannot be credible unless it believes in and practices good project management. An initiative or project office is a great place to model desired behavior. One delightful benefit of being part of such a group is systematically practicing, or at least attempting to practice, worthy processes that get only lip-service elsewhere.

The initiative team published a proprietary catalogue of products and services and used direct e-mail and a Web page to inform internal customers about its offerings. A decisive competitive advantage of an internal initiative team versus outside vendors is access and distribution capability to the user base through global electronic databases and networks.

The Project Management Council

The members of this council were practicing project managers and representatives from major organizations throughout HP. They were peers of the initiative staff members, not of higher-level managers. Their responsibility was to represent the broad scope of needs for improving project management techniques in their organizations. What does the CEO expect from councils? According to CEO Lew Platt: "Make decisions!"

The council met several times a year. Reports were made about representatives' efforts in their organizations to understand the needs of people who manage projects and to help them get value from the initiative's products and services. Representatives reviewed and prioritized project plans such as new courses, studies on inhibitors to adopting best practices, professional development, certification, benchmarking, and sponsorship. They also provided feedback on pilot courses and made decisions about which activities of the initiative provide greatest value to the company. They reviewed early drafts of proposed publications, served as support staff for the project management conferences, assisted in retrospective analyses, and took on assignments or assisted as guest speakers at the transitions course.

Consulting Services

Consulting services from members of the Project Management Initiative guided teams through the project start-up process. A project start-up workshop is a quick way to lay the foundation for a high-quality, credible project plan. It defines relevant practices and processes and explains the development of initial project plans. The workshop involves the entire project team and should occur early in the project planning process; it is powerful for both planning and team building.

The project start-up workshops of some vendors have a two-day agenda, but the service provided by the initiative aimed to understand the needs of the team and help execute the team's agenda, not to bring in a preset agenda. Facilitation and project management skills, the knowledge of relevant practices, and examples from other entities were some of the contributions offered by the initiative consultant. Exposure to other companies by speaking at or attending professional conferences brought additional ideas to the table. Clients of the consulting service made these comments:

> "The initial meeting we had with you was beneficial because it generated enthusiasm and excitement about the program."
>
> "The planning process was quite beneficial. It also helped us divide the tasks effectively."
>
> "I will incorporate this process into future projects and expect to use your consulting services again. It is extremely worthwhile."

As an example of the consulting function, a marketing person from one of the business divisions had attended the project management fundamentals course and was preparing her first project. She called and requested assistance to get the project started. An initiative consultant spent two days at her site and facilitated her team of "volunteers" through a start-up meeting. The morning focused on developing a shared vision. In the afternoon, the team set up its infrastructure, work breakdown structure, schedule, action items, owners, and due dates. She was very appreciative of the assistance because it helped her start fast and stimulated enthusiasm for the project by all members of the team. "The performance we experienced before [the consultant's] involvement was 20 percent," she said. "The performance currently achieved is 60 percent."

General consulting on other practices of project management were also available. It took such forms as tutorial sessions, project management maturity assessments, project plan reviews, reengineering efforts, event planning, metrics, conferences, best practices, vendor management, prioritization, and tools. One of the most powerful sessions focused on assisting upper management and project teams in establishing their purpose, vision, and mission. Another was helping a group manager and business team select, weight, and apply criteria to prioritize and decide on its portfolio of projects. Certain tutorials drew on experiences and documentation of best practices. Whatever form they take, consulting sessions' objectives are set by the client, and a project management consultant facilitates, guides, or provides leverage for an individual or team to achieve timely and excellent results. The initiative staff either performed these services personally or taped qualified outside consultants. The push was toward doing more strategic consulting such that interventions gained highly leveraged results. Many leads for consulting came from exposure of the initiative staff during courses and from meetings with upper managers during targeting and funding sessions.

One consultant on the initiative team was fully funded by the business organization where she originally worked. That business had targeted project management as an area for improvement and wanted her to be in regular contact with the initiative staff. Thus, all her efforts went toward understanding, proposing, and implementing initiative activities within that organization. She got upper management support for specific programs, facilitated the meetings that drove those programs, and scheduled project management courses for all existing and new project managers. First to participate in these courses were members of the upper management staff.

Training Resources

Courses and workshops were available to everyone in the company to learn about the practices of project management and how they work at HP. Open enrollment is the means whereby any individual, with the consent of his or her manager, may enroll in a training course on-site or at another location. A project management curriculum matrix depicted courses arranged by experience level and by topical areas. Offerings addressed everyone from project participants, to new and experienced project managers, to executives. The idea of depicting all courses on one matrix was received favorably by project managers, who wanted a comprehensive list of available training. Data sheets on each course were available to employees in hard copy and on the HP internal Web page. The initiative sponsored courses worldwide.

Courses in this curriculum addressed the problems encountered in creating an environment for successful projects. The transitions course helped in the selection and development process of new or potential managers. Topics such as team infrastructure in the fundamentals course helped to define core teams. The behavioral process covered in the workshop addressing operating across organizations helped develop relationships and define communication paths for greater information flow. An advanced course provided practice on techniques that reduce anxiety about schedules and risks when creating something new or working with new partners. One workshop identified common success factors for time-constrained projects. Forums allowed participants to learn from their colleagues about best practices, such as work breakdown structures and estimation.

One value of the initiative was its provision of an integrated curriculum that links with other activities in the company. Companies often lament the functional silos that keep units from working together; HP has its silos too. The initiative, however, made a point of reaching out to other corporate or division groups. The curriculum listed courses available from corporate product marketing and personnel that are valuable, or "core," to project management. Publications pointed to contact names in other functions. The initiative team tried to get participation in its conferences from various groups, the intent being to foster cooperation instead of the competition too often brought on by charter or turf wars. These activities provide value to users because they get wider access to training resources.

The initiative team also tried actively to understand the offerings of other departments. For example, the initiative team offered project management training, and a process engineering group provided project management training to the information technology (IT) area. Why were there two separate groups doing project management training? Because the training offered to IT was entirely focused on the IT community and the massive Y2K program; it was methodology rich, providing detailed life cycles relevant only to that community. The initiative provided generic training and models applicable to all projects. The two offerings actually complemented each other.

Participants say they especially appreciate the personal understanding they got and the sharing of in-house experiences they received when initiative staff members facilitated courses. Their course evaluations often included comments like this one: "The instructor's ability to share real-life HP experiences is a strength of this workshop." HP's culture is a distinct competitive advantage; the initiative leveraged that by sharing HP examples that emphasize the effective ways people work together. These are not always unique, but a culture that tells its stories vividly and consistently remains strong because the examples explain the whys and hows that motivate others to higher performance.

Many training courses were conducted under open enrollment, where individuals or their managers registered to attend the course. People interacted with others from different parts of the organization and learned how they do business. It became increasingly apparent, however, that greater business impact was possible by conducting courses with intact teams. When this is done, the consulting or facilitative skills are applied with a critical mass of people who hear the same things at the same time and can apply them to the challenges of their specific project. This practice helps avoid the problems of a sole individual single-handedly trying to change the ways of an organization. The manager of one team that went through training together reported these results: "The class was well presented, and each of us took away action areas for improvement in our respective project management roles. We recently reviewed our list of individual improvement goals that we documented in the class in a recent team meeting and significant accomplishments were recorded by each individual in the team. [The instructor from the initiative team] was very easy to work with and flexible in setting up the class and working around our team meeting schedule. The feedback from the class was very positive overall."

The need to develop upper managers on project management became increasingly apparent. These managers most likely did not receive training on project management earlier in their careers, when projects usually were completed by brute force—"just do it." As newly trained project managers venture forth from training rooms, they send feedback on the difficulties of implementing a project discipline. Management does not always understand the language or value of the time it takes to plan the project, fully develop the team infrastructure, improve the estimation process, build a credible schedule, and do contingency analysis. The HP initiative expanded its horizon to help develop a better support structure up and down the management chain.

One expansion area was the Engineering Management Program (see Figure 9.3). The target audience for this was managers of project managers and up. The Project Management Initiative itself got started by offering a conference, so one of the first offerings of the new program to upper management was a conference

FIGURE 9.3. EXPANSION OF THE PROJECT MANAGEMENT INITIATIVE.

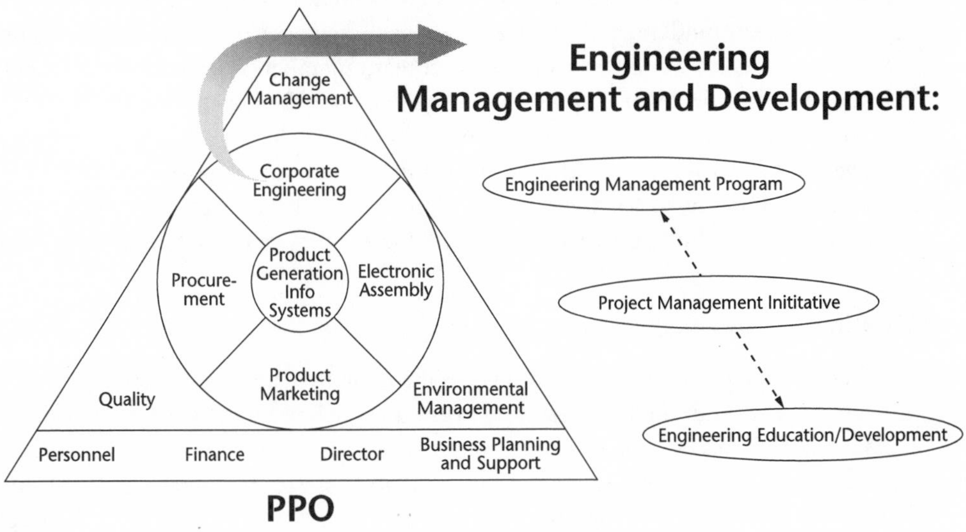

where peers from around the world could get together, listen to world-class external experts, and network among themselves to discuss common concerns (more about this later in the chapter). Another offering was a project management overview for executives. This course highlighted the terminology and practices being taught to project managers. Project management for executives provided the opportunity for upper management teams to reinforce the practice of project management fundamentals within their organizations. This course presented the project management fundamentals course structure, relationship of this course to other existing courses, management issues, and an overview of project management processes—what they need to do to support the process and what they receive in return for their investment. Managers said, "From this overview, I realize our division's functional areas have been using divergent process terminology and therefore confusing the troops. We need to use the same process terminology." This course plus other initiative workshops were deliberately offered in the same week as the upper management conference; the target audience was upper managers from remote sites who were in town for the conference.

Increasingly, however, it appears that an overview course for executives is not sufficient because they do not experience the work involved in doing project management. An overview is intellectual instead of experiential. A far more effective approach is to have upper managers go through the same or a slightly abbreviated course that project managers do and then add a discussion period about what the upper managers need to do to create a supportive environment.

Project management initiatives were conducted within a number of divisions where the upper management team as a group went through a three-day project management fundamentals course. Then each manager did it again with his or her intact team. No longer would project team members question management support of project work; upper managers demonstrated by getting trained first and by being there for the team training that they believed in the project management process and would support it. One general manager reported, "This course helped me to see areas where I can remove obstacles to the project team and how to create a successful framework for our project managers."

Information Resources

Documenting best practices began when the initiative team surveyed project managers throughout the company to determine which practices were most important to their success. Topics scoring the highest, such as scheduling and estimation, were researched to find ideas and best practices and to share them widely. Both the initiative staff and the project managers around the company documented these practices and made them available to others in hard copy and on-line using a Web browser. Interested individuals were tracked on a database so best practices and success stories could be disseminated to a known audience of practitioners. Preparation of these documents had the added advantage of bringing the knowledge of the initiative staff about each topic to a peak. At first, binders with these documents were free to anyone interested. Later, in response to self-funding pressures, charges were added for both the initial binder and annual updates. The professional staff viewed this funding decision as detrimental to the more noble cause of getting widespread sharing of the practices.

A project manager's survival kit of instructional materials was assembled to help new and seasoned project managers perform their jobs better. It is recommended that each project manager get a personal copy so the material may be marked up, easily accessed, and used repeatedly.

The survival kit contained the following components:

- A computer-based training course on project management
- An audiocassette program that discusses ways to improve communication, managing, and time management skills
- Videotapes of interviews with successful HP project managers
- Books on effective meeting skills, the project manager's work environment, coping with time and stress, and the implementation of project management
- Bibliography of additional resources
- Project management training curriculum outline

Questions arose about the certification of project managers. One member of the Project Management Council pushed for a recommendation on whether certification should be required and enlisted members of the council to prepare a proposal. However, the effort stopped when CEO Platt responded that he was more interested in managers' getting results than getting certified. Individuals interested in certification were referred to the program sponsored by the Project Management Institute (PMI). PMI's Project Management Professional (PMP) certification program is recognized worldwide as the standard for measuring an individual's core knowledge and understanding of project management principles. Increasing numbers of large organizations are incorporating PMI's PMP certification into the career path requirements for individuals seeking project responsibility. Stating that the basic elements of managing projects are universal to all project types, PMI provides the official *Guide to the Project Management Body of Knowledge* (Project Management Institute, 2000).

The field professional services organization is more emphatic in requiring this certification because external customers are reassured by knowing that the project managers they are paying for are certified as project management professionals. Internal organizations do not generally exhibit concern about whether a project manager is certified. Some entities—those where management has specified that instructors must be certified—are starting to require formal training for all project and program managers.

Project Management Conferences

Every two years, a project management conference brought together HP people who manage projects around the world. The 1994 conference theme was "Applying Proven Practices for Project Success, Today!" This recognized that timely, excellent results from projects are vital to HP's success in a globally competitive environment. It is not necessary to reinvent all new processes when a proven body of knowledge about project management is available, so participants were invited to learn techniques and practices that others have successfully applied to the challenges facing HP projects today.

The purpose of the conference was to do the following:

- Improve professional knowledge about project management.
- Share best practices for managing projects at HP.
- Learn from external experts about project management.
- Network with other HP people involved in managing projects.

In his address to the conference, HP's CEO answered questions submitted by conference participants about his views on project management at HP. "What issue is he most concerned about and what should we as project managers do about it?" was one question. He chose the issue of complacency and recommended practicing "healthy paranoia." External speakers were chosen for their knowledge about project management as well as their effectiveness as speakers. They were briefed by the initiative staff and requested to submit materials to be published, along with HP internal papers, in the conference proceedings. Each internal paper was reviewed in advance by five or six peers in order to improve its ability to share valuable lessons. This review process tremendously improved the quality of the papers; the exciting contents also got reviewers even more fired up to attend the conference. Paper submitters were solicited by general announcements sent out to electronic distribution lists of the target audience. Reviewers were solicited by mailings to early registrants for the conference.

The two-day conference provided a broad mix of topics and formats. External speakers typically addressed the entire audience. Up to four HP papers were presented concurrently; attendees had the option of picking topics of most interest to them. The papers were grouped not by business or discipline, such as printers, software, or manufacturing, but rather by topics of project management, such as metrics, partnerships, and success factors. The initiative team sponsored several conferences, so the process was well documented through a work breakdown structure, retrospective reports, and statistics. In fact, this documented process provided corporate engineering with higher scores during its quality maturity system audit.

The 1996 conference theme, in recognition that project managers are at the heart of the action that makes things happen—new products and processes, integrating customer projects—was "Manage the Action." How do you manage that action to get better results? There are things to learn, skills to sharpen, best practices to share, and tools to adopt, adapt, and apply. To emphasize this, management professionals from other companies were brought to the conference to share their approaches to project management. Consultants provided compelling stories about the role of project management, whether delivering products to market, climbing Mount Everest, or tapping creativity within teams. Papers were presented by project managers from all businesses, factory and field, and across the globe. Optional courses at the conference allowed travelers to experience a full week of training experiences. HP's executive vice president answered questions at one session; he clearly indicated the need to focus on fewer projects and shared his thinking about partnerships, influencing without authority, and field professional services.

Conferences are an excellent opportunity to share stories and reinforce the culture of continuous improvement and learning from each other. Attendees highly valued the opportunity to network with peers during breaks and discussion sessions, which may explain why three times more people registered for the 1996 conference than for the 1992 conference.

The conference became a victim of its own success: the need to watch expenses led upper management to cut attendance to a minimum. The expense control targets were met, but project managers uproariously protested being limited in their attendance. This sent a difficult message about the priority of training and networking, but otherwise the responses to the conference reflected favorably on its value and the work of the initiative. The economic situation led the initiative to suspend further attempts at sponsoring large conferences.

The initiative modified its networking approach by implementing a series of regional training events. Over a two-week period, all courses were offered nearby major company facilities, such as Fort Collins, Colorado; Atlanta, Georgia; Portland, Oregon; Singapore; and Stuttgart, Germany. In addition to minimizing the travel component for most attendees, this traveling training program became very popular to help project managers complete their development programs.

Another innovation was adding WebShops as distance-learning events. People registered (and paid) for on-line sessions lasting ninety minutes to two hours on topics such as, "If project management were easy, anyone could do it" and "Speaking truth to power." The initiative team again worked extremely well together to produce outstanding programs by panels of presenters that brought awareness of issues to a broader audience in a cost-effective manner. All concerned knew, however, that these sessions add to but do not replace in-person skill-building training room sessions. The use of on-line polling questions and typing in questions or comments in real time created more effective interactive sessions.

Upper Management Conference

Only about twenty people can take a course at one time, but organizational change will not occur until a larger critical mass of people is exposed to and follows the practices espoused in the course. Early participants often forget the course material by the time a critical mass is reached; thus, it is important to reach the people who may be interested in it as quickly as possible. The outside experts that some upper managers seem to prefer as catalysts or change agents are expensive, so using them can be justified only if the audience is large. Before HP's first upper management conference, there was no format for upper managers to network and learn from each other.

The initiative team had already been very successful with its project management conferences. Knowing that the information imparted at these now needed to proceed up the organization, the team decided to conduct engineering management conferences. In preparation, the staff ran a survey to determine in-

FIGURE 9.4. CONFERENCE DISCUSSION THEMES.

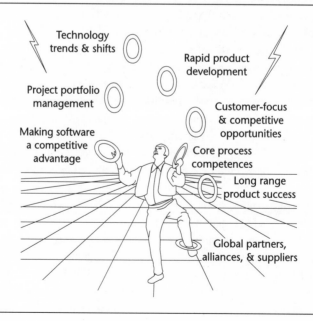

terest in the concept. The overwhelmingly positive response indicated that section and function managers wanted a two-day conference featuring external world-class experts, HP executives, workshops, and networking. They did not want HP papers or a parade of speakers describing the current status of their business. Extensive interviews were conducted with managers around the company to assess the main issues they were facing that a conference might address. These issues guided the selection of speakers and topic areas for facilitated discussion groups (see Figure 9.4), and a vision statement and conference theme were developed based on them (see Box 9.1). It became quite clear that upper managers sensed a void in the training and networking opportunities available to them.

BOX 9.1. HP's Upper Management Conference.

The vision statement guiding the planning of the upper management conference was this:

> Participants come from all areas of HP. Stimulating world-class experts and proprietary exchanges provide exposure to more usable ideas per hour about product and process development at HP than any other forum. The conference environment supports exploration of major topics of concern by participants while temporarily moving operational decisions into the background. New contacts and sources of information are developed. Participants get real solutions they are enthusiastic about applying to product and process activities in the entities.

Accordingly, the conference theme was "Product and Process Strategies for Future Success." This was elaborated on in the conference proceedings as follows:

> Our surveys and interviews with HP middle managers indicate you are concerned about the "big picture" view of strategies that HP needs to pursue for success into the 21st century. You recognize that changes are rampant and affecting every aspect of your job. You need to accelerate product development and improve processes. You want to network with peers and learn other ways to cope with changing roles.
>
> The cover of these Proceedings illustrates our theme [see Figure 9.4]. The juggler is trying to handle the many challenges and opportunities you face. Each of the eight rings he's tossing is a topical area for needs you want to address during the Conference. The grid reaches into the future—a big question in your minds about what's ahead and what your role should be. The lightning bolts are a stark reminder, riveting your attention in the present, transitory moment, to take action now.

The conference objectives were to:

- Share concerns with peers in other parts of the company.
- Discuss major challenges to the "HP Way" (the standards for excellence formulated by founders Bill Hewlett and Dave Packard).
- Learn from external experts about trends, ideas, and strategies.
- Look at big picture threats as well as opportunities to develop or maintain businesses.
- Make mutual discoveries about what can (or must) be attained for the company to prosper.
- Convert lessons learned into high-impact actions.
- Probe the thought processes of executives.
- Pick up survival tactics for entering a new millennium.
- Improve skills for managing operations and people.
- Get away from the maelstrom, and think about other ways to do things.

Professional speakers were selected whose credentials indicated high knowledge of the topic areas and who were known to be excellent communicators. The conference coordinators were or became familiar with the message each speaker conveyed. The speakers were briefed to address a worldwide audience where the focus is on global working relationships, not just on making the United States more competitive. The speakers' topics included creating a learning organization, competing for the future, strategic alliances, successful habits of visionary companies, fast cycle times, managing project managers, and advanced product development.

Advance questions were solicited from participants about issues they wanted addressed by a senior executive. A humorist (representing the court jester) talked after dinner about humor in the workplace. Overall, the conference featured an HP senior vice president, the director of corporate engineering, nine external speakers, one demonstration by a lab manager and team on bringing in the voice of the customer, and an HP customer who addressed the question, "Can an organization known for its engineering excellence provide superior customer satisfaction?" Facilitated discussion groups where conference participants shared their experiences were conducted toward the end of each day.

After the conference, one participant noted: "The outside speakers were fantastic . . . and worth the time and cost of the conference. The humorist (and topic) was a good choice for an evening speaker." Another said the after-lunch speaker "was exceptional. He offered new insights and attempted to shake the foundations of complacency. He had evidence and appropriate, relevant anecdotes. His models enabled new thinking." However, a third attendee observed, "Given the [excellent] quality of the external presentations, I would have preferred short workshops to get people together to talk about the key ideas which were presented and how we might apply them within our organizations."

Other courses or workshops—on topics such as managing across organizations and models of systems thinking—were scheduled around the two-day conference such that a complete week of training experiences was available for managers from out of town. One of the leadership workshops was a simulation based on "The Complete Project Manager" (Graham, 1991). A participant commented: "The simulation helped me understand that team development, although viewed as valuable, tends to be underestimated under the pressures of the schedule. Learning the importance of human (and my) behavior on project outcome was valuable." Another noted learning several important points: "[Do] not use arbitrary deadlines, support my teams without meddling, manager is an information source, establish core values/objectives early." And a third said the simulation provided "tremendous benefits—bottom line. [I learned to] have people excited about our projects while meeting business objectives. I can and will use the concepts on an ongoing basis."

Experience with the Initiative Process

An important paradigm shift for the Project Management Initiative after several years of being funded by corporate allocations was an organizational requirement to become fully self-funded. A new corporate functions initiative required that certain groups provide products and services that internal customers value by purchasing them on a pay-as-you-use-it basis. The change meant that the team had to begin satisfying the needs of specific customers, not just work on projects that it believed were good for the company. Prior to this change, the initiative staff paid minimal attention to the courses or to extensive promotion of its activities; its time was consumed by publications and conferences.

One effect of being self-funded (being part of the internal market program) was an increased drive to get closer to internal customers and understand their needs. The efforts spent promoting the courses and publications resulted in record numbers of participants signing up; courses filled rapidly, and waiting lists developed. Instead of vendors' delivering all courses, team members took over direct delivery of some. They developed workshops on other topics and provided consulting on project start-up processes. As experienced project managers and skilled facilitators, they relished the opportunity to be among their peers, sharing ideas and encouraging others to greater professionalism. Evaluation scores and feedback were extremely positive.

Being a self-contained business means having to improve the efficacy of processes. Some labor-intensive aspects of conferences provided less than spectacular results; the approach was therefore simplified. Other processes with no potential revenue stream went on the back burner.

The downside to self-funding is the difficulty of conducting research and development on project management with no clear source of revenue to pay for it. A short-term mentality results. When an idea comes up—such as a suggestion from the CEO to do competitive benchmarking—it is almost impossible to move on it without funding. This is particularly frustrating for team members whose motivation for moving from an applications or functional organization was to help develop new practices or sources of information that could have widespread significance for the corporation over a longer term. The pendulum still swings on this issue. Several years later and under a new CEO, a workforce development group consumed many of the corporate functions. It became funded by corporate and offered "free" instead of transaction-based services.

The initiative as a group did not survive the aging process, a new CEO, and a major shift in the business situation. Several members took an early retirement or severance package or left to pursue other opportunities. One would hope that with fulfilling its purpose over a twelve-year period that the project management discipline would now be inculcated across the organization. Probably like many other stories, this is partly truth and partly fiction. The natural order that causes change does not negate the many learnings and contributions made by this group.

Since the initiative began, so much more information, training, and trained project managers are now available that as these elements become more common, mature organizations change their approach. Following best project management practices is the important focus, not forming organizational structures for their own sake. A more formal approach may be downsized. Newer project-aware organizations learn to accelerate their approach to projects based on these learnings.

Results of HP's Project Management Initiative

Managers throughout the company found value in the Project Management Initiative. People adopted, adapted, and applied practices of project management to their work environments. Feedback from internal customers showed that they are learning the processes and using them; participants predicted that the value placed on improved results from applying the training over their careers is enormous. Self-assessment scores indicated that team performance can more than double by using the knowledge gained through exposure to the products and services of the initiative. When the founding sponsor of the initiative reflected in glowing terms on the huge impact it has had on the company, as quoted in Chapter One, it is rewarding.

Upper management teams that used consulting services from the initiative concluded sessions with clear action items on two or three key areas of project management that they selected for improvement. Project teams finally gained consensus on a vision that clearly directed their work in new ways—ways that all members were excited about pursuing. Intact teams received training on processes that all could apply and from which all could reap the benefits of common language and understanding. Whole organizations became consciously skilled in the practices of project management.

One key metric certainly indicated success and the value offered by the initiative: people who used the products and services provided enough revenue to fully fund the initiative—at least they did except under extreme cost-cutting measures. Courses were fully booked and had waiting lists. Most courses were scheduled because business groups pulled them in for their own benefit. In the beginning, the initiative team was rarely pulled in; it had to push to get businesses to allow them to present the courses. As in any other business, it takes hard work to develop products and promote them to achieve this status. The self-funding model of an organic organization lets the initiative team, within certain constraints, act like its own small business with a large captive market. It feels good when customers respond.

The quality of the initiative offerings did not go unnoticed. A number of influential managers in the company referred to the initiative team as a model self-funded group. Positive testimonials popped up in news groups and in meetings between people familiar with the materials. Participants continually reported leaving training sessions with tangible tools and skills that have immediate relevance. Other managers who rely solely on personal services for revenue called the initiative to get ideas; their people are always on the road, so they are looking for other products to develop that can generate revenue independent of requiring highly skilled people to deliver them.

Of course, we would be pleased to report that initiative offerings directly resulted in many new products or services offered in record times with fewer people and lower budgets. Probably it has, but that is difficult to prove. So many factors influence product success that it is problematic to establish meaningful metrics that reflect solely on one variable. Desirable as it might be to better measure such direct contributions to the bottom line, developing a metric to do so did not rise to the top of the priority list. There were too many other opportunities to make a contribution, phones to answer, and meetings to go to! Instead, the initiative team relied on its customers to measure its success (see Box 9.2).

The merger of HP and Compaq has benefited project and program management in several ways. Compaq brought a wealth of commitment and tools to this discipline. Professional services has adopted the Compaq project management methodology. HP now shows up in highly visible ways at Project

---

**BOX 9.2. Comments on Courses
Offered by the HP Project Management Initiative.**

Here are testimonials from satisfied users:

- Using the estimation skills learned, one software group said it used data from previous projects to produce more accurate estimates of cost, resources, and time. By using task decomposition to see increased detail, the group got more accurate estimates, produced an accurate schedule, caught project "gotchas" (errors, defects, and miscues, for example), and planned in advance for project hurdles.
- "I picked up quite a few techniques that I can apply immediately to a cross-organizational project, so my time was well spent."
- Ten project managers indicated that they saved a minimum of sixty project days as a direct result of the scheduling, planning and project management skills they learned in a course on project management fundamentals. This resulted in direct benefit to HP in the form of timely product releases.
- "The success factors prompted me to leverage off an existing product, so we saved half an engineer's time over our three-year project."
- "This course has caused me to think about which career path I really want to pursue, project management or technical contributor."
- "I really resonate with the job of the project manager. It's definitely what I want to do."

Management Institute conferences, sponsoring keynote speakers and a booth in exhibit areas, largely driven by the Compaq influence.

Robert Napier (2002), former chief information officer (CIO) of Compaq, is now CIO of the combined companies. His agenda on the merger, from an information technology (IT) standpoint, was to have common goals, common values, and common language. They needed to have enough team building done that they had developed enough trust before day one of combined operations, at least in his direct reports and in their direct reports. He led many team-building meetings that took the time to examine the cultural perceptions of both companies and to figure out the norms about how they operate. They sat together and defined what they wanted the new culture to be and what they thought their common values should be.

To achieve a common language, Napier is a proponent of a standardized global IT program management function or office: a common IT methodology, a common way of reporting, a common way of setting priorities, a common way of doing metrics. Everybody who is an IT professional needs to speak the language of program management and project management. It is all about planning to win.

In the premerger Compaq, everybody in the IT organization had been through formal project management training. Napier put the same methodology discipline into the new organization. He calls it speaking the same language—the language of project management. Whether it is a $10,000 project or a $10 million project, about provisioning and implementing infrastructure or about implementing a new software release, everyone approaches the problem in the same methodical process way. Napier's advice about the number one thing to achieve in leading to cost savings during the merger was to simplify the application portfolio.

The Compleat Upper Manager

The serious development of project management practices requires effort by upper management to establish or support a staff group that helps create an environment for successful projects. Concerted efforts like this always require support from senior management. With this backing, the staff group can be charged with assembling an advisory group such as a council and with developing training, consulting, and information resources. This group needs to devise methods for continuing development such as conferences and dissemination of best practices using various communication technologies. Developing this group allows the idea to be permanent, outlasting the initiator and changes in management. The initiative becomes a repository of information conducive to creating a learning organization. Managers throughout the company need to encourage their project managers to participate in the activities sponsored by the initiative.

A project management initiative is one form of a project office. It offers a generic methodology, and trains, mentors, and consults with project managers. (See Englund, Graham, and Dinsmore, 2003, for details about how to approach and design a project office that fits the current project culture and guides it toward an enterprise project management concept.)

The successful complete upper manager:

- Determines the importance of project management in an organization and enlists senior management support.
- Makes a point of getting support across the organization from people interested in project management.
- Clarifies the purpose, vision, and beliefs that lead a change toward more effective project management.
- Develops a program with a dedicated staff to address key issues of project management.
- Focuses a concerted effort on a program that can make a positive impact across the entire organization.

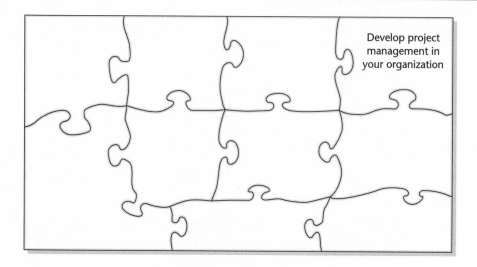

Develop project management in your organization

R ecognizing the variance in organizational culture among the companies mentioned in this book, this chapter suggests a process for implementing project management in your organization and gives some examples of how it was done in others. The first step is developing senior management support. This can be done through the use of a project inventory. With this commitment, the next step is to develop a structure of interdepartmental input. With this input, develop a process for project selection, and then develop upper management's ability to manage project managers. As this is being done, it is important to establish a project manager development program. Other steps are to change the career track to make project management a career option and also develop a project learning organization.

CHAPTER TEN

CREATING AN ENVIRONMENT FOR SUCCESSFUL PROJECTS IN *YOUR* ORGANIZATION

Amid pressure of great events, a general principle gives no help.

HEGEL, *PHILOSOPHY OF HISTORY*

Bold moves are needed to develop project management in most organizations. The person leading the change is likely to be going against tradition, fighting inertia, and attempting to overcome fierce resistance to change. Many organizations halfheartedly attempt to add project management to existing organizations. But to do it right requires that someone in senior management wants the change to happen. Without the backing of at least one person in senior management, any number of excuses can be found to justify not making the change; but it is also true that if only one senior manager wants to implement proper project management, and wants it badly enough, then it can happen. At Hewlett-Packard (HP), the chief operating officer made excellence in project management a priority, and it came to pass. One senior manager, definitely committed to the process of implementing project management and bold enough to begin it, may bring forth all the power and magic necessary to pull it off.

This chapter outlines a process of implementation and provides examples, many of which are from large organizations. However, the process can also be used in smaller organizations, though the project management office may not be as extensive and the project manager's development curriculum may need to be purchased rather than developed.

Implementation Process Overview

The overall implementation process is shown in Figure 10.1, where the ovals are steps in the process and the arrows indicate the consequences of not successfully implementing a step. The process begins with developing senior management support. If this is not accomplished, most of the succeeding steps will fail and the organization will require new senior management. The next step is to develop a project management process using interdepartmental input. Without this input, the process will fail because the departmental cooperation needed for good project management will probably not be forthcoming. The next step involves developing a process for project selection. If this is not done correctly, there will be massive fights for resources among competing projects. The following step involves developing upper managers' abilities in managing project managers. Without this, there will be a return to the old ways of managing and not an advancement to project management. Subsequent steps involve developing a project management

FIGURE 10.1. A PROCESS FOR SUCCESS AND DEFAULTS FOR NONACTION.

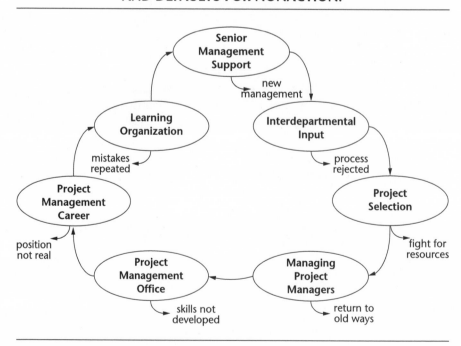

office to accelerate progress up the project management maturity scale, determining a project management career ladder so that the position is considered real, and creating a learning organization to leverage strengths and help ensure that past mistakes are not repeated.

Step 1: Developing Senior Management Support

If the managers at the top echelon of an organization are forward looking, this first step, developing senior management support for a project management program, should not be too difficult. If upper managers, the people at the middle levels of an organization, are not forward looking, they usually become enlightened after several project failures. For example, at Chevron, a project management program was developed after a benchmarking study found that, on average, Chevron projects were taking longer and costing more than those of competitors (Cohen and Kuehn, 1996). At NCR, a project management program was started after several projects lost money (Kennel, 1996). The organization may follow the path of the revitalization process (see Chapter One) and enter the period of cultural distortion before realizing that significant effort is needed to break people out of their old departmental management habits and instill practices that support project management. However, it is not absolutely necessary to wait for a large failure in order to develop senior management support and senior management resolve. There are other ways.

Ways to Develop Support. One possibility is to hold a project inventory meeting. To do this, have all senior managers list the projects in process in their organizations. When all the projects are put together, the managers may be amazed at how much total project work is going on in the organization. Determine how many projects there are in total, and then list those that were recently finished or canceled. Understand why the canceled projects were canceled. Are there any runaway projects? Have any languished for years, never canceled but never finished, always with an excuse? Experience indicates that the senior management group may be struck by how many total projects exist and how much money is being wasted on poorly run ones. In addition, there may be several potential runaway projects—projects that have the potential of wasting still more money. A runaway project is described as one that has one or more of the following characteristics:

- It is way behind schedule.
- It is grossly over budget.
- When and if it is finally implemented, it subjects the enterprise to the risk of a substantial financial loss.

Research by Martin (1994) suggests that at any time, there is a runaway in every Fortune 200 company and that one-third of all companies have a runaway in progress. Usually technology is conveniently blamed as the cause of the runaway. Blaming one factor is an example of the "man on the dock" approach to explaining organizational catastrophes, as discussed in Chapter One. However, technology is usually not the only cause; more than 80 percent of the time, organizational, planning, or management problems are responsible. Thus, project runaways are much more of an upper management issue than they are a project management issue. Projects that have run away, languished, or been recently canceled will probably lack a project sponsor (see Chapter Two), indicating that no one in senior or upper management really wanted them to happen. Do any current projects lack an upper management sponsor? If so, you might as well cancel them now; they will probably be canceled later anyway.

However, remember that the function of a project inventory meeting is to examine the state of projects and the management of the project portfolio. The next step is to look at how many person-years each of those projects requires annually and find the total person-years being consumed by the entire inventory. Are that many person-years available to be devoted to projects in your organization? Are there that many person-years in total in your organization? The normal result of a project inventory is that senior management sees for the first time that too many projects are being attempted, that they are not coordinated in any way to reach organizational goals effectively, and that they cannot possibly be accomplished with the resources of the organization.

Now examine how important project management is in your industry. In a commodity industry that produces standard off-the-shelf products that rarely change, project management may not be very important. However, if many projects are already under way in your organization, it is a sign that project management is becoming very important in your industry. If you are experiencing increasing changes in products with a corresponding decrease in product life cycles and increasing need for product quality and customer acceptance, then project management is certainly becoming essential to your organization's survival. It is time to embrace the tenets of a project-based organization.

The normal result of a project inventory is that senior management realizes that management of the project portfolio is essential for the survival of the company, that the current portfolio probably does not represent the optimum use of resources to reach organizational goals, and that a coordinated effort to properly manage the portfolio of projects as well as the individual projects themselves is necessary for future survival. With this realization, senior managers should be ready to support a project management response.

An alternative to having a project inventory is to hire someone into senior management who has worked in another company and understands what needs to be done to have more effective projects. For example, an insurance company that was having trouble with information technology projects (IT) hired a senior manager from a leading computer firm as its IT director. This person convened a senior management meeting to discuss IT project problems and how they had been solved in the computer firm. A consultant was brought in to discuss the role of upper management in creating the environment for successful projects and to indicate how these problems had been solved in other organizations. This approach got senior management attention, and a project management program was begun.

Another approach is to have upper managers attend training courses with the project managers and then create a senior management review based on the comments from those courses. This can work well. In designing a project management course for an engineering firm, for example, the members of the technical committee (who were upper managers) were challenged to attend the course, one at a time, with the project managers. Thus, they heard the pain caused by upper and senior management firsthand from the lower-level participants. A survey instrument was also used to generate data about how bad things were in this company. Summarized and presented to the senior managers, these experiences and data allowed them to see the problems through the eyes of their own project and upper managers, and the project management program was expanded throughout the organization.

If your organization does not have a tradition of challenging upper management, you may not get good results from having upper managers in courses. In organizations where open communication is not the norm, the presence of upper managers in courses tends to restrict conversations and the true expression of perceived problems. If this is the case, having a project inventory or getting the view from a respected outsider may work better. It is much less threatening to have an outsider talk about senior management problems in general than to have data from insiders reveal senior management problems in particular. Remember that the important result of this step is to focus attention on a problem, not to threaten the senior management team. Choose a method that will work in your organization.

If you are not able to get senior management support at this time, simply wait. Project failures will continue to grow; competitors that have adopted a project management approach will begin to develop superior products, better customer response, or better product service in much less time. Your organization will founder as its sales decrease and it enters the period of cultural distortion. Then a new CEO will be appointed who will no doubt trumpet the virtues of project management, and you will then have senior management support for change.

Using PEAT to Develop Upper Management Support. Following publication of the first edition of this book, people asked how they could benchmark their project environment against the best project organizations. They realized that if they could show their managers they were far behind the best organizations, they could use that result to get upper management attention and action. As a result we developed, first with the Strategic Management Group, Inc. and now with the Optimal Performance Network LLC, a project environment assessment tool (PEAT).

PEAT is designed to measure how well organizations support project management. It is not designed to measure the success of projects themselves. We did not ask project and upper managers how well they *think* the organization supports project management. Rather, we identified about seventy practices that organizations follow when management has created an environment for successful projects. We asked managers if those practices happened on their current project. For example, one question asks if "the upper management of the organization acted as a team to select this project." In best practice organizations, upper managers act as a team when selecting projects. In other organizations, they do not. PEAT was thus designed to measure how well the best practice organizations practice the best practices. PEAT was also designed as an assessment tool so other organizations can see how they compare to the best. Managers then assess how their organization compares to those that have created an environment for successful projects.

Eight organizations participated in this survey: HP, IBM, NCR, Chevron, Boeing, Motorola, 3M, and Lucent Technologies. HP had its Project Management Initiative group, which was charged with developing project management skill across the organization. IBM has a similar organization, the Project Management Center of Excellence, as did Motorola and 3M. HP and Motorola were both cited by Kerzner (2001) for excellence in project management. The NCR project management group has developed a well-known methodology, GlobalPM, and their executives earned the PMP certification. The Chevron group is also known for its Chevron Project Development and Execution Process, CPDEP (Cohen and Kuehn, 1996). Boeing is famed for the Boeing 777 program, and a Lucent Technologies project was honored as PMI Project of the Year in 1995. Given this level of dedication to excellence in project management, this group certainly approximates the best of the best.

Eight areas comprising environmental success factors were measured:

1. *Strategic emphasis.* This factor measures the degree to which the project is aligned with business strategy. In the past, projects often proliferated without regard to strategic importance. Now, over half of the activity in most organizations is done through projects. As projects gain importance, they need to be selected based on contribution to business strategy. Sample questions for this factor are, "I

know how this project is linked to other projects to help implement business strategy" and "The upper management of the organization acted as a team to select this project."

2. *Upper management support.* This factor measures the degree to which upper management behavior supports project success. One important factor in project failure is the lack of upper management support for project management. To increase chances of success, upper managers need to support the project management process and behave in ways that increase project success. Sample questions for this factor are, "Upper managers are more interested in project results than they are in project control" and "I feel that the upper managers fully understand the project management process."

3. *Project planning support.* This factor measures the degree to which upper managers encourage and support proper project planning. One of the most important factors in project success is having team members develop the project plan. In less successful project environments, this step is often skipped or not given enough emphasis. Sample questions for this factor are, "The core team was involved in the development of the project plan" and "Key 'stepping stones' from the beginning to the end of the project (milestones) have been identified and scheduled."

4. *Customer/end user input.* This factor measures the degree to which customer and end user input is considered during project planning and execution. This is important because the final product can rarely be specified at the beginning. Successful projects need close contact with customers and end users in order to get a pulse on the market and to know what features are best to include. Sample questions for this factor are, "The end users were consulted early in the project planning process" and "There are clear measures in place for customer satisfaction."

5. *Project team development.* This factor measures the degree to which organizational practices support project team development. The successful environment should help to support and motivate project team members. A well-functioning team is one of the best indicators of a good project environment. Sample questions for this factor are, "(Most) project team members work full-time on this project" and "A core team has been established to work from the beginning to the end of the project."

6. *Project execution support.* This factor measures the degree to which organizational practices support project execution. The successful project environment is designed to support project execution. The novice environment often trumpets project beginnings with much fanfare and then starves them to death during execution. Sample questions for this factor are, "The project is staffed with all necessary resources" and "There is a person or group in charge of improving project management in this organization."

7. *Communications and information systems.* This factor measures the degree to which the organization enables good communication among project team members. Communication is the lifeblood of effective teams. An effective environment makes communication easy among members of specific teams *and* across different project teams. Effective environments also enhance communication by performing project reviews and making that information available to all current and future project teams. Sample questions for this factor are, "Updated project information is readily available to all stakeholders" and "The results of this project review will be made available within the organization."

8. *Organizational support.* This factor measures the degree to which organizational factors such as the reward and promotion system support project management. Good project environments are reinforced when the organization as a whole supports the best project management practices. Sample questions for this factor are, "The organization will reward the team members if they are successful on this project" and "The project manager for this project has received adequate training for the task."

Readers can see the results of this survey and see how their organization scores using the sample questions by accessing survey.peopleview.net/peatdemo (or www.englundpmc.com) on the Web.

Step 2: Develop a Structure for Interdepartmental Input

It is important to develop a project management program, often called a project management office or initiative, to guide the development of project management practices throughout the organization. Because the program affects all parts of the organization, all parts of the organization should be represented. Therefore, the first step is to develop cross-organizational teams that can help guide and implement the project management effort.

Two important levels of questions will probably require two different levels of teams. The first level has to do with what projects to attempt; address these questions by a senior or upper-level management team. The second level is more operational, concerned with which project practices to adopt and how they will be implemented; answer such questions by a team of upper managers and project managers.

HP uses the council concept as one mechanism to establish a strategic direction for projects spanning organizational boundaries. A council may be permanent or temporary, assembled to solve strategic issues and thus typically involving upper managers. Standard council roles are setting directions, managing multiple projects or the project portfolio, and aiding in cross-organizational issue resolution.

3M also developed an interdisciplinary team to help improve project management. The company held a focus group with some top project leaders from different parts of the organization to find out precisely what problems they were experiencing on projects. From this came a list of more than eighty areas of difficulty grouped into ten major categories of "critical success factors." These factors became the basis for developing a project management process (Storeygard, 1995).

A financial services firm realized it had a problem after several software project failures—a classic way to get management attention. Case studies were developed for these projects, and a senior management team, including the CEO, was convened to study the causes and cures. As a result, a team of senior managers from the IT, operations, and management development departments was established to research solutions. It developed and supported a cross-organizational project management program. (See Graham, 1993, for additional details.)

The important point here is that any sort of cross-departmental effort requires input from the different departments involved in order to help ensure its eventual acceptance. For people in various departments to embrace any set of standard procedures, they must first have voice in the design of those procedures. Some project management practices may not make sense from the point of view of an individual department, but if department representatives were part of a team that developed those practices, they could explain the rationale to members of their department. Understanding the reason for recommended practices is critical to cross-departmental acceptance, so facilitate it from the beginning by forming cross-departmental teams to help define the total project management program.

Examine your organization to see how cross-departmental efforts are coordinated. Many organizations have a council structure that can be used; others use ad hoc teams. Whatever structure is available, it can help gain input from those who will be affected by the output. Without performing this important step, the people affected do not own the resulting process, and the probability of failure of the final effort is greatly increased.

An enabling factor to improve input and subsequent actions is an effective information system. Terry Cooke-Davies (2002), managing director of the Human Systems network, a research-based consulting group dedicated to expanding the knowledge and practice of project management in organizations (www.human systems.net), says:

> People in many different positions in organizations contribute to effective decision-making about priorities within a portfolio. What this means is that the data on which the decisions are based must be derived from common and compatible raw data, but presented in a variety of different formats that are relevant to strategists, line managers, capacity planners, project and

programme managers, and project and programme support offices. Sadly, evidence from surveys that are currently being conducted on behalf of the Human Systems' networks indicates that few organizations have management information systems that are yet up to this challenge [p. 3].

One member organization in this network reports that the organization is managed at the top level on just three key measures. They found that:

- Metrics must provide information, not data.
- Best-run project-based businesses use a taxonomy of consistent metrics from top to bottom of the organization.
- The stream of metrics can be tailored to have impact and provide clear messages at different levels in the organization.
- There is considerable scope for reducing cost and effort in gathering and reporting metrics in most organizations.

Other best practices to surface include:

- Not asking for measures for which there is little or no use (it costs money and time to develop and collect measures).
- Metrics alone may not stimulate senior management actions. Stories can be more successful.
- Develop a Web-based tool accessible to all, but capable of reporting different metrics available to suit different needs.
- Use a journalist to write key messages in an understandable way.
- Communicate performance using a single sheet of metrics, updated at appropriate intervals, which can be pinned on senior managers' office walls. Use a traffic light (red, yellow, green) approach to convey key information.

A benefit that one company achieved when using these tools for portfolio management was to reduce its project portfolio by 75 percent, which resulted in a 500 percent increase in delivery in the first year. A key skill learned is how to kill projects, not just wound them.

Step 3: Develop a Process for Project Selection

Project selection will normally be done by an upper management team, which ensures that the projects selected are those that best fit the organizational strategy. First, they determine which types of projects will be supported; not all projects will be R&D types that break new ground or develop new product platforms, and not all projects will be add-ons that modify current products or procedures. The team of senior and upper managers decides on the mix of types of products for both the long and short terms.

The Pillsbury Project Portfolio Management process seeks to develop a mix of projects that represent balance, business benefit, and alignment (Abraham, 1995). Balance is defined as the trade-off between urgency and importance, short term and long term, and developing competences and core competences. The business benefit assesses the profit potential for all activities, calculating the return on the joint R&D-marketing investment. Alignment questions consider the degree of shared objectives, cross-functionality, common understanding of requirements, and ability to integrate into the total business plan. This is one example of a management team's determining the most important criteria for selecting projects to meet the goals of the organization.

Once the criteria for projects are determined, potential projects are prioritized according to their ability to meet the desired objectives. The upper management team assesses the ability of each project to meet the stated goals. Pillsbury does this with a priority assessment form. For each project to be considered, the team lists the project goal, the strategic basis for interest, the business benefit, the R&D investment needed, the implementation timing, toughest hurdles, and odds of success. Based on these assessments, priorities are assigned to each of the potential projects.

NCR looks at a risk-to-payback analysis in evaluating potential professional services projects. An upper management team from project management, sales, professional services, and risk assessment, plus technical subject matter experts, prepares a risk analysis. This package describes the project opportunity, risks, a high-level technical design, and a business case. Sales and professional services management then decides whether to pursue the project by weighing the rewards against the risks.

Many organizations use a business case approach for each potential project. The business case includes a project narrative and a financial analysis. The narrative explains the business process the project is designed to address, the linkage to corporate strategy, the time frame of the project, resource requirements and risks, and issues associated with the project. The financial analysis provides a project cost summary by year reflecting the costs required to complete a proposed project. In addition, it reflects on the financial benefits that successful accomplishment of the project will achieve. Finally, the analysis calculates the net present value, the return on investment, and the discount period based on the cost and benefit streams. The purpose of the business case is to provide the senior management team with an overview of the project that enables it to make go/no-go decisions on projects submitted for approval.

Other organizations use the priority assessment method described in Chapter Two. Chevron uses the Chevron Project Development and Execution process: multifunctional teams meet during the initial phase of the process to test project ideas for strategic fit. Many other methods are probably in use as well. The point is that upper managers determine the most important criteria for project selection and then rank potential projects accordingly. The rank of a particular project then becomes that project's priority. Once the projects are in priority order within categories of project types, they are selected according to the available resources. Use the in-plan/out-plan document for recording this selection, as described in Chapter Two. When a project is selected, assign a project sponsor, as discussed in Chapter Two.

If an organization's project selection process is not properly executed, its strategy suffers because too many projects will be launched in a scattershot manner. This causes a massive fight for resources among competing projects, a Darwinian scenario where those who fight the hardest get resources for their projects and the other projects die. "Survival of the fittest" would not appear to be the appropriate upper management tactic for implementing organizational strategy. Projects should be chosen for their contribution to strategy, and it is upper management's responsibility to make that happen.

Step 4: Develop Upper Managers' Abilities in Managing Project Managers

The most critical step in implementing the chosen projects is developing upper managers' abilities in managing project managers. Without success here, all other efforts are wasted. Throughout the land, project managers complain that upper managers will not let them do what they are trained to do. As a result, all the time, effort, and training that go into developing project managers are wrecked on the rocky shores of some upper manager's mismanagement. Yet despite its importance, this is the step most often forgotten or ignored. Ignore it at your peril.

Developing abilities can be done only over time. Even if upper managers realize the importance of project management and follow the project selection step just described, they must not think their influence is over. The behavior of upper managers has a profound effect on project success, and they need education on best practices. For example, the NCR executive team responsible for implementing the GlobalPM methodology attended executive project management education and attained certification as project management professionals (PMPs). The team understood that leading by example was the best measure of success, and they expected nothing of their associates that they did not expect of themselves (Kennel, 1996). In this way, the NCR team members increased their skills in managing project managers and showed that they can "walk the walk" as well as "talk the talk." Start any training program with upper managers first.

Like project managers, upper managers need time to practice any new skill they learn. The most likely vehicle for learning best practices is some combination of courses, conferences, refreshers, and discussions. To begin, develop a course or executive overview as a part of the project management office. This course could cover all the ways that upper managers help the project management function, as discussed in Chapters Three and Four. Normally, this includes what upper managers should ask for in terms of a project plan, goal statement, staffing plan, and so on. The HP Project Management Initiative discussed in Chapter Nine developed such a course. The course might cover why upper managers are so important in the change to project management and explain best practices so that the upper managers can support the project management process.

An interesting way to teach best practices is to let the upper managers discover the effects of their actions themselves. One approach taken at HP was to have upper managers go through the "The Complete Project Manager" simulation (Graham, 1991) as if they were project managers. This simulation helps project managers learn to deal with team building, stakeholder management, and other project issues by solving a sequence of problems that affect project success. As the upper managers went through the problems in the simulation, they became just as angry and upset as real project managers normally get at the problems caused by the upper managers in the simulation. In the feedback discussion, they were asked who causes these problems in their organization. Of course, it is themselves. Because they were angry and upset at the simulated problems they encountered, they could easily understand how their actual project managers could also be angry and upset. It was important for upper managers to go through the simulation themselves and experience the frustrations. Otherwise, discussion of the problems they cause is just an intellectual exercise that they do not internalize. Having experienced the problems themselves in the simulation, they were ready to listen to solutions and best practices.

Another way to develop upper managers' abilities is to hold an upper management conference like the one described in Chapter Nine. Conferences gather together many upper managers to network among themselves and listen to some of the best experts discuss problems and suggest solutions. When properly designed, these conferences are well attended and even sought out by upper managers.

If management conferences are not normal procedure in your organization, it may be best to hire a consultant to help upper managers understand how they affect project success. Experience indicates that upper managers tend to listen to outside experts more than they do to insiders with the same information. This is especially true if the consultant has experience in other organizations that are similar to yours. The consultant interviews upper managers and project managers to see which practices are prevalent in your organization and then describes the consequences of those practices in other organizations. The consultant can show the results achieved from applying best practices in the best organizations.

The important point is to note that upper managers need to change along with project managers in order to make the move to project management successful. This cannot be done by executive fiat, so a development plan is needed. Develop a plan that fits the customs of your organization. If none of the above methods seems to fit, consider developing an internal upper manager–project manager team charged with developing a list of best practices.

If this step is not successfully implemented, the benefits of the first three steps will not be realized. This is because a change in practices must be reinforced by upper management on a daily basis. If upper managers say they want new practices but continue to use old practices, the project managers sense this lack of integrity and revert to old practices too.

Step 5: Establish a Project Manager's Development Program

Motorola undertook a very large system development project involving satellite communications. It represented a significant shift away from familiar military projects into work for hire on a massive commercial project. A senior manager initially established self-managed teams, believing they were empowered to make all decisions unhindered by management meddling and delays. Chief planner Darrell Blackburn (1994) described the resulting scenario as similar to team members inside a large number of tubs lashed together by long ropes. The mission was for all tubs to reach the other side of a wide river. Everybody rowed like crazy to complete the mission, but without project and program managers, each tub went off in its own direction, fighting the current as best as it could. Members were fiercely loyal to their mission but impervious to the needs and wishes of other teams. The long tethers occasionally snapped, and people were jolted by miscues of poor communication.

They corrected this situation by positioning project managers in each project and establishing a program management office. This shortened the ropes between project "tubs" so that project managers took ownership not only for their own projects but for the whole program as well. They served as communication liaisons between projects and to the program office. All became closely synchronized, the efforts of each were supported by the efforts of others, and rapid progress for all became evident.

Upper managers need to determine attributes that they think are most important for potential project managers and then inculcate them through training. This is usually the job of a project management development office, a group like the Project Management Initiative at HP that is most often staffed by experienced project managers. However, it could also be part of regular training and development; if so, it could be done more cheaply because there is no need to establish an entirely new group, and project manager development becomes part of regular management development. But done this way, certain possibilities may be missed, such as project management conferences, the ability to incorporate the latest developments, and having people who have "been there" transfer knowledge based on experience. If these are not important to your organization, do project manager development as part of the organizational development program.

A good example is 3M's development of its competence model and curriculum, as discussed in Chapter Six. Honeywell is also developing a total curriculum, as is Chevron. Lucent Technologies had a project management department to oversee project management development and project management practice. All these companies put together a development program and course curriculum. All have a basic course in project management fundamentals and further courses that develop other skills, including business skills. Project management curricula tend to feature courses in the following areas:

Project techniques. Project management fundamentals courses teach basic project planning, estimating, and risk analysis techniques. When participants finish such a course, they know how to put together a project plan.

Behavioral aspects. These courses cover such areas as team building, motivating team members, developing effective project teams, and dealing with upper managers, contributing department managers, and other stakeholders. Many of these courses use simulations to help teach the effects of management behavior on team development and other matters.

Organizational issues. These courses cover techniques for managing across organizations when the project manager has all the responsibility but none of the authority. They teach participants how to get projects done in spite of the rest of the organization.

Business fundamentals. Many project managers have a technical background but lack basic business knowledge. These courses teach the business of the organization, how decisions affect the bottom line, and how to run a project as if it were a business.

Marketing and customer issues. In the end, there must be a market—a set of customers—for the final product of the project. This is true even of internal projects. Courses on these issues focus on the techniques of defining and developing a market as well as understanding the needs and desires of the customers and end users.

Not all courses must be developed from scratch. Some project management skills are similar to regular management skills, so it may be possible to use courses that already exist in the organization to teach project managers about such subjects.

Project managers need to know the company's business if they are to act as if they are managing their own business. They understand business better if they have had a variety of assignments before becoming project managers; in designing any curriculum, it is important to understand what skills current project managers have and what they lack.

Project forums are an opportunity for practicing project managers to get together to discuss a particular topic, such as work breakdown structures. These can be informal luncheons or half-day sessions to review basics, cover advanced applications, and discuss problems with application in the organization.

Another possibility is to develop project management conferences, as discussed in Chapter Nine. The ability to do this depends on the culture of your organization. The idea is to design meeting places where project managers can learn from the experiences of one another. Increasingly, there are Internet forums on the Web where people can share experiences. Be careful, however: do not expect impersonal technologies to take over for the personal touch that people need.

Smaller organizations may not have the resources to develop the competence models and complete curriculums described here. An alternative is to examine the models given in Chapter Six in some detail and modify one for use in your organization. The curriculum can then be developed by choosing from the array of public courses that are readily available. Encourage people to attend universities that offer a master's degree in project management. Many organizations offer complete curricula and will tailor them to fit the needs of smaller organizations. The easiest way to determine available courses is to attend a national project management conference such as the annual seminar and symposium of the Project Management Institute and visit the vendor displays. In this way, smaller organizations can develop the same caliber of project management as larger organizations do.

Step 6: Make Project Management a Career Position

Any organization that is serious about projects will make project management a career position, not just an add-on to peoples' regular responsibilities.

At NCR Professional Services, for example, project management is now defined as a career position. Project managers run all aspects of their projects using NCR's GlobalPM methodology. They are assigned to their position at the end of the concept phase of proposal development, and they remain on the project until the end. The best performers have superior skills in specifying project requirements, meeting customer needs, and managing change. To handle larger efforts, NCR has defined the program manager role. A program is a set of individual projects that are integrated to accomplish a customer's objectives. The program manager oversees the multiple projects that are included in the program, supports the project managers, and resolves conflict as needed. The program manager also provides a planning and control function to ensure that individual projects come together as needed at completion (Kennel, 1996).

A project management career track based on the roles just mentioned was established to emphasize the value that NCR places on project management skill. Project managers are expected to advance their capabilities through ongoing company-supported formal training and certification. Certification as a project management professional is mandatory for individuals aspiring to rise on the project management career track.

Many organizations draw project managers from the ranks of technical or engineering professions. AT&T (Ono, 1990), in contrast, assembled a large section of professional project managers drawn from various areas of the company. Upper manager Dan Ono developed a distinct career position for people aspiring to advance within the organization. They make significant contributions by focusing strictly on project management issues to coordinate cross-organizational projects. Many of them did not have advanced professional training before joining this organization; they followed a course of study leading to the project management professional certification given by the Project Management Institute. They continue advancing in the profession by completing a series of increasingly complex projects and by attending conferences and networking with other project managers.

In the field of e-commerce, many businesses are scrambling to develop Internet-specific business practices. There is an explosive growth in the need for system integrators who can provide services ranging from reselling hardware and software to architecture design and business process consulting. Businesses sometimes look to integrators to assume total responsibility for their business applications and the business processes they support. There is a question about how ready businesses are to turn over mission-critical functions to outside firms, and the answer often lies in talking to people who have been through a similar experience. In an extensive survey of information systems managers, *ComputerWorld* (1996) gathered the criteria into three categories: business practices, project management, and technical performance. Project management expertise, according to the survey, becomes significant when clients are looking for a global integrator that can attack a worldwide challenge with a common set of methodologies and practices while being sensitive to cultural differences.

These projects pair hundreds of professionals together from client and consulting firms, handling project management, applications development, business function analysis, and technical support. The projects require more than passing interest from upper managers; without a sense of urgency and enough full-time people on the integration job, "projects tend to fail," according to one participant. Said another about a positive experience: "Management backed the project with dollars and freed up senior people in the organization to make it happen."

Project management criteria in the survey broke out into areas such as integrators' knowledge of clients' business, integrators' project management skills, integrators' systems integration experience, and integrators' level of flexibility. Even the business practices criteria included project management areas such as integrator communication processes and problem resolution processes. Technical performance criteria included actual versus scheduled completion time and compatibility with other systems.

If project management is not made a career position, it will not be perceived as a job of importance to the organization; the best people will not be drawn to it and the organization will most likely revert to the accidental project manager approach, a recipe for failure. Upper management needs to ensure that project management is a desirable position and that it is indeed a school for leaders.

Step 7: Develop a Project Learning Organization

Developing a project learning organization is something that everyone agrees is important but that few attempt. Learning through projects could be the responsibility of a project office, but that requires project reviews, many of which are sporadic at best. Some organizations require reviews of all projects, but the information is shared only within the team. Few organizations have a mechanism to share the learning of one team with another. One organization solved this by requiring project managers when starting new projects to research previous findings and report to the upper management team what was learned and will be applied to the new project.

Information is basically free at the end of a project, and everyone seems to agree that sharing it is an important way to increase project management skills in the organization. Yet few organizations actually avail themselves of this free yet priceless information. Why not?

One reason is organizational perversity. Some upper managers say they want people to learn from other projects but do not reward or support the necessary reviews of those projects. Ideally, they would ask for reviews of all projects and support the idea and process of sharing learning with other project managers.

A more important reason may be that although people learn from their mistakes, sharing project learning also reveals project mistakes. Only the rare organization rewards people for mistakes, so most people hide them and try only to show their triumphs. Most people have a public self that they show to others and a real self that they hide from public view. Because organizations comprise people, they too exhibit a public persona and a private persona. The public persona usually requires that everything be done right—that there be no mistakes. Thus, any mistakes tend to be hidden from customers and others, who are fed a steady stream of the "right stuff." Employees learn this from senior managers, and if the senior managers are seen hiding the truth, they tend to do the same. This reinforces the notion that hiding behavior is natural, which is another example of organizational perversity: what is desired is a learning organization, but what is rewarded is covering up mistakes.

Too few organizations reward learning because true learning requires leadership of the kind that goes against well-established norms and that rewards what is really best for the organization. O'Toole (1995) describes this as value-based leadership, which is based on what is morally right even if it goes against the norm. For example, Jesus Christ is often considered a value-based leader because his message of forgiveness went against the norms of his times. So is Mahatma Gandhi, whose message of nonviolence went against the behavioral norms of his time and place in the twentieth century. Yet both were able to effect massive social change, mainly because their message was morally right and they stuck to it despite assaults from all sides. Says O'Toole, "In complex, democratic settings, effective leadership will entail the factors and dimensions of vision, trust, listening, authenticity, integrity, hope and, especially, addressing the true needs of followers. Such a philosophy must be rooted in the most fundamental of moral principles: respect for people" (p. 11).

For the value-based project management leader, imagine the vision as an open organization where mistakes are openly discussed and the learning value of the error is appreciated. This is particularly necessary in a project organization where people are constantly doing something new, which is where mistakes are most likely. Mistakes, as we come to understand them, are merely after-the-fact judgments of decisions made with incomplete knowledge. The line between hero and goat is often very thin; a decision may be a big success or a huge failure depending on how subsequent events unfold. So the first step in developing true learning from experience is to avoid labeling erroneous decisions as mistakes; instead, consider them as decisions that did not work out as planned. Beyond that, center discussion on why things went other than as planned: from this understanding, learning occurs.

Developing trust in this vision is difficult. If the company has a long history of berating people for mistakes, it may be almost impossible. Trust builds only after a long period during which upper managers repeatedly and consistently discuss mistakes with an open mind and with the goal of maximizing learning from them and not maximizing the guilt of some scapegoat. Honestly examining the reasons that a decision did not work out is the best way to ensure better decisions in the future. Hanging a scapegoat merely ensures that the reasons for failure will never be discovered; the same mistake might be made again and again. Upper management will not be trusted until it sees that people who discuss "mistakes" are no longer made the scapegoats.

The change to open discussion must be made with authenticity and integrity, or it will never take hold. Organization members are very well tuned to the "flavor of the week" approach to management: if upper managers do not really mean what they say about understanding the reasons for "mistakes," people will assume that the new management style is just a fad and that things will soon return to normal. In other words, no change will happen.

Integrity in this context means that upper managers do something with the project learning information they receive to help make things better in the future rather than fire or otherwise berate the messenger. They adopt new learnings into their values and belief systems, adapt them to the current situation, and apply them consistently—not just until a new idea or crisis comes along. Authenticity and integrity mean that upper managers really want what they ask for and will do what they said they would do. It seems so simple, but many organization members seem to think that their upper managers lack authenticity and integrity. When that feeling is prevalent, trust cannot possibly develop, and the learning organization remains a fiction.

The final part of value-based leadership is meeting the true needs of organizational members. Most project managers and most people in general truly need little more than the authenticity and integrity just described.

Pillars to Arches: A Metaphor

Evolution of a project management culture in any organization can parallel the development of early architecture. Greeks used a column and beam system (see Figure 10.2 (a)), which greatly restricted the width of each span. The heavy spans were difficult to make and expensive, and they prevented Greek architects from building big, tall, gaudy, or spacious structures.

FIGURE 10.2. USING A METAPHOR OF ARCHITECTURE.

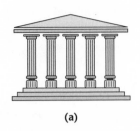

(a)

(b)

Major advancement accrued to the Romans, who adopted and expanded columns with the arch (see Figure 10.2 (b)). The semicircular arches form large, open, ornate vaults and domes with tremendous strength and stability.

Where Greek structures were spiritually modest, Romans opened up new political and imperial vistas. They benefited by having fewer limitations or obstacles. Arches are even more difficult to construct, but they span greater distances and support greater loads. A shift from pillars to arches clears clutter and opens new possibilities. What they conceived they could build.

Organizations advancing along a project management maturity model toward enterprise project management can be viewed as a pillars-to-arches evolution. Enterprise project management is an organizationwide managerial philosophy, based on the idea that company goals are achievable through a web of simultaneous projects, which calls for a systemic approach and includes every and all types of projects. Ideally, the discipline of project management is ingrained in the hearts, minds, and souls of all participants.

People in organizations with lower levels of maturity typically erect a number of pillars or columns to put project management in place. One pillar may be a champion, another a sponsor, then a steering committee, and finally a project office. Viewers note much hubris, such as methodologies, training courses, project life cycles, templates, and thick binders. Managers wonder about overhead costs and whether this "project management stuff" contributes to shareholder value.

As astute managers learn what works or not, they stop doing non-value-adding activities, such as detailed reports and extensive metrics. They work smarter, not harder, so fewer or different people are required to staff project support activities.

The three-inch binder is replaced by a one-page summary of key issues to resolve (as happened with the HP Phase Review Process). The streamlined portfolio process has clear goals to select the critical few projects instead of the trivial many. This new "arch culture" minimizes obstacles and keeps focus on value-generating activities. Removing clutter reveals new vistas or possibilities.

Here is how you can create an arch culture, otherwise known as *enterprise project management:*

1. *Start with the foundation.* Adopt and adapt a project management discipline, methodologies and techniques, policies, processes, procedures, and tools.

2. *Put necessary structures in place.* Support project management champions and evangelists, formally title and train project managers and sponsors, form a project management council or steering committee, and involve functional management in project selection and program reviews. Implement a project initiative that drives a concerted effort to pull everything together.

3. *Simplify.* Appreciate what works in the organization and build on its strengths. Dismantle activities, structures, reports, and metrics that detract from rather than support progress. Conduct controlled experiments, such as whether anyone reads the eighty-page report or if certain metrics make any difference in decision making. Remove "pillars" that are no longer useful or needed, and morph them into a fewer set of "arches" that support heavier loads. Stop doing nonproductive activities. Find elegant solutions to annoying problems. Select people enthusiastic and knowledgeable about project work so that core teams accelerate their progress from forming to performing.

4. *Expand capabilities.* As the organization becomes more effective and efficient, capacity is generated to take on new business, bid new projects, and add products. This happens because "opportunities" quickly sort into opportunistic, strategic, or distracting buckets; simplified, repeatable, consistent processes ensure that success is achievable; people know their roles and responsibilities and take accountability for success of the whole. Generate new knowledge and share new best practices that expand the realm of what is possible both within the organization and with outside partners.

5. *Implement a strategic program office.* The program management office is the linchpin for implementing and maintaining a project approach across the organization. It is a gigantic building block for shaping enterprise project management into reality and sustaining its vitality. The project management office adds value by ensuring that projects are performed within procedures, are in line with organizational strategies, and are completed in ways that add economic value. A strategic program office supports the vision, construction, and maintenance of the "arches" for the organization.

The Compleat Upper Manager

Former HP executive vice president Rick Belluzzo (1996a) expressed his commitment to project management at HP by his presence, his words, and his willingness to answer the tough questions presented to him at the company's Project Management Conference. This event provided him the opportunity to share his values, beliefs, hopes, and concerns with those closest to managing the action throughout the company. He emphasized the "concept, belief, strong principle I have about focus. It can be applied to everything we do. There is so much more value that if there are ten things you can do, pick one or two to do extremely well, and then go on to the third one. This is so much more valuable and so much more rewarding than trying to cover everything and doing a mediocre job." In his statements, he demonstrated values-based leadership, shared his thought processes, provided one answer to the issue of doing too many projects, and empathized with the desire of all to accomplish great results through projects. It is heartwarming when we can point to managers who act with authenticity and integrity.

The successful complete upper manager:

- Conducts an inventory of all projects under way and optimizes the project portfolio.
- Examines how important project management is to the organization.
- Develops a project management program or office.
- Uses an assessment and prioritization process to select projects.
- Gets training or outside assistance to improve the ability to manage project managers.
- Recognizes the profession of project management and invests in training project managers.
- Learns from mistakes, avoids organizational perversities, and builds a trusting, open organization.
- Builds a strong project management culture.
- Acts with authenticity and integrity.

*S*ince this book was first published, we have continued applying, researching, and learning about what it takes to build a project-based organization. This Epilogue summarizes additional work that integrates change management processes into the project manager's toolkit.

EPILOGUE: LEADERSHIP IN EVOLVING PROJECT-BASED ORGANIZATIONS

Time cannot be stored or stretched and is unidirectional. Time integrates the Universe. Our culture of appreciating time needs a total re-orientation.

ADESH JAIN, 2003

As the director of the Centre for Excellence in Project Management and editor of the *Indian Project Management Journal,* Adesh Jain points out that today the rate of change is unprecedented, resulting in the need to manage complex and nonlinear transition processes. Project management is emerging as a key profession to deal with change effectively. We need leaders who can step up to this challenge (Englund and Jain, 2003).

Project management is the art and science of converting *vision* into *reality* and *abstract* into *concrete.* Christopher Columbus's vision was to discover the undiscovered; his reality was the "discovery" of America. The new frontier of project management includes a vision to make citizens and corporations happier and more productive; the reality involves applying and improving scientific project management processes. These steps require leadership in a changing and fast-moving environment. Through project management, an organization addresses the issues of change and transition throughout a life cycle.

All projects involve change; thus, every project manager and team member becomes involved in an organizational change process. We want to address modern change agents—those in the quest for knowledge about specific actions that can create and sustain a project-based organization (PBO). Because a PBO approach is vital to most organizations, every reader in almost every endeavor can benefit by following the process we describe. The objective is to share concepts and practices that help project participants at all levels of an organization make sense of the change processes they need to lead.

People may come to a leadership role accidentally, by default, by choice, or by ambitious intent, but sooner or later, all professionals find a leadership role thrust on them—a team to lead or a project to accomplish with others. To be successful in this environment requires people and organizational skills. Greater success comes to those who define, develop, and refine a plan to be successful. These people ultimately embrace the journey or process of changing an organization to be more efficient and more profitable by developing an organizationwide project management system, often called enterprise project management. Wise are the persons who choose a proactive path, employing a change management process, rather than wishing retrospectively that they had done so.

The path includes many uncertainties. *Leadership is a key to managing uncertainties.* And modern project management provides effective strategies to reduce uncertainties throughout the project life cycle.

Leadership has different dimensions than management does. Few people get anointed with the title and authority as a manager. We speak here not of a "great man" approach to leadership but rather of an every person situational role. Each person on a project team inevitably has an opportunity at some time to express leadership. Opportunity comes to those who are ready for it—in this case, to those who understand and can apply a change management process.

Change is not an isolated phenomenon. It engulfs every living being within organizations. Often we close our minds to new things and look for precedents as if tomorrow is an extension of today. The compression of time and the unprecedented challenges we face mean that only those companies that have project management processes in place and are proactive in managing change will survive. If companies and people adopt a reactive mode in facing change, they cannot survive, leave alone thrive.

An imperative is to support enterprisewide change. The boundaries of a modern enterprise need to include customers and contractors. Support does not just happen—it must be elicited. Effective leadership includes the art of eliciting support. Figure E.1 illustrates a process (path) to get support and achieve results.

The enterprise approach to managing projects is a managerial philosophy based on the principle that company goals are achievable through a web of simultaneous projects. In today's race against time, there can be little meaning to managing single projects in isolation or operating in functional silos. This calls for a systemic approach. The concept is based on the idea that prosperity depends on adding value to business and that value is added by systematically implement-

FIGURE E.1. A PROJECT-BASED ORGANIZATION CHANGE MANAGEMENT PROCESS.

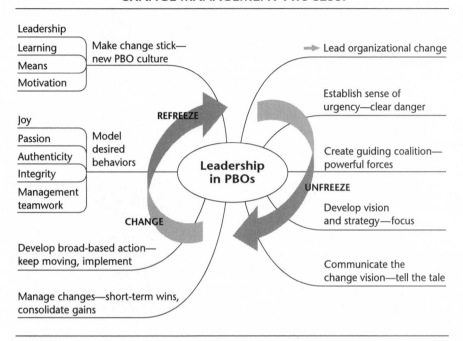

Source: Adapted from Englund, Graham, and Dinsmore, 2003.

ing projects of all types across the enterprise. If projects are managed more effectively, then the company's bottom line is greatly enhanced.

The aim we espouse is to develop a group of change agents whose efforts are enthusiastically applied throughout the organization in a way that brings about real change to it. Ultimately, organizations have to balance the ratio of the investment in new projects to ongoing operational investments. The higher the ratio is, the more importance must be placed on visions of futuristic aspects for making organizations sustainable.

Lead Organizational Change. Begin the journey by determining what needs to be done to lead real change in the organization. View the organization change process from a different slate. Be careful not to get bogged down by current constraints. Look at new processes without bias. Often, the existing boundaries create roadblocks in viewing new things objectively and developing new commitments. Appreciate the positive qualities and examples that exist and led to current levels of achievement. Instead of a reorganization (which is often incorrectly the first rather than one of the last things done), what is needed is to recreate an organization to build on the existing strengths.

Start any change process by assembling a group of people who share a common core and believe that change is possible and desirable. Demonstrate how the change is good for the organization, and then work to have this change adopted throughout the organization. A PMI *PM Network* article, "Implementing the Project Office for Organizational Change," described this "Quaker" approach to organizational change (Englund and Graham, 2001). Early Quakers set up farms near Native American territories and went about their business of growing crops, producing bountiful harvests. Hungry Natives came to ask, "How do you produce such bounty?" Educating indigenous peoples to new agricultural ways was much easier once the benefits were clear.

The successful movement to develop a project-based organization will eventually lead to radical change in organization practices. As with any other radical change process, those in the vanguard will often feel like missionaries introducing new practices into a hostile environment. It is essential that the approach be aligned with organizational culture. Much of this will be missionary work: trying to convince people they will be better off if they change to new ways. The metaphor of the Quaker approach to organizational change is a valuable reference point to consider. It is one end of a continuum about how to implement a project office.

As Figure E.2 illustrates, the other end of the continuum is the old hierarchy, command and control, "Attila," do-what-I-say approach. As a leader, Attila the Hun was able to get people to do what he commanded, mainly through his aggressive, ambitious, and arrogant nature. He was a savage conqueror who compelled those not destroyed by combat to serve in his armies. He caused vast suffering and died, possibly by those he commanded, before his invasion plans could be carried out.

Change agents and their sponsors can assess where they are on the continuum based on the current organizational culture. Design a plan resonant with that

FIGURE E.2. A CONTINUUM APPROACH
TO IMPLEMENTING CHANGE.

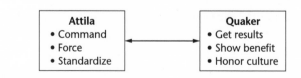

position, and possibly aim to shift direction over time. A hybrid strategy may be very effective: start with a grassroots small success that is comfortable for everyone concerned, and then enlist upper management support to mandate its use across the organization.

Establish a Sense of Urgency—a Clear Danger. A first step in creating the conditions for change in any organization is to establish a sense of urgency for the change. Learning new processes and doing things differently can become difficult transition problems for many members of the organization. People do only those things they value.

A management myth exists that people naturally resist change. That is not quite accurate: people tend to resist change that they feel is not in their best interest, but they embrace changes that they believe are in their best interest and they are in a position to shape. Establishing a clear sense of urgency and identifying consequences of nonaction makes it clear that this change is in their best interest.

The merit of a change must be fairly well established in the financial plane and be governed by market conditions. Be clear about the problem that needs solving or the consequences of maintaining the status quo. Focus on significant long-term issues, not just a current fad or temporary fire.

Create a Guiding Coalition. Develop a group of people across the organization who will help to define the changes needed and ultimately aid the implementation process. These people need position power and must act as a team. Develop a formal organizationwide group of people who are interested in implementing a project-based organization and will help guide the implementation process. Do a stakeholder analysis, and identify how to approach each stakeholder individually. Understand the power structure and sources of power, and then develop a political plan.

Develop a Vision and Strategy, and Focus Your Thinking. The vision is a picture of the future; the strategy is developing a project-based organization to get there. Enlist a guiding coalition that can help to determine the vision of both the future organization and the strategy for achieving that vision.

Many project management efforts begin by building organizational capability, usually by developing standard project management practices for the organization. From this base, they can develop more advanced functions such as project manager training and career development, as well as training all members of the organization. Then they can move to a strategic project office and develop capabilities for project selection and business skills for project managers, and they can develop venture project management where each project is truly managed as a business venture. Vision includes change away from narrow measures of success to broader measures of business performance. Integrate the vision, and ensure that it supports the corporate vision and strategy.

Communicate That Change Vision—Tell the Tale. Communicate the vision and strategy to all parts of the organization. Communication, communication, and communication are key to effecting changes with comparative ease. Communication should be perceived by all partners in the change process as true and transparent. If there is even a small bit of doubt in the way a message is communicated, distrust spreads very rapidly, destroying the process of change. Distrust multiplies without logic and faster than trust, and it takes more time to establish trust. Trust is not digital and one time; it is analogous and continuous.

For you to have any real effect throughout the organization, communicate not only the overall vision but also how the implementation of that vision affects the way people do everyday work. Understand, at every level of the organization, the problems they face, the procedures they currently use to solve problems, and the ways in which the project approach will help them solve problems easier, better, and faster. This is what people want to hear.

It is important to appreciate the perceptions of people formed over the years. There is often a reality disconnect between what we want them to see and hear and what really happens in real life. Bridging the gap is a prerequisite in bringing about a change faster and better with less heartburn. When we communicate the change processes, what we think and what we say and what we do need to be aligned as much as possible. This alignment brings high credibility to the communication process without doubting the reasons for bringing a change.

Make Change Happen—Contact. Change happens in any organization when there is a critical mass of people who change their behavior to match the new vision. Build on small wins. Recognize and begin to eliminate the organizational barriers to change, often classified in terms of structures, skills, systems, and supervisors.

Illuminating the barriers to change will be a daunting task. Developing skills will be the easiest part. Newly developed skills soon fade without supporting changes in structures, systems, and supervisors. Changing structure is a political land mine, for it includes a shift in power with the creation of a chief project officer. Without a very strong sponsor and support of other organizational officers, change will be impossible. Changing systems is also difficult because much has been invested in the current systems, and the people who run them probably favor the status quo. Finally, getting the support of department directors has been notoriously difficult over the history of the project management movement. It is here that many change processes fail. Even when the procedures have proven to be effective and the necessary skills have been developed, structures, systems, and supervisors do not yield to change, and the process fails.

Know that *no plan survives contact with reality.* Be ready for resistance: be flexible and adaptable, all the while staying true to the spirit of the vision and to your values. View the resistance from a positive angle, and understand that often it occurs because of misaligned perceptions between a person who is a change agent and other people who are targets of the change process. Perception matching reduces risk considerably.

Recognize also that control is an illusion, and chaos is a natural phenomenon. Tame rather than control the chaos through strong, shared purpose and vision statements supported by ample opportunities across the organization for innate talents, desires, and capabilities of people to interact, grow, and work together.

With short-term wins under your belt, you are positioned to consolidate these gains and take more broad-based action, especially when you attract the attention of key stakeholders who notice the impressive results and want to spread the practices across the organization. Use the leverage that this increased support offers to keep moving and implement more elements of the grand vision.

Model Desired Behavior. A leader's values come across like peeling an orange: easily detectable, even when out of sight. A project-based organization is successful when people sense value in the environment created by people's actions. These largely come from joy, passion, and enthusiasm, which are contagious across an organization. These traits represent patterns in the chaos that surrounds us; people universally respond to them. To be effective, leaders need to believe in what they are doing and be authentic, so say what you believe. Practice integrity—do what you say for the reasons stated. "Integrity crimes" cause many projects to lose momentum because people sense the lack of resolve from leaders and lose energy themselves.

Consider measuring attributes of organizational project management maturity along a people-based scale: ad hoc, ritual, compulsive, leadership, visionary, passion based.

Another imperative for management is to work together as a team. The ancient Hermetic principle of correspondence says *as above, so below.* The idea is that the world is a mirror of heaven—a reflection. Dissension in the ranks of management will be reflected in the behavior of project teams. By working together, especially on project prioritization, instead of bickering across the organization, leaders model the behavior they desire from project teams. Getting people involved in change processes is the antidote to avoid or ameliorate the political behavior that erupts when a change is introduced.

Change Organizational Culture. The teamwork and cross-organizational co-operation necessary for enterprise project management are antithetical to the re-ality experienced in most organizations. For this reason, it is a good bet that the changes that are necessary to implement enterprise project management will be quite incompatible with the organizational culture. Even if systemic changes are made in the organization, the old ways will still be just below the surface for many organizational generations. Sustained leadership is imperative.

Culture change is an extremely long and complicated process. It means changing the way people construct their reality. People must experience the con-nection between new action and performance improvement on many different occasions and over a sustained period of time. The changes must be passed on from one generation to another, and this will probably have to happen several times before the organizational culture adjusts to the new reality. Constantly ap-plying L^2M^2 (leadership, learning, means, and motivation) improves the proba-bility of success.

Establishing a strategic project office provides the ability to follow a project from its inception all the way through until the end of the product that was produced by the project. Success probably requires a changed accounting system, where the ac-counting for the project investment as well as the return on that investment come together in one place—a strategic project office positioned high in the organization. This information will help develop portfolio management and project selection proce-dures, as well as pave the way for developing a venture project management pro-gram where project managers feel responsibility beyond the completion of the project and until the completion of the project product.

With this approach, project management will be seen as much more than just a set of techniques to complete projects on time and on budget. Project manage-ment practices become totally intertwined with business management practices such that project and business management are seen as the same thing. Project management in essence is change management, and project managers are change agents. Project management brings vision into reality through many steps in defin-ing, executing, controlling, and establishing a change. The steps in project and change management processes are universally effective. We challenge each per-son to adopt, adapt, and apply them. Achieve success on small projects, build your ability to influence others, and dream big about effecting greater impact across your organization.

REFERENCES

Abraham, T. "Leveraging the R&D Marketing Interface: Finding and Exploiting the 'C' in R&D." In *Proceedings of the Product Development and Management Association International Conference 1995*. Bloomington, Minn.: Product Development and Management Association, Oct. 14, 1995.

Anderson, E. S., Grude, K. V., Huag, T., and Turner, R. *Goal Directed Project Management*. London: Kegan Paul, 1987.

Baker, B., Murphy, D., and Fisher, D. "Factors Affecting Project Success." In D. Cleland and W. King (eds.), *Project Management Handbook*. New York: Van Nostrand Reinhold, 1983.

Belbin, R. M. *Management Teams: Why They Succeed or Fail*. Oxford: Butterworth-Heinemann, 1996.

Belluzzo, R. Presentation at the Hewlett-Packard Project Management Conference '96, San Diego, Calif., Apr. 1996a.

Belluzzo, R. Untitled presentation at the IDC European IT Forum, Paris, Sept. 1996b.

Benton, R. "Platform-Based Development: A Case Study and Measurement Evaluation." Unpublished master's thesis, National Technical University, 1995.

Birchall, D., and Lyons, L. *Creating Tomorrow's Organization*. London: Pitman, 1995.

Blackburn, D. R. "And Then a Miracle Happened: Cost/Schedule Performance Management on the Iridium Program." In *Proceedings of the Project World Conference*, Session D-4. Santa Clara, Calif.: Project World Conference, Dec. 14, 1994.

Block, P. *The Empowered Manager: Positive Political Skills at Work*. San Francisco: Jossey-Bass, 1987.

Boehm, B. *Software Engineering Economics*. Upper Saddle River, N.J.: Prentice Hall, 1981.

Bowen, K. H., Clark, K., Halloway, C., and Wheelwright, S. "Make Projects the School for Leaders." *Harvard Business Review*, Sept.–Oct. 1994a, pp. 131–140.

Bowen, K. H., Clark, K., Halloway, C., and Wheelwright, S. *The Perpetual Enterprise Machine: Seven Keys to Corporate Renewal Through Product and Process Development.* New York: Oxford University Press, 1994b.

Brooks, F. *The Mythical Man Month: Essays on Software Engineering.* Reading, Mass.: Addison-Wesley, 1975.

Burkhard, R. *Good People, Bad Habits.* Fifteenth International Project Management Association World Congress, London, May 2000.

Cadillac. *Information Book.* Detroit: Cadillac Motor Company, 1991.

Campbell, J. *The Hero with a Thousand Faces.* Princeton, N.J.: Princeton University Press, 1990.

Carlisle, A. E. "MacGregor." *Organizational Dynamics,* Autumn 1995, pp. 68–78.

Cialdini, R. B. *Influence: Science and Practice.* (3rd ed.) New York: HarperCollins, 1993.

Coblentz, C. *The Blue Cat of Castle Town.* Woodstock, Vt.: Countryman Press, 1974.

Cohen, A. R., and Bradford, D. L. *Influence Without Authority.* New York: Wiley, 1989.

Cohen, D. J., and Graham, R. J. *The Project Manager's MBA: How to Translate Project Decisions into Business Success.* San Francisco: Jossey-Bass, 2001.

Cohen, D., and Kuehn, J. "Navigating Between a Rock and a Hard Place: Reconciling the Initiating and Planning Phases to Promote Project Success." Paper presented at the Project Management Institute Twenty-Seventh Annual Seminar/Symposium, Boston, 1996.

Cohen, E., and Gooch, J. *Military Misfortunes: The Anatomy of Failure in War.* New York: Free Press, 1994.

Collins, J. C., and Porras, J. I. *Built to Last: Successful Habits of Visionary Companies.* New York: HarperCollins, 1994.

"Company Sets Industry Standard with Limerick Refueling Outage." *Perspectives: PECO Energy Company Newsletter,* Feb. 1996.

ComputerWorld, Feb. 26, 1996, pp. SI/14–19.

Cooke-Davies, T. "Portfolio Management: Delivering Business Strategy Through Doing the Right Projects." *Project Manager Today,* Feb. 2002, pp. 1–3. [www.humansystems.net].

Cooper, R. G., Edgett, S. J., and Kleinschmidt, E. J. *Portfolio Management for New Products.* (2nd ed.) Boulder, Colo.: Perseus Publishing, 2001.

Cooperrider, D. L., Sorensen, P. F., Whitney, D., and Yaeger, T. F. (ed.). *Appreciative Inquiry: Rethinking Human Organization Toward a Positive Theory of Change.* Champaign, Ill.: Stipes Publishing, 2000.

"Corporate Culture." *Business Week,* Oct. 27, 1980, pp. 148–154.

Davidow, W. H., and Malone, M. S. *The Virtual Corporation: Structuring and Revitalizing the Corporation for the Twenty-First Century.* New York: HarperCollins, 1992.

de Geus, A. "Planning as Learning." *Harvard Business Review,* Mar.–Apr. 1988, pp. 70–74.

DeMarco, T. *Why Does Software Cost So Much?* New York: Dorset House, 1995.

Desatnick, R. L. *Managing to Keep the Customer.* San Francisco: Jossey-Bass, 1993.

Dinsmore, P. C. *Winning in Business with Enterprise Project Management.* New York: AMACOM, 1998.

Edgemon, J. "The Right Stuff: How to Recognize It When Selecting a Project Manager." *Application Development Trends,* May 1995, pp. 37–42.

Ellis, R. "The Importance of Infrastructure in Complex Projects." In *Proceedings of the Project World Conference,* Session C-4. Santa Clara, Calif.: Project World Conference, Dec. 14, 1994.

Englund, R. L., and Graham, R. J. "From Experience: Linking Projects to Strategy." *Journal of Product Innovation Management,* 1999, *16,* 52–64.

Englund, R. L., and Graham, R. J. "Implementing a Project Office for Organizational Change." *PM Network Magazine,* Feb. 2001, pp. 48–50.

Englund, R. L., Graham, R. J., and Dinsmore, P. C. *Creating the Project Office: A Manager's Guide to Leading Organizational Change.* San Francisco: Jossey-Bass, 2003.

Englund, R. L., and Jain, A. "Leadership in Evolving a Project-Based Organization." *Indian Project Management Journal,* Jan.–Mar. 2003, pp. 4–6.

"Expert Choice." Pittsburgh, Pa.: Expert Choice, 2000. Software.

Expert Choice Inc. *Voice,* May 1996, *6*(1), 1.

Frame, J. D. *The New Project Management: Tools for an Age of Rapid Change, Corporate Reengineering, and Other Business Realities.* San Francisco: Jossey-Bass, 1994.

Frame, J. D. *Project Management Competence: Building Key Skills for Individuals, Teams, and Organizations.* San Francisco: Jossey-Bass, 1999.

Gadeken, O. C. "Project Managers as Leaders: Competencies of Top Performers." In *Proceedings of Internet '94.* Oslo, Norway: World Congress of Project Management, 1994.

Gerstner, L. *New York Times,* Mar. 10, 2002, p. Bu-11.

Goleman, D., Boyatzis, R., and McKee, A. *Primal Leadership: Realizing the Power of Emotional Intelligence.* Boston: Harvard Business School Press, 2002.

Graham, R. J. "Give the Kid a Number: An Essay on the Folly and Consequences of Trusting Your Data." *Interfaces,* 1982, *12*(2), 40–44.

Graham, R. J. "Management Lessons from the Industrial Revolution: A Comparative Study of Industrial Innovation in England and France, 1066–1850." *Human Systems Management,* 1984, *4*, 189–200.

Graham, R. J. "Organizational Culture Change and Revitalization at AT&T." Unpublished master's thesis, University of Pennsylvania, 1985.

Graham, R. J. *Project Management As If People Mattered.* Bala Cynwyd, Pa.: Primavera Press, 1989.

Graham, R. J. "The Complete Project Manager." Philadelphia: Strategic Management Group, 1991. Software. Multimedia updated as "Project Leadership," 2003.

Graham, R. J. "A Process of Organizational Change: From Bureaucracy to Project Management Culture." In P. Dinsmore (ed.), *The AMA Handbook of Project Management.* New York: AMACOM, 1993.

Graham, R. J., and Englund, R. "Communicating with Upper Management: The Problems with Speaking Truth to Power." In *Proceedings of the Project Management Institute: Twenty-Sixth Annual Seminar/Symposium.* Upper Darby, Pa.: Project Management Institute, 1995.

Graham, R. J., and Englund, R. "Speaking Truth to Power: The Project Manager as Revolutionary." In *Proceedings of the Project Management Institute: Twenty-Seventh Annual Seminar/Symposium.* Upper Darby, Pa.: Project Management Institute, 1996.

Gulliver, F. R. "Post Project Appraisals Pay." *Harvard Business Review,* Mar.–Apr. 1987.

Hamel, G., and Prahalad, C. K. *Competing for the Future.* Boston: Harvard Business School Press, 1994.

Hammer, M., and Champy, J. *Reengineering the Corporation.* New York: HarperBusiness, 1993.

Hardin, G. "The Tragedy of the Commons." *Science,* 1968, *162*, 1243.

Heckscher, C., and Donnellon, A. *The Post-Bureaucratic Organization: New Perspectives on Organizational Change.* Thousand Oaks, Calif.: Sage, 1994.

Hegel, G.W.F. *Philosophy of History,* 1832 (quoted in H. Pachter, *The Rise and Fall of Europe.* London: David & Charles, 1975).

Hirschman, A. *Exit, Voice, and Loyalty: Responses to Decline in Firms, Organizations and States.* Cambridge, Mass.: Harvard University Press, 1970.

Hobbs, B., and Ménard, P. "Organizational Choices for Project Management." In P. Dinsmore (ed.), *The AMA Handbook of Project Management.* New York: AMACOM, 1993.

Jain, A. *Indian Project Management Journal,* Jan.–Mar. 2003, p.2.

Juran, J. M. "Managing for World-Class Quality." *PM Network,* Apr. 1992, pp. 5–8.

Katzenbach, J. R., and Smith, D. K. *The Wisdom of Teams.* Cambridge, Mass.: Harvard University Press, 1995.

Kendrick, T. *Identifying and Managing Project Risk—Essential Tools for Failure-Proofing Your Project.* New York: AMACOM, 2003.

Kennel, J. "Creating a Project Management Culture in a Global Corporation." In *Proceedings of the Project World Conference.* Santa Clara, Calif.: Project World Conference, Dec. 1996.

Kerr, S. "On the Folly of Rewarding A, While Hoping for B." *Academy of Management Executive,* 1995, *9*(1), 7–14. (Originally published 1975.)

Kerzner, H. *Strategic Planning for Project Management Using a Project Management Maturity Model.* New York: Wiley, 2001.

King, C. G. "Multi-Discipline Teams: A Fundamental Element in the Program Management Process." *PM Network,* 1992, *6*(6), 12–22.

Kleinfield, J. "Stryke Force: How Ingersoll Rand Beat the Clock." *New York Times,* Mar. 25, 1990, sec. 3, p. 1.

Koroknay, J. W. "Global Information Technology Project Management Initiative." Paper presented at the Hewlett-Packard Project Management Conference '96, San Diego, Calif., Apr. 1996.

Korten, D. C. *The Post-Corporate World: Life After Capitalism.* San Francisco: Berrett-Koehler, 1999.

Kostner, J. "Why Empowerment Doesn't Go Far Enough on Remote Teams and What You Can Do About It." Paper presented at the Hewlett-Packard Project Management Conference '94, San Jose, Calif., Apr. 1994.

Kostner, J. *Virtual Leadership: Secrets from the Round Table for the Multi-Site Manager.* New York: Warner Books, 1996.

Kumar, V., and others. "To Terminate or Not an Ongoing R&D Project: A Managerial Dilemma." *IEEE Transactions on Engineering Management,* Aug. 1996, pp. 273–284.

Leonard-Barton, D. *Wellsprings of Knowledge.* Cambridge, Mass.: Harvard Business School Press, 1995.

Marshall, L. J., and Freedman, L. D. *Smart Work: The Syntax Guide for Mutual Understanding in the Workplace.* Dubuque, Iowa: Kendall/Hunt, 1995.

Martin, J. "Revolution, Risk, Runaways: The Three R's of IS Projects." In *Proceedings of the Twenty-Fifth Annual Project Management Institute Seminar/Symposium.* Upper Darby, Pa.: Project Management Institute, 1994.

Martino, J. P. *R&D Project Selection.* New York: Wiley, 1995.

McGrath, M. E. (ed.). *Setting the PACE in Product Development: A Guide to Product and Cycle-Time Excellence.* (Rev. ed.) Newton, Mass.: Butterworth-Heinemann, 1996.

Mead, R. *Cross-Cultural Management Communication.* New York: Wiley, 1990.

Meyer, C. *Fast Cycle Time: How to Align Purpose, Strategy, and Structure for Speed.* New York: Free Press, 1993.

Miller, L. *American Spirit: Visions of a New Corporate Culture.* New York: Morrow, 1984.

Moore, G. A. *Crossing the Chasm: Marketing and Selling Technology Products to Mainstream Customers.* New York: HarperBusiness, 1991.

Moore, G. A. *Inside the Tornado: Marketing Strategies from Silicon Valley's Cutting Edge.* New York: HarperBusiness, 1995.

Moskowitz, R. "Workplace of the Future: Telecommuting at the Office, Redesigning the Office to Replicate the Telecommuter's Environment." *Microtimes*, Nov. 4, 1996, pp. 64–66.

Munns, A. K. "The Potential Influence of Trust on the Successful Completion of a Project." *International Journal of Project Management*, 1995, *13*(1), 19–29.

Napier, R. "Q&A with Robert Napier, CIO at Hewlett-Packard." *CIO Magazine*, Sept. 15, 2002, pp. 1–8.

Neihardt, J. G. *Black Elk Speaks*. Lincoln, Neb.: University of Nebraska Press, p. 5.

Ono, D. "Implementing Project Management in AT&T's Business Communications System." *PM Network*, Oct. 1990, pp. 9–19.

O'Toole, J. *Leading Change: Overcoming the Ideology of Comfort and the Tyranny of Custom*. San Francisco: Jossey-Bass, 1995.

Packard, D. *The HP Way: How Bill Hewlett and I Built the Company*. New York: HarperCollins, 1995.

Platt, L. Untitled address to the Hewlett-Packard Project Management Conference, San Jose, Apr. 1994.

Platt, L. "Turning Our Thinking Around." *MEASURE, Hewlett-Packard*, Mar.–Apr. 1996.

Project Management Institute. *Guide to the Project Management Body of Knowledge*. Upper Darby, Pa.: Project Management Institute, 2000.

Rogers, E. *Diffusion of Innovations*. (3rd ed.) New York: Free Press, 1983.

Roosevelt, T. *American Ideals and Other Essays, Social and Political*. New York: Putnam, 1897.

Rosenau, M. D. (ed.). *The PDMA Handbook of New Product Development*. New York: Wiley, 1996.

Rubinstein, J., Meyer, D., and Evans, J. "Executive Control of Cognitive Processes in Task Switching." *Journal of Experimental Psychology: Human Perception and Performance*, 2001, *27*(4), 763–797.

Russell, L. *The Accelerated Learning Fieldbook*. San Francisco: Jossey-Bass/Pfeiffer, 1999.

Russell, L., and Feldman, J. *IT Leadership Alchemy*. Upper Saddle River, N.J.: Prentice Hall, 2003.

Russell, P., and Evans, R. *The Creative Manager: Finding Inner Vision and Wisdom in Uncertain Times*. San Francisco: Jossey-Bass, 1992.

Saaty, T. L. *Decision Making for Leaders*. Pittsburgh, Pa.: RWS, 1990.

Sarna, D. "The Institute for Project Management Development." Paper presented at the Project Leadership Conference, Chicago, June 1994.

Schmidt, W., and Finnigan, J. *The Race Without a Finish Line: America's Quest for Total Quality*. San Francisco: Jossey-Bass, 1992.

Senge, P. *The Fifth Discipline: The Art and Practice of Learning Organizations*. New York: Doubleday, 1990.

Senge, P. "Collaboration Is Key to Organizational Change." *Leverage Points*, no. 34. [www.pegasuscom.com]. 2003.

Shooshan, H. M., III. *Disconnecting Bell: The Impact of the AT&T Divestiture*. New York: Pergamon, 1984.

Smith, P., and Reinertsen, D. *Developing Products in Half the Time*. New York: Van Nostrand Reinhold, 1991.

Stacey, R. D. *Managing the Unknowable: Strategic Boundaries Between Order and Chaos in Organizations*. San Francisco: Jossey-Bass, 1992.

Steele, L. *Managing Technology: The Strategic View*. New York: McGraw-Hill, 1989.

Storeygard, R. "Growing Professional Project Leaders." In *Proceedings of the Project Management Institute: Twenty-Sixth Annual Seminar/Symposium*. Upper Darby, Pa.: Project Management Institute, 1995.

Stoy, R. "Experiment with Reducing Cycle Time." In *Proceedings of the Project World Conference, Session C-11*. Washington, D.C.: Project World Conference, Aug. 9, 1996.

Tarnus, R. *The Passion of the Western Mind.* New York: Ballantine, 1991.

Trudel, J. D. "Book Review: Creating an Environment for Successful Projects." *Journal of Management Consulting*, 1998, *10*(2).

Turtle, Q. C. *Implementing Concurrent Project Management.* Upper Saddle River, N.J.: Prentice Hall, 1994.

Vidans, M. "Cross Cultural/Cross Functional Project Management: An Experience with a Japanese Automotive Supplier." In *Proceedings of the PMI Seminar/Symposium*, Sept. 21–23, 1992, pp. 81–84.

von Hippel, E. *The Sources of Innovation.* New York: Oxford University Press, 1988.

Wallace, A. *Culture and Personality.* (2nd ed.) New York: Random House, 1970.

Westney, R. E. *Computerized Management of Multiple Small Projects.* New York: Dekker, 1992.

Wheelwright, S. C. "The Roles of Leadership in New Product Development." In *Proceedings of the Product Development and Management Association International Conference 1996*. Orlando, Fla.: Product Development and Management Association, Oct. 14, 1996.

Wheelwright, S. C., and Clark, K. B. "Creating Project Plans to Focus Product Development." *Harvard Business Review*, Mar.–Apr. 1992a, pp. 70–82.

Wheelwright, S. C., and Clark, K. B. *Revolutionizing Product Development: Quantum Leaps in Speed, Efficiency, and Quality.* New York: Free Press, 1992b.

Wheelwright, S. C., and Clark, K. B. *Leading Product Development.* New York: Free Press, 1995.

Wheelwright, S. C., and Hayes, R. H. *Restoring Our Competitive Edge.* New York: Wiley, 1994.

Wilson, J. M., and others. *Leadership Trapeze: Strategies for Leadership in Team-Based Organizations.* San Francisco: Jossey-Bass, 1994.

Wood, S. "Everest: To the Summit and Beyond—Dare to Achieve." Paper presented at the Hewlett-Packard Project Management Conference '96, San Diego, Calif., Apr. 1996.

"Y2K Leader Receives Jenett Award." and "Survey Reveals Members' Key Needs." *PMI Today: A Supplement to PM Network*, June 2001.

Zells, L. "Total Employee Involvement." *PM Network*, May 1992, pp. 32–35.

INDEX